Swiftynomics

Swiftynomics

HOW WOMEN MASTERMIND AND REDEFINE OUR ECONOMY

Misty L. Heggeness

UNIVERSITY OF CALIFORNIA PRESS

University of California Press
Oakland, California

Library of Congress Cataloging-in-Publication Data

Names: Heggeness, Misty L. author
Title: Swiftynomics : how women mastermind and redefine our economy /
    Misty L. Heggeness.
Description: Oakland, California : University of California Press, [2026] |
    Includes bibliographical references and index.
Identifiers: LCCN 2025027254 (print) | LCCN 2025027255 (ebook) |
    ISBN 9780520403116 cloth | ISBN 9780520403123 ebook
Subjects: LCSH: Women—United States—Economic conditions |
    Caregivers—United States—Economic conditions | Celebrities—United
    States—Economic conditions | United States—Economic conditions
Classification: LCC HD6053.6.U5 H44 2026 (print) | LCC HD6053.6.U5 (ebook) |
    DDC 331.40973—dc23/eng/20250912
LC record available at https://lccn.loc.gov/2025027254
LC ebook record available at https://lccn.loc.gov/2025027255

Manufactured in the United States of America

GPSR Authorized Representative: Easy Access System Europe, Mustamäe tee
50, 10621 Tallinn, Estonia, gpsr.requests@easproject.com

35 34 33 32 31 30 29 28 27 26
10 9 8 7 6 5 4 3 2 1

*For Magdalena and Santiago—may the world present
you with deeper compassion, energy, and equity than
I have ever known.*

*In honor of my ancestor Lisbet Nypan and all the other
misunderstood women of this world. May their fierce courage,
independent economic nature, and ability to thrive in an
environment never created for them live on in the rest of us.*

"Swiftynomics" is the power of harnessing women's experiences and voices to advance economic growth, development, and equity.

CONTENTS

I have memories of getting lost in rows of freshly sprouted garden greens. Trailing behind my grandmother on blisteringly hot summer afternoons, I'd watch her pull carrots and cut peonies for the house. We'd listen to the sweet melody of songbirds hidden among the looming American elm trees of her expansive yard nestled in the heart of the Dakotas.

My grandmother and I would enter her cozy, dimly lit 1950s rambler. I would squint my eyes to adjust from the scorching summer's midday sun. A rectangular turn-dial radio covered in tanned leather and dark mesh sat on the kitchen table. A thin metal antenna protruded from it, the kind easily broken with a slight pressure. Next to it lay a partially finished crossword puzzle from the daily newspaper, wrinkled and folded in quarters, held down by a crisply sharpened number-two pencil. Eraser shavings ran across the tablecloth. The radio sent out sounds of classical music and opera from a local public radio station.

My grandmother would sit down, inviting me to join her. Her bent arthritic fingers folded over each other. Her beehive hairdo encompassed irrational volumes of height, not moving an inch while she spilled the stories of her youth, who she was growing up. How she trained to sing opera before she got married, describing to me who she had wanted to be and who she had become. On those days, she revealed family mysteries, taboos, and triumphs. Her patience was infinite as I asked her to retell, again and again, the stories of her past so I could crystalize them in my present—to tell me who she was and how she became the woman and grandmother I knew her to be.

Pushing boundaries runs in my family. My other grandmother left her family farm on the scorched earth of the Dakota plains to get an education in town. She received weekly boarding and a high school education.

Venturing toward economic independence, she then studied at a teachers' college and became a teacher in a one-room school, Laura Ingalls Wilder–style. At the age of twenty-one, she boarded a train alone, headed toward Tacoma, Washington, to marry my grandfather, who was in the US Army. She left her job, birth family, and everything she knew to start a family of her own.

I come from a long line of strong, resourceful women, which explains my love affair with understanding how gender shapes the world and the economy. The women from the deep, dark roots of my family tree have been grafted onto my being. My memories of them are as vivid as a florescent summer sky radiating sunlight across a Midwestern lake. Whether they toiled at household chores so their families could flourish or worked for pay in jobs outside the home, they knew when and how to play their hand.

They were a tether binding our family together in love and war. They crafted and framed their own lives within the constraints that governed them. They broke through barriers to achieve that which was important to them and pushed back on traditional gender molds that suffocated them. Grit and determination defined them. And if there was anything they had wanted to achieve but could not, that made them determined to make sure I would not be held back. These voices from my childhood have always echoed in the back of my brain, reminding me that I could achieve anything, anywhere, whenever I wanted to, no matter what.

In the pages of this book, I focus on the untold economic stories of the women around us. I explore the disproportionate ways in which their economic lives have been ignored, dismissed, or undermined. This book is about the generations of women who have harnessed intellect, wit, and perseverance to ensure they and the world around them flourish. With Taylor Swift as my muse, and armed with underreported, newly developed statistics, I challenge ingrained thinking about the economic situation of women and the challenges we face as we strive for gender equity. I correct misperceptions of the role women play in our economy and highlight the abundance of economic activity occurring in the daily lives of women throughout history.

Through this exploration, I hope that you identify how to break through traditional molds when they do not work for you, thereby allowing for a life based not on what others expect, but rather on what you need so you can flourish. Using Taylor Swift as a lens, I dig deep into the power of women as economic agents. Along the way, I address the gender wage gap, the motherhood penalty, and other gender-based inequities. I focus on the current choices available to modern women and retell their stories from their perspective, just as my grandmother did for me as we sat at her kitchen table on sunny weekend afternoons.

I hope that readers of this book who benefit from their gender or care status increase their awareness and become better allies of women and caregivers, and that they help make the invisible economic lives of women more visible. I aim to inspire us all to tend to the often ignored yet fascinating stories of the women in our own families and lives, and to lift up our communities so that we can all live fully guided by our preferences and personal life goals, now and into the future—no matter our gender.

. . .

All around us, men are labeled using "Mr.," "Dr.," or "Professor," titles that imbue them with authority. Women are also called "Dr." or "Professor," but people are quicker to omit their titles when addressing them. They often are not afforded the same respect as men. In this book I challenge this norm by presenting individuals, women and men, by their first names. This removes authority and prestige and brings in an informality that some may find uncomfortable. But if we were living in a woman's world, a world really built by women, this is what it would feel like. In this vein, I pay my respects to the individuals discussed in this book with the use of their first names.

Binary gender words are used throughout this book, not to intentionally exclude, but rather because most of the research and data I draw on is based on a binary dichotomy. Still, I hope all readers see themselves reflected in these pages.

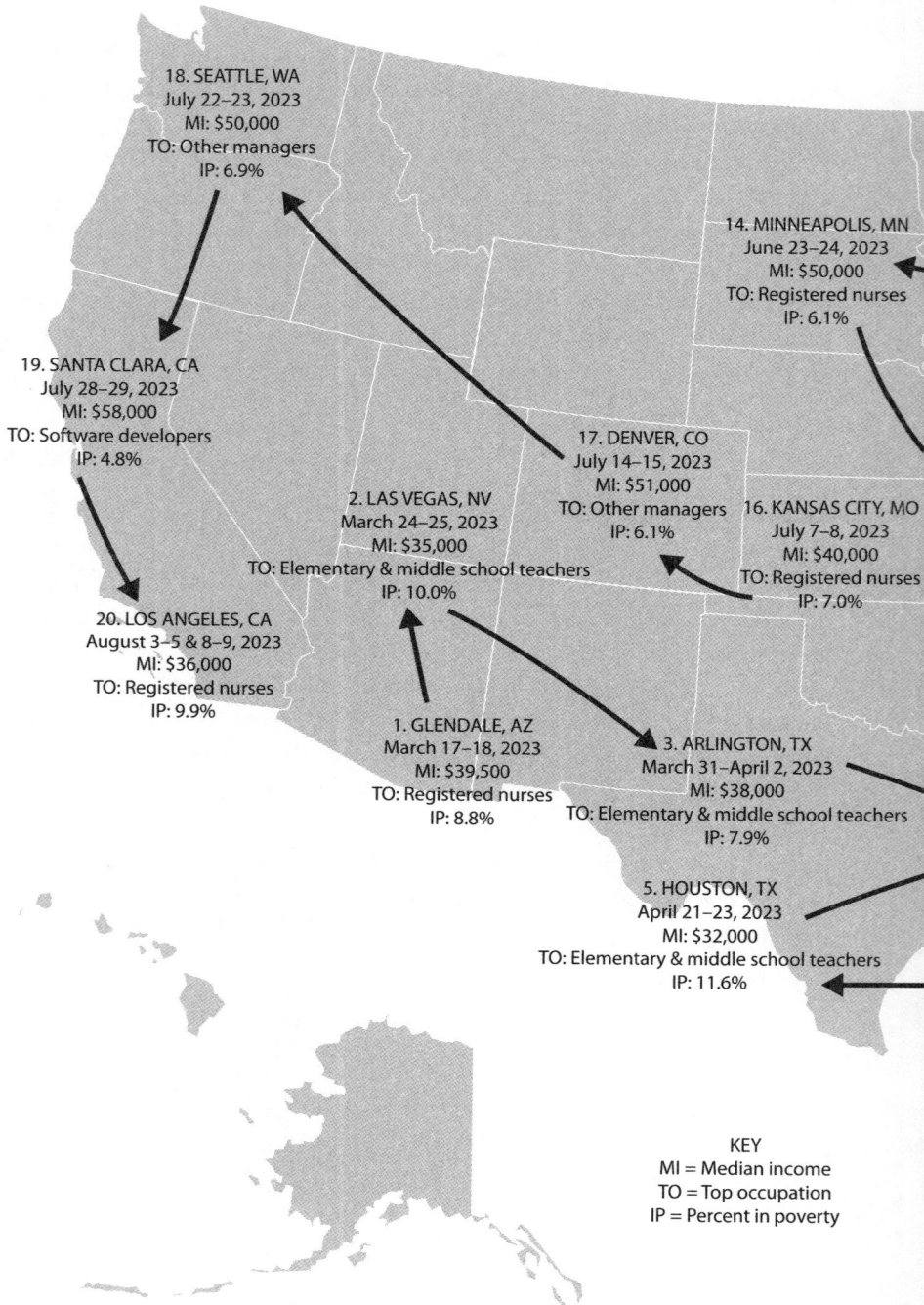

MAP 1. Prime-age women (25–54) in metropolitan areas along the Eras Tour, 2023: median income, top occupation, and percent living in poverty. Source: Author's calculations using the 2023 American Community Survey, US Census Bureau, ipums.org.

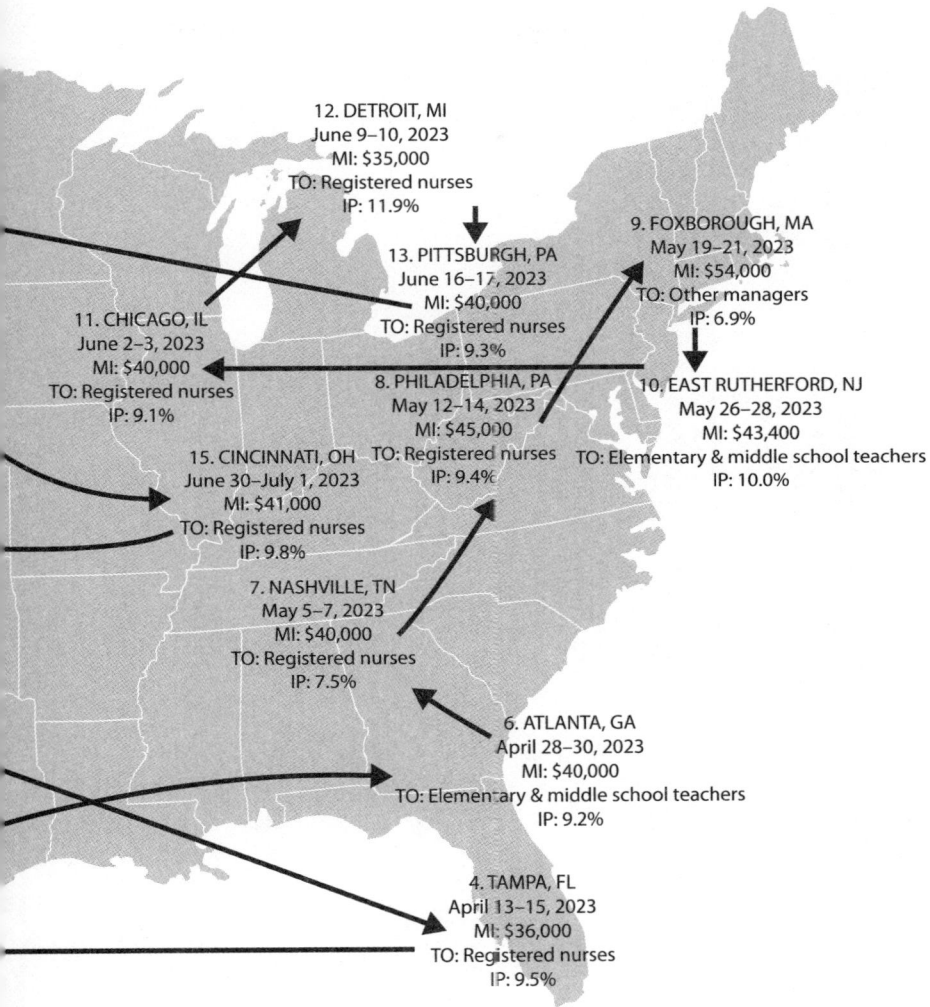

12. DETROIT, MI
June 9–10, 2023
MI: $35,000
TO: Registered nurses
IP: 11.9%

13. PITTSBURGH, PA
June 16–17, 2023
MI: $40,000
TO: Registered nurses
IP: 9.3%

9. FOXBOROUGH, MA
May 19–21, 2023
MI: $54,000
TO: Other managers
IP: 6.9%

11. CHICAGO, IL
June 2–3, 2023
MI: $40,000
TO: Registered nurses
IP: 9.1%

8. PHILADELPHIA, PA
May 12–14, 2023
MI: $45,000
TO: Registered nurses
IP: 9.4%

10. EAST RUTHERFORD, NJ
May 26–28, 2023
MI: $43,400
TO: Elementary & middle school teachers
IP: 10.0%

15. CINCINNATI, OH
June 30–July 1, 2023
MI: $41,000
TO: Registered nurses
IP: 9.8%

7. NASHVILLE, TN
May 5–7, 2023
MI: $40,000
TO: Registered nurses
IP: 7.5%

6. ATLANTA, GA
April 28–30, 2023
MI: $40,000
TO: Elementary & middle school teachers
IP: 9.2%

4. TAMPA, FL
April 13–15, 2023
MI: $36,000
TO: Registered nurses
IP: 9.5%

Introduction

OUR ECONOMIC POWER ERA

> And what has existed since the dawn of time? A patriarchal soci-
> ety. What fuels a patriarchal society? Money, flow of revenue,
> the economy. . . . If we're going to look at this in the most cyni-
> cal way possible, feminine ideas becoming lucrative means that
> more female art will get made. It's extremely heartening.
>
> TAYLOR SWIFT, *Time*, 2023

TAYLOR SWIFT BREATHES LIFE INTO LYRICS. She articulates lived
experiences and perspectives that hover deep in her soul. When we get lucky,
she shares those stories. We see ourselves reflected in them, and our relationship with Taylor the artist grows.

Artists are known for writing, speaking, and singing their truth. Female
artists leave breadcrumbs of their real lives as women loosely sprinkled
throughout their music for fans to devour. Through this artistry, they peace-
fully protest a society built for others. This activism guarantees that women's
stories are seen, heard, and remembered.

Their voices are relatable. They document our legacy. Through their art,
we know we exist. Through our purchasing power, we exercise an economic
strength consuming their art because the art defines us. The Taylor Swift Eras
Tour represented the epitome of our modern-day economic power: millions
of us purchased an experience that was relatable and gave us joy.

Taylor arrived at precisely the right moment. She stood tall and proud on
the peak of this mountain of economic power and agency. She waved down
at us from her stage; "Oh, hi," she would say. She was living her best era yet.
The rest of us stood below, shouting with excitement because she was us, and
we were her. When we rose, she rose, and vice versa. This is representative of

what I call "Swiftynomics," a reality in which women reclaimed a power that had been theirs all along and in which their economic influence in every aspect of society would not go ignored.

OUR SONG

Want to understand the economic power of women today? Listen to Taylor Swift. Even if you are not attracted to all the glitter, cat hair, and pop undertones, listen anyway. Listen to her lyrics intentionally. They will tell you about common lived experiences, from start to finish. They might even help explain why those not interested in the Taylor fandom struggle to understand it, so much so that some are caught off guard as to why and how she wields so much market power.

If this is you, then I invite you to absorb her lyrics, which are filled with meaning. Listen to them closely, or read them, and you will likely find an entirely new, deeper perspective—one that has character and vibrancy and a perspective of hope, frustration, and perseverance. The lyrics tell real stories of what it is like to be a woman in the world, stories we do not often hear in mainstream media, movies, or music and that spark a determination to reclaim space in the world—a demand to be heard, seen, and accepted.

We women are in our economic power era. The secret no one is telling you is that we have always been in this era and still are, including within the results of recent elections. Women have had economic power since the beginning of time. It is not always obvious because our stories are not recorded, not measured, not told, or not told from our perspectives.

Our stories, from our perspectives, are left out of history books. Our stories, when passed down, are retold from someone else's point of view, not ours. In this book, we travel back to the women of our past to gain a roadmap for the future. As our muse, we draw on Taylor Swift, who has repeatedly written and spoken about women through her own lens, sharing a female perspective with passion, power, and economic strength.

My hope is that you see yourselves in these pages and discover how economically powerful you have been all along. During a turbulent time, when the pendulum has swung back toward loud chest-pounding bro-ism in the national media and political circles, it is more important than ever to remember our own strength, the power we have, and the economic contributions we make. We are here and have economic power. We always have. It just might look different than you think.

Taylor's discography is a collection of lived experiences. Her early albums—*Taylor Swift, Fearless, Speak Now,* and *Red*—tell stories from the perspective of a young girl trying to find her way through relationships and life. They explain what it is like to have simple and straightforward desires and expectations of those around you. They describe what it is like to be taken advantage of by someone wiser and older than you. They carry the weight of naïveté and ignorance, the rage that builds with awareness, and the peace that comes from acceptance. They speak to an evolving understanding of independence, work, family, and first loves experienced by so many of us.

As Taylor ages, the lyrics become fuller, more complex. Listen to the words from the next series of albums, where she jumps from country music into pop with *1989, Reputation,* and *Lover.* These lyrics command attention yet are written for no one other than a girl with a guitar. They are a diary of womanhood detailing, first, an explosion into independence and the awareness that comes from realizing the one holding you back from a more desired path might just be yourself. Then the lyrics move on to all the pain that cuts deep when we become aware of others who are intimidated by our success and willing to undermine our worth and value. Structural constraints become clearer. Finally, in *Lover,* we move from high school romance and first-love naïveté to the more deeply complex and freeing relationships of our twenties, relationships that today have more to do with equality of shared space and similar likes than the formalities of marriage and children.

Gen X fans like me waited with open arms for her next foray, with *Folklore, Evermore, Midnights,* and *The Tortured Poets Department (TTPD).* We could not be prouder of who and what these albums represent. We love the active revival of tortured (read: economically successful) women of the past, like Idina Sackville, Rebekah Harkness, and Clara Bow, as seen through the eyes of someone who relates to them deeply, who sees their truth and values their worth enough to share stories from their perspectives in lyrical form.*

* Lady Idina Sackville (1893–1955) lived in England and, eventually, Kenya. She was nicknamed "the bolter" for the number of times she divorced and remarried. It is speculated that her story, written from Idina's perspective, appears on *The Tortured Poets Department* in the song "The Bolter." Rebekah Harkness (1915–1982) is the protagonist of "The Last Great American Dynasty" on the *Folklore* album. A divorcée who married an oil company heir, she inherited his fortune when he died. She was blamed in social circles for not protecting his

Not only does Taylor Swift open the lens of what it is like to walk through the world as female by retelling these women's stories in her lyrics, she also speaks her own truth. Take the song "Who's Afraid of Little Old Me," which screams out a correction of who controls the narrative, who decides crazy, and who is responsible for her fighting those looking to hurt or maim her reputation, her story, and her path in broader society. *The Tortured Poets Department* was introduced to the Eras Tour on May 9, 2024, in Paris, France, with Taylor welcoming her audience to "Female Rage: The Musical." She filed an application to trademark that name two days later.[1]

Taylor's ability to enlighten us and hold our feet to the fire by retelling truer versions of old tales—tales spun by a society that wanted women to be seen and not heard, controlled and not free, dominated and not dominating—is exactly why we should listen closely to her storytelling. She tells us what is critical to know about women in the world. She unrolls stories that are often hidden or pushed into corners and under cobwebs. She exemplifies how girl power has pushed beyond the sisterhood and into the larger economy we all live in.

If you have a teenage daughter, you get it. Given the pressures of social media influencers and a hyperawareness of today's trends, teen girls and young women are pedal-to-the-metal driving consumption patterns, including by spending on music and concerts.[2] And Taylor is smack-dab in the middle of this whirlwind, thriving in the best possible way.

LOVER

When I first started paying attention to Taylor Swift, she was already well past her *Reputation* era and immersed in promoting her album *Lover*. I was intrigued by this megastar who was telling everyone to calm down and making a music video about someone called "The Man." She seemed to have layers of self-confidence, ambition, and wisdom beyond her years. She was unique and unusual in her ability to speak her truth, from her vantage point, and her fans soaked it up. She was authentic, against the odds. Tall, gangly, awkward,

---

health and for burning through his fortune with a group of friends from her youth she called the "bitch pack" in wild parties at their home after his death. Clara Bow (1905–1965) was a famous silent movie actress who became known as "The It Girl" after starring in the movie *It*. She appears in the song bearing her name on *The Tortured Poets Department*.

sparkly, and girly—she had all the characteristics that society so easily dismisses in women. At first blush, one might wonder what she might possibly have to teach me, a professional economist who studies women and work. Turns out, a lot.

More than half of the US adult population (53 percent) claim to be Taylor Swift fans.[3] But even if you are not—maybe you got tired of her showing up at your favorite football team's games or raining down fan-driven consumer spending in hotels and restaurants as her tour landed in your city— I encourage you to read on anyway. Those dismissing her power do so at their peril and lose the opportunity to learn about the changes and adaptations women are making to survive and thrive. She is the modern economic woman's muse. Undercut the strength in her sparkle, assume it to be powerless and shallow, and the joke may just be on you.

With a PhD and more than a dozen years of experience under my belt as a research economist in the federal government, I surround myself with academic economists and economic policy wonks. Many see women narrowly, their view clouded by stereotypical tropes that brand a woman's labor supply (read: the time she spends working for pay) as complex. It is considered complex because women are assumed to be choosing simultaneously between caring for their partners, caring for their family, and paid work. Their choice set, which is full of emotional responsibility, is considered more "difficult" to model.

Men, on the other hand, are seen by economists as simpletons who can always be assumed to be maximizing their time spent in paid work. These assumptions are so strong in economics that the labor economists of the 1970s simply tossed women out of their samples when developing models that predicted or explained labor supply trends in the United States, a practice that lingers in studies today.[4]

Luckily for us, economists like Nobel Prize* winner Claudia Goldin get their hands dirty digging through historical data on women and work. Sleuthing like data scientists turned archeologists, they find data highlighting that the women of today expect—in fact, demand—to have both careers and families at the same time, just as men always have.[5] But even with Claudia as our guide, the broader profession of economics has yet to adapt its models

---

* What is often referred to as the Nobel Prize in Economics is technically called the Sveriges Riksbank Prize in Economic Sciences in Memory of Alfred Nobel. It was first awarded in 1969.

of the home and paid labor into broader macroeconomic thinking that incorporates women's experiences. We have yet to recraft our theories to be representative of the script driving women's agency and economic activity.

IT WAS RARE TO BE THERE

Back in the summer of 2023, I stood in line waiting for a shiny souvenir mirror ball. Everywhere around me, people sparkled. We were in an unabashedly masculine concrete structure, a football stadium with seating for up to almost 80,000 passionate spectators. The group of four school teachers in front of me began a conversation. We exchanged favorite songs and told personal stories about the meaning certain lyrics held for us.

It was early July. The women in line had travelled to Arrowhead Stadium in Kansas City, Missouri, for this once-in-a-lifetime event. They were there for the glitter, good music, and feelings of shared joy and happiness. They were there for the experience, one that would uniquely mark, if not define, this exact moment of their lives.

As we waited for our $20 mirror ball cocktails, suspense grew. Members of the concessions staff looked nervously at each other, calling in desperation for their manager. We arrived at the head of the line to disappointing news: they had filled their last mirror ball cup, the unique souvenir vessel sold in stadiums along the tour. Rumors of a manager frantically searching the stadium for more cups passed through the line. None ever arrived. Even though the concert had not yet started, the demand for anything and everything tour-related was on fire. This energy ran through the entire stadium.

All along the Eras Tour, whether purchasing tickets, merchandise, drinks, or getting into the venue, fans waited patiently in long lines. Even the 1.5 million Ticketmaster users* lucky enough to receive a verified presale fan code waited in historically long virtual waiting rooms to get their tickets.[6] I was one of them.

BAD BLOOD

I was driving to a doctor's appointment the morning of November 15, 2022, when I remembered it was the day ticket sales opened for verified presale fans.

---

* There were 3.5 million fans who registered, the largest registration ever for Ticketmaster.

After almost missing my opportunity, at 10:00 a.m. I jumped in the online cue from the parking lot of my doctor's office. I waited in that virtual cue in what seemed like forever, accidentally booting myself out twice because of clumsy thumbs and a small phone screen. But eight hours later, at 6:00 p.m., my turn finally came. I purchased six tickets for $99 each. I felt like I had won the lottery.

The entire rush to purchase was a fiasco. With extraordinarily long Ticketmaster lines, even some fans who had presale codes showed up on social media crying hysterically because they were not able to purchase tickets. The chaos was so enormous that the US Congress held hearings on the monopolistic aspects of Ticketmaster. A handful of politicians attempted relatability during the hearing by quoting Taylor song lyrics in their speeches and in their questions to Ticketmaster.[7]

Everyone wanted a ticket, an opportunity to enjoy what could be argued was the most thrilling cultural event of our post-pandemic lives. Presale tickets for the concert sold out in two days, with only a subset of verified presale fans being able to purchase them. By November 17, Ticketmaster had cancelled the public sale of tickets that was set to start one day later, on November 18, saying there was not enough inventory left.

Taylor responded publicly on Instagram, saying that "we asked them, multiple times, if they could handle this kind of demand, and we were assured they could. It's truly amazing that 2.4 million people got tickets, but it really pisses me off that a lot of them felt like they had to go through several bear attacks to get them."[3] The long lines and insatiable demand continued through all aspects of the concert experience. The price of resale tickets skyrocketed into the thousands. Merchandise sold out at location after location, as did mirror ball drinks.[9] This was as true in Kansas City, a stop toward the end of the first leg of the US tour, as it was on day one of the tour.

THE 1

Four months after verified fan presale tickets sold out, the Eras Tour began in Glendale, Arizona. It was March 2023.[10] Taylor Swift began singing, dancing, and skipping her way across the country in enormous stadiums historically known for raw, masculine, knock-down drag-out sports brawls. Taylor, along with her dancers, band, and crew, sparkled onto the stage like fireworks on Independence Day. Everywhere she went, media reports followed, documenting the tour's advantage to local economies.[11]

Fans made friendship bracelets to wear and trade, a signature born of her song "You're on Your Own Kid" from *Midnights*. Sales of craft store beads and jewelry categories skyrocketed more than 300 percent in cities with tour stops.[12] Fans traveled long and short distances. They forked out hard-earned money on airfare, gas, hotels, restaurants, and beverages[13]—all for a chance to experience a tour covering all of Taylor Swift's musical eras or, perhaps more accurately, all the critical milestones of a girly life fully emotionally lived.[14]

Fans not lucky enough to get tickets found gigs at stadiums.[15] They sold drinks, ushered people to their seats, and worked security just for a partial glimpse of the show. Others without tickets stood outside stadiums listening to the concert and singing along. Seismographs picked up tremors in Seattle, Washington, and in and around Edinburgh, Scotland, when fans began jumping up and down, dancing with joy.[16] In Munich, Germany, fans camped out on park hills outside the venue, culminating in an additional 40,000 to 50,000 fans without concert tickets listening each night.[17]

As the first leg of her United States tour came to an end in 2023, Taylor made an announcement on *Good Morning America*.[18] With a desire to give those not able to attend the concert live an opportunity to see it, she announced that a three-hour Eras Tour concert film was landing in movie theaters across the US. It would eventually expand to theaters across the globe. Ticket prices were $19.89 for adults and $13.13 for children and seniors, referencing both Taylor's *1989* record album (and the year she was born) and her lucky number thirteen (the day she was born).[19]

The following day, media outlets reported that *Taylor Swift: The Eras Tour* broke AMC Theatres' single-day ticket sale record, with more than $26 million in presale tickets sold in one day.[20] Two weeks later, theater owners were predicting a record $100-million opening for the Eras Tour movie.[21] At least five other movies changed their release dates so as not to compete with the scheduled release on Friday, October 13. The start date for *The Exorcist: Believer* was moved up a week, with producer Jason Blum writing on X (formerly Twitter), "Look what you made me do. The Exorcist: Believer moves to 10/6/23."[22]

The most unanticipated chatter surrounding the movie announcement was the hollow scream of Hollywood executives who were excluded from the deal between Taylor Swift and AMC.[23] Taylor's team had quietly negotiated a deal directly with AMC instead of going through a Hollywood studio broker, cutting studios out of a portion of the profits and demonstrating that theaters had leverage to bring big names to their cinemas without depending on Hollywood. Taylor and her team had single-handedly reinvented the process, blowing up what for decades had been standard protocol in the movie industry.[24] This was not the first time her influence had broken industry protocols and expectations, and it wouldn't be the last.

WE WERE HAPPY

In a multiplier effect of female consumerism, groups of women attended the live concerts and the movie, reiterating the experience with other groups of friends and family members on different dates in other cities. As the fall of 2023 approached, the *Wall Street Journal* zeroed in on the generalized phenomenon of women's accelerated spending power.[25] While it might be simple to chalk this activity up to fandom, the summer of 2023 can best be defined as the summer of the economic woman. With entertainment like the Eras Tour, the *Barbie* movie, and Beyoncé's Renaissance Tour, the purse-string flex that women brought to a town near you was loud and proud and impossible to ignore.

Women's economic might was showing up everywhere. P!nk performed acrobatic stunts across stadium skylines while rocking out to a set list of girl-power songs in her Summer Carnival tour.[26] The US Women's Open tennis championship highlighted the spectacular talent of Coco Gauff, and 3.4 million viewers tuned in to watch, compared with 2.3 million for the US Men's Open.[27] At the FIFA Women's World Cup, fans forked out unprecedented amounts of discretionary spending to travel to Australia and New Zealand to attend games, only one year after women in the US won equal pay in professional soccer.[28]

That summer Beyoncé shone on stage on the Renaissance World Tour, where her daughter Blue Ivy debuted her hard work and talent. Fans everywhere dressed the part in sparkling cowboy hats and silver shine from head to toe. *Renaissance* was an ode to Beyoncé's late cousin Jonny, whom she called her uncle, and to the pioneers of LGBTQIA+ club culture.[29] She was doing something worthy: dominating the music industry while explicitly acting through inclusion, using her fame to push priorities that mattered to her and demonstrating that she is economically powerful enough to control her own narrative.

Beyoncé's tour passed through cities around the world and eventually landed in movie theaters as a concert documentary highlighting the challenges and opportunities of being a Black mother CEO in charge of her own concert tour. Meanwhile, the entertainment industry was preparing to release a movie exposing often toxic gender-driven behaviors that hold women back (and propel others forward): *Barbie* would gross over $1.4 billion globally and turn Greta Gerwig into a household name as the highest-grossing female producer of all time.[30] Around the country, girls and boys, friend groups and couples dressed in their favorite Barbie and Ken pink took in the movie at their local movie theaters.

The marketing geniuses of *Barbie* joined forces with those of *Oppenheimer*, avoiding a clash of the gender titans by suggesting fans see both, and the "Barbenheimer" phenomenon was born. The difference in tone between the two movies could not have been more pronounced. *Barbie* acknowledged a world in which the roles of women and men were rigid yet reversed—in Barbie Land, women ruled the world. But when the characters ventured into the "real world," their experiences of rigid but opposite gender roles were explicit and obvious. The movie leaned into the challenges women face living in a world built for men's advantage through these two juxtaposed worlds. *Oppenheimer* unconsciously demonstrated how we often see the world just through the lens of male privilege by completely ignoring the critical role women played as mathematicians and scientists involved in the atomic bomb's creation. Women's roles in Oppenheimer were restricted to stereotypical supportive roles. The movie, through its dominant male perspective, made it clear that while women shone bright in the summer of 2023, there was, nonetheless, unfinished business.[31] *Oppenheimer* grossed around $850 million worldwide, around 60 percent of *Barbie*'s grossed total.[32] The purse strings were pulling for female content and stories that exposed women's hidden experiences living in a world not built for their advantage.

The excitement continued into the fall with women's collegiate sports. On August 30, the universities of Nebraska and Omaha paired off their women's volleyball teams in Memorial Stadium in Lincoln, Nebraska, home to the men's football team. It was a record-setting event for women's sports, amateur or professional, with more than 92,000 fans in attendance.[33] In a neighboring state, fans broke attendance records at the University of Iowa when more than 55,000 showed up at a preseason exhibition game to watch Caitlin Clark.[34] The mood and hype followed Caitlin through her season and straight into her Women's National Basketball Association debut. Sports bars focusing solely on women's sports began sprouting up across the country, bars like *The Sports Bra* in Portland, Oregon, and *A Bar of Their Own* in Minneapolis, Minnesota.[35]

THAT'S WHEN

Barbie was not without controversy.[36] While it lit up the summer with pink sparkles, traditional award shows remained lukewarm on it, snubbing *Barbie* while raining down awards on the manly aura that was *Oppenheimer*. Be it the Golden Globes, Grammys, British Academy Film Awards, or Screen Actors Guild awards, *Barbie*'s cast and crew won only a third of the time.[37] When nominated for the People's Choice Awards, based on votes by the public rather than industry leaders, *Barbie* won two-thirds of the time.[38]

Almost two decades earlier, the actor Geena Davis took notice of the issues women experienced interacting with leaders in the entertainment industry. In 2004, she created the Geena Davis Institute on Gender in Media. Its purpose is to fund research on bias in Hollywood decision-making after she observed the rigid stereotypical assumptions directors used to cast actors in Hollywood, assumptions that limited everyone, but especially women.[39]

The stark contrast between the preferences of traditional leaders of the film industry and those of the public also sheds light on the reason Reese Witherspoon began leading change. Reese won an award in 2015 for Woman of the Year from *Glamour* magazine. In her acceptance speech, she challenged everyone to think about the limited roles women were allowed to play in Hollywood and highlighted a common line said in a high, squeaky voice by women in movies, a line portraying a damsel in distress: "What are we going to do now?!" She then challenged the audience to think of the real women in their lives and come up with a time when their mothers, sisters, grandmothers, friends, and coworkers had been faced with a problem and responded with a helpless "What are we going to do now?!"[40]

Reese passionately wanted Hollywood to represent the real, lived stories of women. She acted on that goal in 2016, when she co-founded Hello Sunshine, a production company that gave depth and meaning to women's roles in movies and streaming series through the production of *Where the Crawdads Sing*, *Big Little Lies*, and *The Morning Show*, among others. Her latest venture, announced June 13, 2025, at Cannes Lions, is Sunnie, a production company focused on highlighting the voices of Gen Z women with an advisory board of teenage girls.[41] Reese's passion for representation of real women in the entertainment industry knows no bounds. We see more women today in lead roles in movies and streaming, roles that have depth and meaning, thanks to the efforts of Reese and other women who want change.

Historically, women's perspectives have rarely dominated content in the entertainment industry, and the same is true in the media. This was the reason Emily Ramshaw and Amanda Zamora joined forces to start the newsroom The 19th*, founded after Hillary Clinton's loss in the 2016 presidential race.[42] The 19th* was named after the Nineteenth Amendment of the Constitution, which gave women the right to vote. The asterisk in its name denotes the fact that there was still work to be done for women of color in terms of voting equity after the amendment passed. The 19th* is a nonprofit dedicated to covering news stories affecting women and the LGBTQIA+ community, stories that often go untold in mainstream media.

These intentional pathways to more informed news of and knowledge about women's real, lived perspectives have sprung up as women's economic might has grown and taken up more space in the marketplace. Women are demanding more from a society that has historically not taken them seriously and that has regarded their contributions and spending power as bound to purchasing goods for the household and as otherwise irrelevant. But as we will see, women's talent and stories are anything but unmarketable and irrelevant.

Anu Duggal, one of the founders of the Female Founders Fund, sees opportunity in investing in women's ideas, just as Taylor Swift saw value in singing about teen experiences early on in her career. Anu invests early in untapped innovations she thinks are likely to return a profit, mining the fresh concepts and talent that society has traditionally undervalued due to sexism, implicit bias, and misogyny. Like Anu Duggal, Taylor Swift, Beyoncé, Reese Witherspoon, Geena Davis, Emily Ramshaw, and Amanda Zamora have all tapped into this space with vigorous energy and seen positive returns.[43] They bet on women's potential. They see real women, document their realities in meaningful and profound ways, and invest in and help develop their good ideas.

But even these strides exist within the reality of a dominant culture that has historically minimized women's experiences, a reality that has allowed a convicted felon guilty of sexually assaulting women the privilege of rising to the office of the US presidency.[44] A reality that allows a male comedian to make distasteful sexist jokes that write women off or minimize their power, like the comments made about the *Barbie* movie and Taylor Swift during the 2024 Golden Globes.[45] Some are still betting on society as a whole to accept misogyny as unobjectionable and even funny—perhaps because it might be all they know.

TELL ME WHY

Society generally has a narrow view of what economists do. We are not all experts in finance, or macroeconomic masters like Claudia Sahm, famous for inventing the Sahm Rule, a tool that helps the Federal Reserve identify incoming recessions.[46] Macroeconomists inform decisions about whether to raise or pull back interest rates to stabilize prices and when and how to encourage full employment, but they are only a subset of economists. Other economists study marriage, education, parenthood, poverty and inequality, games, sports, and even gang behavior.[47] The breadth of our studies is vast.

Economists are passionate about modeling human behavior. We care about big-world views, like understanding how families make decisions within the real constraints of their household budgets, or how businesses thrive by minimizing expenses in order to maximize utility and profits.* We excel at finding mathematical derivatives, but some of us struggle to balance a checkbook. Currency, for the economist, is nothing but a means to an end. When you enter a market as a consumer, you often barter and exchange some currency with a producer or seller of a good. Whether you use dollars or trade old baseball cards to pay for the item you want, economists care most about the act of the exchange and your use of the limited resources available to you. The dollar or currency is simply a mechanism or throughway, a means to an end. We also obsess about eliminating waste and being very clear about whether A caused B.

I study microeconomics by researching how people share family resources and how control over the allocation of these resources shifts based on who paid for them or brought them into the home. I study how the social rules embedded in laws and policies that govern major life events like marriage and divorce influence how families distribute resources within the household. I

---

* Utility refers to satisfaction or pleasure derived from consuming goods and services. An individual's preferences for goods and services drive their utility. Households and businesses can minimize costs by focusing consumption on their preferences, which, in turn, maximizes their utility.

examine how structural constraints like sexism change behavior and how control over household resources affects our ability to thrive. In a nutshell, I study how businesses, households, and cultural expectations encourage or discourage women's well-being.

In these pages, I employ the tool of economics, broadly defined, to understand women in society—how they show up for themselves, their friends and family, and the larger community. If I stopped at that, this book might not be engaging enough for you to want to keep reading. So I am combining my two biggest passions, pop culture and economics, to demonstrate how women have been masterminding and redefining the economy all along. Our muse for this adventure is none other than the talented superstar Taylor Swift.

This book covers other major themes, including reinvention, survival, misogyny, invisible labor, generational transmissions, motherhood, self-investment, and negotiation and planning. It explores "Swiftynomics," which I define as the power of harnessing women's experiences and voices to advance economic growth, development, and equity. I highlight the ways in which bold, brave women are reshaping industries, highlighting inequities, and living their best lives, against the odds. Whether women work in the formal labor market or not, women as economic actors are all around us. We merely need to open our eyes to see their daily activities as economic in nature.

This book is about the everyday woman as much as it is about the famous women blazing trails around us. We should all see ourselves in these stories. This is the magic of Taylor Swift. She is untouchable yet relatable. She succeeds because we see ourselves in her lyrics. She tells the world the stories of how women thrive economically every day.

In these pages, you will read about famous artists and not-so-well-known women. I explain how they survive and thrive, and what commonalities we share in thinking about how women across the globe engage with the world around them. Women are continuously masterminding and reinventing themselves. Era to era, they evolve. We all have this in common. We all reinvent. We all mastermind when we cannot get what we want or need in the moment. It is what keeps us alive. It is what keeps us present, and it is the heart of "Swiftynomics." Welcome to the journey.

———

ONE

Reinvention

(TAYLOR'S VERSION)

And now I realize this is just what happens to a woman in music
if she achieves success beyond people's comfort level.

TAYLOR SWIFT,
2019 *Billboard* Woman of the Decade Award Speech

AT THE END OF THE MUSIC video for her song titled "Look What You Made Me Do" from her *Reputation* album, fifteen different Taylors appear next to each other in an airplane hangar, in front of a black plane with "Reputation" spray-painted on it.[1] There are Red Taylor, 1989 Taylor, and Debut Taylor, to name a few. Each has her own persona and style. The lyrics of this song speak to drastic, determined reinvention, including lyrics boldly claiming a rise from the dead, or that the old Taylor is unavailable because she is dead. These reinvented Taylors provide evidence of how Taylor the artist transverses life, at least in her public persona, shedding one skin to harness the next layer of transformation.

Taylor has continuously reinvented her own image and whole-heartedly leaned into reinvention as a superpower. Women in societies across the globe understand the continual need for reinvention because we do it all the time, for survival and to advance in our careers and families. In this chapter, I cover what reinvention means and why women reinvent for survival. Reinvention is, in fact, our best secret weapon. It has propelled many of us forward and led us to increased economic agency.

LOOK WHAT YOU MADE ME DO

Taylor's career officially began in country music. She was a teenager who had been obsessed with pursuing a singing career since her childhood.[2] She was not influential at first; she had to work for that, and knowing she wanted to be a singer so early in life did not protect her from having to reinvent herself, repeatedly.

At the age of sixteen, Taylor made her mark on the Nashville country music scene with a debut album, but country music could not contain her for long.[3] After releasing subsequent albums every two years, in 2014 she took a big risk with *1989*, her first big step toward reinventing herself by moving into non-country genres.

As an early reinventionista, she proceeded with caution, first playing her new songs for friends and family in her home, then hosting *1989* secret sessions with superfans in New York, Los Angeles, Nashville, and London.[4] Country artists at the time did not transition into other genres, yet Taylor had success moving into pop music.[5] This would be just the beginning of Taylor's reinvention story.

Whether it was a musical genre or her image, as Taylor aged, she continued to reinvent. Perhaps her most drastic reinvention happened after the 2009 Video Music Awards, when a male singer got up on stage and unexpectedly took the microphone away from her to say that Beyoncé should have won the award.[6] It did not stop there. The male singer hyper-focused on Taylor and in 2016 brought his wife, Kim Kardashian, into the fold; he and Kim falsely accused Taylor of lying in a phone call about getting permission to use Taylor in the husband's lyrics, and she called her a snake.[7] This eventually led to Taylor reclaiming snake imagery on her *Reputation* album. That entire episode led to a lengthy break out of the spotlight, but Taylor came back swinging with a new album, *Reputation*. She worked through all that had happened to ruin her reputation, and a bold I-deserve-this-space Taylor came back fighting and won.

Then, in 2019, Taylor's label was purchased, and the masters of her first six albums, including *Reputation*, were sold without her consent.[8] Unhappy that others in the industry were controlling her artistry and music, she spoke out publicly, directly to her fans, first asking them to help convince her prior label to allow her to sing a medley of songs from her first six albums at the American Music Awards ceremony—where she was going to be acknowledged with the Artist of the Decade award—and second, to allow her music to be used in an upcoming Netflix documentary titled *Miss Americana*.

After public encouragement from singer Kelly Clarkson and others, Taylor decided to regain control of her music by rerecording her first six albums.[9] Owners and leadership at her old label tried to negotiate with her, offering to give her access to her albums "if she didn't record 'copycat versions' of her old songs and if she stopped talking about them altogether."[10]

Taylor again took to social media, saying, "The message being sent to me is very clear . . . be a good little girl and shut up. Or you'll be punished."[11] Taylor was not willing to negotiate access to her autonomy and moved forward with the laborious act of rerecording old albums to regain control of them.

Taylor's reinvention story has always been driven by a belief in her artistry and a refusal to be bullied or controlled by those with legal paper rights to her catalogue but no rights to her talent. She focused on communicating her issues publicly to garner support after private discussions failed. Fans and the larger community stepped in to support Taylor's fight. Rerecorded albums carry the same name as the original followed by *(Taylor's Version)*. Radio stations began playing *(Taylor's Version)* albums instead of the originals, and fans began listening to them on streaming services. Against the odds, Taylor had won, again.

On May 30, 2025, after rerecording four of her early albums, and backed by the financial success of the Eras Tour, Taylor announced that she had bought back the rights to her originals and now, finally, owned her entire music catalogue. Fans celebrated by streaming the music they had been boycotting for so long. *Reputation* moved to number one on iTunes, and Taylor's old music dominated at least four spots in the top ten. By June 9, 2025, *Reputation* the album reentered the top five on the Billboard 200. After all the struggle, reinventions, and masterminding, Taylor had successfully reclaimed both her *name* and *reputation*.[12]

Taylor continues to incorporate her struggles into her music, and fans continue to show up for her because her struggles are relatable. The prior owner of her earlier masters, on the other hand, retired from his role as a music manager on June 17, 2024, after losing other high-profile clients like Ariana Grande and Demi Lovato.[13]

Taylor Swift, Beyoncé, Mon Laferte, and P!nk, to name a few, are current-day examples of women who take control of their talent and power to rewrite the script of an entire industry, including the script of how they merge motherhood with work. P!nk's latest documentary shows how she balances concert touring with her spouse and children.[14] Beyoncé's recent concert film talks about the challenges of combining motherhood and touring, and about her decision to allow her daughter to have a job and role on stage.[15] Mon Laferte, a Chilean living in Mexico, recently produced a Netflix documentary highlighting how she blended pregnancy with work and touring.[16]

Women artists are successful because others see themselves in their artistry, buy their albums, attend their concerts, purchase their merchandise, and follow them on social media. They succeed because they are active agents in determining how they will balance family and children with career, often choosing a nontraditional path that allows their roles as mothers to fluidly interact with their professional personas. They are nimble and flexible because the constraints imposed on them by their industry are rigid.

"Swiftynomics," the art of escaping the confines that limit women's economic fulfillment, recognizes women's power and autonomy and encourages women to follow their gut. Because we live in a world overwhelmingly constructed for the convenience of men, women must often change paths in order to overcome barriers to success and fulfillment. Eve Rodsky, author of the *New York Times* bestseller *Fair Play*, a book about invisible labor in the home, is one of many women leaning into reinvention.

A PLACE IN THIS WORLD

When I first met Eve, I knew immediately that she was cool and spunky, with a burning desire to make change. Eve is a Harvard-trained lawyer who left a demanding career to better balance work and family. Her "greedy job" at a high-powered law firm—a job that was inflexible, that required to be her first priority, and that demanded long hours at the office—pulled at her time and restricted her availability for family. Having two equally demanding jobs, one in the office and another at home, which constantly tugged on the limited hours she had in a day, was not for her.[17] She was determined to forge her own path and not let the challenges of a society built for someone else define her.

Along her path to reinvention, Eve started a movement. She wrote *Fair Play*, which details the disproportionate burden mothers often hold in household management and family caregiving, even when they also have jobs or professional lives. Life experiences can either hold us down or help us advance, and the story of Eve's youth provides insights into the art of escaping traditional societal confines and the power of harnessing our lived experiences to thrive.

The child of a single mom, Eve was in eighth grade when she took on the task of opening the family's mail and managing household bills. One day she opened a truancy letter from the New York City Department of Education. Eve had missed enough school days that the city declared her truant. Her mom did not know she had been skipping class. Eve hid this letter, and her mother never found out.

Some time after that, her mother forced her to take the entrance exam for Bronx Science and Brooklyn Tech high schools. According to Eve, "It wasn't an option. I could be truant. I could be wild. I could do all the things I was doing, but I had to sit for the test. I got into Bronx Science."[18] When Eve told her teachers, they did not believe her. They thought she had cheated.

Bronx Science was two and a half hours from Eve's home. She would have to take the M line and a bus, walk three long avenues, then take the L train and another bus to finally arrive at the school. The night before school was to start, Eve's mother received a notice. Another parent had challenged the scores for a different elite school, one located just across from their home, which resulted in a handful of students being reevaluated for admission. The school was offering Eve a slot.

Eve believes her trajectory changed that day. Living across the street from school led to fewer temptations to skip. Being surrounded by smart, highly motivated high schoolers pushed Eve to take academics seriously. But always the contrarian, as her classmates competed for spots in Harvard's incoming class, Eve choose the University of Michigan.

While her classmates at Michigan partied, Eve focused on studying hard. Having attended an elite high school in New York helped Eve stay on task. According to her, "Being in that [high school] environment for sure was [a] reinvention."[19] Over the years, Eve would reinvent herself multiple times. From college, she went on to law school at Harvard. She graduated, married, took a demanding job in corporate law, had children, got exhausted with the simultaneous demands of home and paid work life, quit her corporate job, wrote a book, started to advocate for gender equality within the home, and founded the Fair Play Policy Institute, a nonprofit dedicated to creating awareness of the effects of unpaid labor on women's lives.[20]

She wrote a second book, led mentoring and mediation workshops for couples, and became the lead in a documentary directed by Jennifer Siebel Newsom, First Partner of California, filmmaker, advocate, and herself a mother of four.[21] The documentary, based on Eve's book *Fair Play*, streamed on Apple TV in July 2022.[22] Today, Eve continues to explore and reach for activities that stretch, pull, and push her, allowing her to live her best blended professional and personal life. She gave up on living a life defined by the boundaries of what is easy for men so that she could successfully live her best life on her own terms, in a world that values her time, effort, and priorities in their entirety.

Reinvention begins with a roadblock. Reinvention happens, for example, when one graduates with a law degree and then has a child and discovers one would rather stay at home with the baby than be in litigation all day long. It occurs when children become adults and stay-at-home parents decide to jump back into the paid labor market. Moving to a more flexible job to manage childcare or eldercare responsibilities can be a reinvention. Reinvention happens when musicians jump genres, like Taylor did from country to pop music. Reinventions drive our leaps from era to era. Most of us have experienced some form of reinvention in our lifetime—a change in the life path we thought we would take.

When women get stuck in life, many reinvent themselves within their careers, families, and communities. My research team and I surveyed around 300 respondents and asked if they had ever reinvented themselves along their career paths.* Weighted to represent the US adult population, nine out of ten adults (89.8 percent) surveyed said yes. Ninety-one percent (90.9 percent) of women with an advanced degree had reinvented their careers (the percentage was similar for men), compared to 81.2 percent for women with less than an advanced degree. The top reasons respondents gave for reinventing were lack of opportunity to advance in the professional direction they desired and experiences that stifled their ability to grow.[23] Others reinvented to better align work with personal life.

Reinvention is a fact of life. In our careers and work, most of us do it. Many women and parents feel shame or disappointment when they need to move on from one job or career to another, but reinvention does not mean we have failed. It means we are alive, moving forward, and growing.

Our economy has evolved from being primarily driven by manufacturing and agriculture to being a demand-driven service economy. This is due to economic growth and development brought about over time by increases in educational attainment and other factors. The jobs of our parents and grandparents are not like the jobs many adults hold today. Our economy continues to reinvent itself. As it does, our capacities, skills, aspirations, and goals evolve with it. It should come as no surprise that with elevated levels of education and innovations in all sectors, employees aspire to more. They also grow with

---

* The survey defined career reinvention as switching employers, bosses, jobs, industries, or education toward a new or different theme, focus, or topic.

these changes in the economy. If employers do not provide them with opportunities, they will find them elsewhere.

Throughout history, women have used their talents, skills, and wits to support issues, ideas, entertainment, and communities that are important to them. Women from regionally diverse areas and experiences all have something in common—a dedication to determining their economic agency in the world, a world that was not built for their convenience.[24] Women are multifaceted and underappreciated in the labor market.

The labor market was built for those with care privilege. Care privilege is the advantage that comes from being able-bodied but having others cover your daily care needs, like making your meals, washing your clothes, cleaning your home, and caring for your children.[25] The care-privileged often have no problem working 9:00 a.m. to 5:00 p.m., Monday through Friday, or longer hours if needed. They do not have to figure out childcare. They are not constrained by school drop-offs and pickups. They advance in what is referred to as "greedy jobs" because others take care of their survival needs.[26]

Women often find themselves in a bind when they attempt to work for pay in a labor market built by and for those with care privilege, because women rarely have care privilege at home. Often, traditional behaviors, expectations, and norms on the part of employers, industry, and even their own families hold women back from maximizing their career potential. When it comes to reinvention as a mechanism that can help us thrive despite misogynistic behaviors in the workplace, we have a lot to learn from Taylor Swift. She has adapted genres and forced big changes in the music and entertainment industries because of her reinventions. These changes have pushed her forward, helping her thrive and advance along her own path. She uses her agency and the support of those around her to improve and reinvent. Many of us could benefit by mimicking her bravery and attitude toward a society not necessarily built for us.

IT'S TIME TO GO

At age eighteen, very few of us know what we want to do with the rest of our lives. Even when we think we do, life often gets in the way. Maybe your partner gets a great job offer in another state and you unexpectedly move, or the labor market is saturated with people seeking jobs in your field once you graduate from college or technical school. Perhaps you have children and your life priorities change, or you cannot find affordable childcare and need to adjust. Life always takes us down unexpected paths. The best we can do is to recognize the need for change, acknowledge that reinvention is a common human experience and an even more common female and caregiver experience and own it.

Reinvention gets us unstuck. It keeps us moving forward when others might like us to stay right where we are so that they can continue to benefit from traditional power structures. Reinvention can make us more productive. It can put us in a fresh environment that better supports our mental and physical well-being. It can even lead to breakthroughs. Failure or change is often a key to eventual success. Just look to science. Scientists generally assume it is necessary to try multiple experiments or paths before finally finding the route to success. The same is true with one's career and life.

The need for reinvention comes about not because the world is divided into men and women, old and young, but rather because people are diverse and come to the table with differing needs, wants, and perspectives. For example, the easy way to explain gender inequality is to believe, simply, that men hold women back. But this view is not empowering toward women and is often wrong. Misogynistic behavior holds women back. This behavior can be found everywhere, including where you least expect it, and to some extent within everyone.

Reinvention, and the belief that "Swiftynomics" is alive and well, exists because there are people in power, of all genders and diverse characteristics, who choose to support women living their fullest life outside of and within traditional gendered expectations when it suits them. Some of my best mentors, people who opened doors for me, have been men who share this belief. Some of my more ardent obstructionists have been women who felt I was too bold and assertive and was not following the informal rules for how I should act; I was acting "too male."

We are driven by the external environmental challenges we face, our responses to them, and, more generally, how we choose to show up on any given day. What we can learn from Taylor, from her ability to reinvent given the challenges she has faced, is the simple idea that our responses to the challenges in front of us matter. How true we are to ourselves, how we respond to each situation we are presented with, big or small, affects both the era we are currently in and our next reinvention.

The more awareness we can develop to anticipate some of these environmental barriers and call them out for what they are—meaning we actively choose not to internalize them or react with shame, as though the barrier is our fault—is very powerful for women and caregivers. It influences our ability to be present and advance with a complete, whole identity. It drives our ability to succeed in the one life we are given. It gets us to reinvention faster by shedding that which does not serve us, increasing the chances that we end up living our best life.

STAY, STAY, STAY

Taylor's continual reinvention has meant that her fan base is wide, diverse, and representative of the US population across various demographics.[27] More than 129 million US adults identify as Taylor Swift fans. Her popularity is driven by the arc of her discography, which encompasses our emotional experiences as we age.[28] Her music speaks of high school romance and tearful breakups, first loves, vengeance and revenge, rage, loss, and forgiveness. As Taylor's music ages and matures, her fans age and mature with her. As she rerecords, younger generations are exposed to her youthful talent, which remains relatable to their experiences today.

It is no surprise that the Eras Tour raked in around $4 billion dollars on its North American tour alone, smashing records and exploding expectations.[29] Taylor reportedly maintained control of around 85 percent of the revenue from her tour—something previously unheard of in the music industry.[30] The benefit to local economies driven by her concerts was well documented.[31]

Communities saw increases in local spending everywhere the tour went. Cincinnati estimated that an additional $48 million flowed into the city around the days of the concerts. Denver declared an additional $140 million. Los Angeles claimed $320 million in revenue-boosting activity.[32] The US Federal Reserve even noted the impact of the Eras Tour on buttressing the local hotel industry in Philadelphia.[33] Across the pond, London gained an estimated $314 million dollars in local spending when the tour descended on Wembley Stadium for a total of eight magical nights.[34] Taylor has proven that, when one stays true to one's authentic self, the power of reinvention is often lucrative.

> The hundreds or thousands of dumb ideas that I have had are what led me to my good ideas. You have to give yourself permission to fail. . . . Go easy on yourself and make the . . . choices that feel right for you.
>
> TAYLOR SWIFT, 2023 iHeart Radio Music Awards Speech

TWO

Survival

MISS AMERICANA & THE HEARTBREAK PRINCE

Somewhere right now your future woman of the year is probably sitting in a piano lesson or a girls' choir. And today, right now, we need to take care of her.

TAYLOR SWIFT,
2014 *Billboard* Woman of the Year Award Speech

LIKE TAYLOR SWIFT, MANY WOMEN who are in their thirties are still in the process of partnering up. Their education, careers, and jobs have allowed them a level of independence that improved their life partner searches and raised the bar they set for a possible match. Instead of partnering with someone for economic survival, as previous generations might have done, these women look for someone with whom they share common interests. They also often search for a match that provides greater equity within the household.

Even as the tradwife lifestyle gains viewership online and influencers tap into viewers' emotional rage by encouraging strict gender roles, young women today tend to look for a partner who has similar consumption preferences, rather than someone who will provide for them financially. This is driven by shifts in social norms, increases in women's educational attainment, and reductions in overt sexism in the workplace. Increased educational attainment of women over the past century has led to increased economic independence and agency.

As more women get college degrees and have access to multiple birth control options and career paths, they put off coupling. Whether intentional or not, this practice increases their economic agency over the entire arc of their lifetime. It gives them more economic power and independence, not only in their twenties, but for the rest of their lives.

While the Eras Tour walks us through the diverse eras of Taylor's life and career, it does more than that. It represents a modern woman's collection of lived experiences. This chapter focuses on how today's Miss Americana survives in an environment built for the Heartbreak Prince. The male-dominated profession of economics serves as an example of how male perspectives often define the world around us, and it highlights the strategies women use to thrive, against the odds, in these spaces. This chapter explores the ways women make professional spaces better, and how they thrive in challenging environments.

To understand the profession of economics, it is important to understand the foundation on which modern economic theory is built: the man, the market, and the invisible hand.

MR. PERFECTLY FINE

Adam Smith, considered a father of modern economics, created the concept of an invisible hand guiding the economy and market activity. Adam argued in his book *The Wealth of Nations* that policies directing the baker to bake and the butcher to prepare the meat are not needed because they will do these tasks of their own free will and agency, selfishly, in order to acquire resources and wealth so as not to perish. The invisible hand guided by human instinct for survival will thus guarantee a functioning market and efficient economy. Adam Smith has had a stranglehold on modern economics, but in 2016, journalist Katrine Marçal published an interesting book titled *Who Cooked Adam Smith's Dinner?*

Adult Adam lived with his mother, Margaret Douglas. She was a strong daily presence in his life. She made his meals, cleaned up after him, and washed his clothes. All this activity, economic in nature if done in the market outside the home for pay, was invisible to Adam in his economic writings. He ignored the activity of his own mother and its role in providing time for the baker to bake, the butcher to prepare the meat, and Adam to write down his theories.[1] How can Adam's mother ever benefit from an invisible hand eliminating gender discrimination from markets if not even Adam incorporates the value of his mother's contributions to the market into his theories?

We struggle with this today. Our modern economic statistics continue to be silent as to the value of unpaid family labor, ignoring the economic contributions of women and caregivers in both theory and practice. The only way we value them in practice is through comparisons to the lives and experiences of men. And here, we often fail.

Modern economic theory has two polarizing perspectives when it comes to gender and the economy. The first is to argue that gender is not a driver of inequality, but rather that inequalities in other characteristics drive observed gender disparities. This argument claims that gendered inequalities will not exist once inequalities among other characteristics are addressed. For example, when women's educational attainment increases, gendered disparities in the labor market tend to decrease. While economists seem to have embraced this perspective, it ignores women's realities by assuming gender inequality will disappear once women begin looking more like men—that is, once their characteristics align with those of men. But women are not men, and economists largely ignore the unique contributions and additive strengths women bring to a productive economy.

A second argument posits that gendered inequalities do exist but that they arise out of efficiency. Shelly Lundberg, Leonard Broom Professor of Demography and Distinguished Professor of Economics at the University of California Santa Barbara, once mentioned that Gary Becker, the 1992 Nobel Memorial Prize in Economic Sciences winner and an economics professor at the University of Chicago, was influenced by his wife when developing his very famous models of marriage and family.[2] He sought to explain in theory what he observed in his own household, which was that his wife was good at household production tasks and he was good at economics. It was, therefore, rational for women to focus on domestic work and men to focus on work outside the home. Each person could specialize and perfect their gendered role and the family would be better off, more efficient.

Our ability to see beyond our own experiences is often limited, and this is just as true for economists as anyone else. The role of gender in today's economy, at least in the dominant traditional schools of economic thought, are driven by economic theory developed in the past by men. We continue to wait for economic theories based on women as economic agents, rather than women in supporting roles envisioned by men, to gain traction in traditional Ivy League schools.[3] Miss Americana is patiently waiting for her Heartbreak Prince to recognize his flaws.

THE MAN

Traditional models of economics originated in the mid-nineteenth century and assumed the existence of a generic non-gendered economic agent called *Homo economicus. Homo economicus* was born in 1836 to John Stuart Mill and was later promoted by other (male) economists of the time.[4] A nineteenth-century ideal, *Homo economicus*'s primary pursuit in life was to minimize costs while maximizing profits or earnings in business. Its goal was to maximize satisfaction or pleasure, called utility.[5] It was ageless, colorless, genderless, and identity-less. To top it off, *Homo economicus* was something of a mathematical wiz, propelling linear algebra, calculus, and real analysis to the front of the classroom, where they became the gold standard in modern economics.

In the twentieth century, *Homo economicus* grew some cojones and began to be known as "Economic Man." Math became prioritized as the most efficient, least biased, and fastest method for accomplishing his primary pursuit in life—minimizing consumption of items and activities he does not like or need so that he can maximize consumption of things he does.

To understand this, think about your own consumption patterns. Your primary consumption goal might be to purchase the biggest, best truck you can. Or maybe it is being able to afford the biggest, best home within a friend or acquaintance group, so you can flex your homeowner status. It might be owning the most parent-approved career, one that gives you leverage over your siblings and parents. For parents, it might be the best education or childcare for your children. For Economic Man, every moment is spent in the pursuit of maximizing pleasure and experiences that bring joy.

CLEAN

Japanese organizing consultant Marie Kondo took the world by storm with the simple, sure-fire strategies outlined in her 2014 book *The Life-Changing Magic of Tidying Up: The Japanese Art of Decluttering and Organizing* and in her 2016 title, *Spark Joy: An Illustrated Master Class on the Art of Organizing and Tidying Up*.[6] If you were drawn to the organizational strategies and cleaning methods of Marie Kondo, you may just be an economist, a great-grandchild of Economic Man.

Marie's method of keeping only those things that spark joy and losing everything else—considering it waste—sums up the entire platform of modern economics. It absolutely nails the original spirit of the men who built modern economics. Note, however, that Marie did not feel the need to flex by using math.

But just as there are limitations to Economic Man's version of modern economic theory, I suspected that Marie Kondo's vision of tidying up could not last. It was not sustainable, mostly because efficiency can be exhausting, overwhelming, and unrealistic in real life, especially for women who juggle multiple roles inside and outside the home. In 2023, after having her third child and while promoting her newest book, Marie admitted to the *Washington Post* that her previously tidy, organized home was now messy.[7] An invisible hand only goes so far when faced with the realities and complexities of the real life of caregivers. A short nine years removed from the wildfire sensation that was the Kondo method, it seems the real world caught up with her. She learned the realities of "Economic Woman," who had been there all along, waiting in the shadows. The strict mathematical efficiency of Economic Man can feel magical and alluring, but it is ultimately unsustainable in real life. Economic Woman has known this all along.

NO BODY, NO CRIME

Modern economic theory rests on a core assumption of neutrality and an "all else equal" attitude. Using math, the field of economics has attempted to remove itself from the need to deal with the messy business of values, biases, and prejudices. But stripping irrationality out of human behavior by acting as if math can represent how humans will act in real-world scenarios has been questioned for some time.[8] University of Chicago economist Richard Thaler, 2017 recipient of the Nobel Memorial Prize in Economic Sciences, in his book *Misbehaving: The Making of Behavioral Economics* quoted Columbia University economist Richard Nelson (1930–2025) as saying, "The purely economic man is indeed close to being a social moron. Economic theory has been much preoccupied with this rational fool."[9]

University of Chicago professor Gary Becker famously used the concept of mathematical optimization to argue that discrimination would go away on its own without state or community intervention because it did not align with the profit-maximizing behavior of firms (and families).[10] One does not have to look far to find examples throughout history in which discriminatory behavior has proven very sticky, maximization and efficiency be damned.

There is never a guarantee that maximizing profits will lead to reduced discrimination even when it makes "economic" sense, unless, maybe, you are Taylor Swift. When Taylor began dating a Kansas City Chiefs' tight end, there was loud backlash from a subset of football fans.[11] These "dads, Brads, and Chads" felt uncomfortable that their bro-gathering sports-viewing sessions were incorporating the megastar entertainer in their coverage.[12] The heat was so intense that the National Football League commissioner, the Chiefs' head coach, and other popular pundits made official statements of support for Taylor's attendance at games and the coverage it generated.[13]

The NFL had for years been focused on increasing its viewership and getting younger generations interested in the game.[14] Taylor is argued to have single-handedly increased viewership among women, younger audiences, and male Swifties who were not into football. Viewership of Chiefs games increased by around 7 percent in 2023.[15] In response, the NFL supported her attendance at games publicly. Taylor brought in fans and revenue the NFL had been unsuccessfully trying to garner since the early 2000s.[16]

The NFL realized that even though a small subset of loud traditional fans complained about Taylor, these fans would not abandon their sports viewership solely because of her attendance at games. Instead, the NFL bet on Taylor's power to drive new fans to the game and their revenues. They continued to refine coverage of her at games throughout the season, a bottom-line-driven business decision.

I BET YOU [DON'T] THINK ABOUT ME

The real world is complex and messy, yet macroeconomic models of the economic behavior of households continue to lack any connection to reality. The original models advanced by economists like Paul Samuelson in the 1950s assumed every person in the household was identical—a twin, if you will—and, as such, behaved in exactly the same way.[17] Think about your friends and family and try to come up with one example where this idea holds—where everyone in the household thinks, feels, acts, and prioritizes resources in exactly the same way. The only realistic example I can think of is a household of one.

After Samuelson, the most entrenched economic models of the household come, again, from University of Chicago professor Gary Becker. Gary quickly moved on from the unsatisfying theory of a household of identical individuals to a model that featured one 1950s, *Leave It to Beaver*–style benevolent dictator, usually a man, in charge of household resources.[18] This model assumes one person in the home controls all household resources but chooses benevolence over selfishness in deciding how to distribute those resources, taking into account the well-being of other adults and children in the household in a "selfless" manner.

Even though there were women and children around these benevolent dictators who might have disagreed that this model accurately represented them, there are many white men in standard-composition marriages and families who probably see themselves as benevolent in their decisions regarding household resource allocation. This might be why this definition made sense to Gary. He himself would have probably defined his own family role as such.

In the mid-twentieth century, the standard stereotypical family was composed of a heterosexual married couple with children. The father worked in the formal labor market (and watched football) and the mother stayed at home (and cooked). These entrenched traditions influence us today in the responses we hear from those who would prefer the NFL not show Taylor, who they see as a sparkly girly girl, on TV when she attends football games.

Gary believed, in his rational, mathematical mind, that this type of gendered division of labor made economic sense—that there was a competitive advantage for women to specialize in homemaking, since they had to stay at home to breastfeed and care for children anyway, and for men to specialize in skills needed to be successful outside the home. It's also possible that Gary believed this not only because it made mathematical sense to him, but also because his wife appeared to enjoy homemaking.[19]

The skills needed to manage a home are not that different from many of the skills needed in the paid workforce. Any job that requires project management, organization, cooking, or people management requires skills that homemakers have in abundance. At the end of the day, the family home environment is nothing more—or less—than the smallest of small businesses.

While traditional economic theory assumes a neutral economic agent unconfined and unconcerned with gender, the conflicting reality is that this same tradition has also assumed gendered preferences when it suits economists. The development of production complementarities in which there is an advantage to becoming skilled at either unpaid work inside the home or paid work outside the home, is just one example. So how do we overcome the misplacement of women in traditional economic theories? How do we move beyond?

As a profession, economists cling to these examples of the world as defined by Economic Man. Most economists are not willing to challenge traditional theories of the household. These traditional theories of the household ignore individual talents and preferences and box us into gendered expectations considered "rational." Gary died in 2014, but his legacy lives on in the field. His theories are so embedded in everything we think we know about the economics of households that when others step up to challenge them, the modern-day economic man bends over backward to explain why they made sense then, even if they might not today.

University of Michigan economists Betsey Stevenson and Justin Wolfers have tried to move us away from production complementarities of household partnership and toward what they call consumption complementarities.[20] According to Betsey and Justin (who live together and are raising two kids but have never legally married), today's higher levels of education, especially among women; shifts in the job market, away from manufacturing and into services; technological innovations that have changed household labor, like the development of washing machines and microwaves; and finally, waves of feminist movements have driven many couples to abandon Gary's worldview and adopt one in which people partner up based on personal likes and dislikes and leisure preferences.[21] Instead of basing joint decisions around the daily workload, couples now maximize leisure activities they enjoy doing together, like when Taylor Swift and her boyfriend took a day trip to the Sydney Zoo in Australia to see the kangaroos during the Eras Tour or vacationed in a little hideout in Italy following the European leg of the Eras Tour in Paris.

This idea of consumption complementarities—that couples partner up today based on similar preferences in leisure activities—has implications for the broader economy. Economists have shown that the increase in women's paid labor and preferences for partnering with someone of similar socioeconomic status account for around 25 percent of the increase in household income inequality today.[22]

When we look at the modern world around us, a view of consumption complementarities makes sense. Yet even in this view there are gendered perspectives that dictate how we show up and how others see us, both inside and outside of the home.

I KNEW YOU WERE TROUBLE

Historical models built on generic interpretations of human beings as all being similar—equally bland and colorless—are bound to be advanced by equally concrete endeavoring measures like math. Such models are, if nothing else, a perfect example of the way things could be. Maximizing preferences is a lofty—some might argue implausible—goal, but one that makes logical sense to analytical thinkers, and this is why the field of economics came to rely so heavily on mathematics in the twentieth century.[23]

It also explains why the field has so often missed the mark when it comes to the effects of unequal power in initial endowments (read: assets like money and wealth at the start of life) and access to resources throughout life. For example, the additional support needed for an individual born into poverty to climb out of it—or, conversely, the ease of staying on the top of the income distribution if born into riches—is not a factor the field of economics handles well. Economic theory has to date been unable to come up with any smooth mathematical models that correct for an unequal start at birth.

Yet the fact remains that unequal endowments exist in most, if not all, economies in the real world and have since the birth of Economic Man. When a new generation is born, some members are born to parents who are flush with resources, some born to parents at the bottom of the economic ladder who are just scraping by, and others born to parents in the middle. This inequality applies to the start of companies (owners versus workers), the start of families (parents versus children), the start of societies (rich versus poor), and even influences the start of global wars. This endowment advantage has, on average, positively affected men and negatively affected women. It explains why women, by the time they make it to the top of their career ladder, are often superstars with glowing accomplishments, while many men at the top are more likely to be average performers.[24]

Modern economic theories of the household, gender, discrimination, and labor markets rarely, if ever, provide satisfying solutions to endowment inequality.[25] While a new school of thought addressing endowment inequality has been brewing in economics,[26] traditional theory generally ignores or minimizes the incorporation of these stubborn real-world facts that are often based on age, sex, race, ethnicity, sexual orientation, or parenthood status.

Unlike Marie Kondo, influential economists have not moved on; they have yet to let go of their idol, Economic Man, in pursuit of more messy, realistic aspirations. Why? One contributing factor is that the profession is still primarily dominated by straight, white, privileged men, many of whom benefit from being born to parents with a larger basket of resources and for whom the invisible labor of caregivers provides a buffer that allows them to fantasize that *Homo economicus* does, in fact, exist.*

* A recent study found that 48 percent of PhD economists have parents who have a graduate degree, and 15 percent of them have a parent with a PhD. About 20 percent of US-born PhD economists have a parent with a PhD. See Stansbury and Schultz, "The Economics Profession's Socioeconomic Diversity Problem."

Imagine if, in September 1897, a curious, budding young economist had sent an inquiry to the *New York Sun* but instead of questioning the existence of Santa Claus, like Virginia did, he questioned the existence of Economic Man. And what if newspaper editor Francis Pharcellus Church had responded—instead of "Yes, Virginia, there is a Santa Claus"—with "Yes, Virgil, there is an Economic Man." Economists might breathe a hefty sigh of relief and decades of future economic thought would be written without batting an eyelash.[27]

Is Economic Man just a relic of the past or alive and well in our hearts today? Is it a worthwhile exercise to ask what Economic Man has done for us lately? For me, I might argue, not much. While a mathematical wiz, Economic Man makes my battle for equality and equity in our economy and in the field of economics challenging. My goals of incorporating ignored and often invisible household labor as visible aspects of our economy are even loftier than they need to be if we believe in Economic Man. If only we could go back in time and ask Francis Pharcellus Church to draft a new response, one that might read, "Yes, Virgil, there is an Economic Man in spirit, but in real life, he will let you down." If we asked Marie Kondo, she would probably agree.

MAD WOMAN

What if today's *Homo economicus* is not a man, but rather a woman, or per-haps someone who identifies as nonbinary? What if she/they had been birthed not by John Stuart Mill or Adam Smith, but rather by Amy Smith, who correctly identified the home as a small business by calling it the family firm? Amy would develop statistics that brought all economic activity within the home into national economic statistics on the country's growth and development.

Economic Woman's life would be extremely busy, much busier than that of Economic Man. Her day would start with a bang: she would coordinate not only her own grooming routine, but also that of her small children or elderly parents, and sometimes (eye roll) that of her spouse. She would prep clothes and breakfast, make sure teeth were brushed and shoes were tied. She would verify that homework was in the backpack and lunchboxes were filled before heading out for the day. She would be responsible for making most decisions about family resources and activities.

While Economic Man might be the bigwig CEO of a Fortune 500 company, he would have delegates, whereas Economic Woman likely would not. While she may also be CEO of a Fortune 500 company and may have a nanny or housekeeper in the home to help with domestic work, she is still stuck with the phone calls from the school or pediatrician. No matter how successful she is outside her home, Economic Woman is more likely to be contacted by her children's school than Economic Man, even when she leaves explicit instructions to call dad.[28]

Just as in Taylor Swift's song "The Man," from her *Lover* album, most women know that advancing is easier as a man. If I were The Man, colleagues would not question my ability to lead. They would not complain to my bosses when I do not do what they want or expect of me. If I were The Man, I would not experience dismissive behaviors, or surprised reactions from colleagues who expect less of me. Some days, it's tempting to daydream about being The Man. But then I am reminded of all his flaws and shortcomings, and it is almost enough to make me a mad woman.

SAD BEAUTIFUL TRAGIC

Female economists do exist. We are best described as sharing a spectrum anchored by two archetypes: pearl clutchers and granolas. Pearl clutchers get ahead by leaning into and flirting with Economic Man. Granolas get ahead by rejecting him.

The pearl clutchers rise in the ranks by stretching to grab ladder rungs built for men—generally too distanced for us to easily climb, especially in a skirt and heels. Pearl clutchers get where they are by acting like Economic Man and conforming to tradition. They are allowed into the club because they mimic the men, so when someone brings up inequality, they get nervous and clutch their pearls. They believe that if they can succeed this way, so can everyone else. They do not want to be identified as disrupters, and they help Economic Man keep women under control. Note that they do this at a serious cost to their own health and well-being.

Pearl clutchers are important, however, because they land in positions of influence and power. They become full professors or hold important titles in government or finance. We need them because even though they sacrificed and disguised themselves to get where they are, they do understand women, and they play an important, sometimes covert role in helping the rest of us ascend—except when they don't.

The challenge with pearl clutchers is that they want power and live their lives in fear of being outed for who they really are—which is not men. They can make it more difficult for young, authentically female economists to ascend. Their fear of being outed means they tolerate little deviation from the norm, making it more difficult for diversity of thought to pierce the glass ceiling Economic Man built long ago.

The opposite of a pearl clutcher is a granola. The granolas grew up in traditional economics but found pretending to agree with economic theory that did not represent their experiences as women exhausting. With a goal of authenticity, they developed their own bubble in subfields like feminist economics. Here they flourished, cackling at how they gamed the system and won by creating their own space. They even created their own annual academic meetings and journals. They became a community for each other.

Their role in the history of economics is also critical. They allowed more female voices and perspectives to be developed, heard, and documented. The challenge is that they are ignored by the dominant players in the field. They have been able to improve their own professional lives but have not had much success in improving the larger profession's ability to incorporate gendered realities.

Most women economists fall somewhere in between pearl clutchers and granolas. I interviewed Julie Nielson, author of *Feminism, Objectivity, and Economics* and *Economics for Humans*.[29] Julie did her undergraduate studies in economics in the 1970s, when she was one of only a few women in her class. Her first publication out of graduate school was in *Econometrica*, one of the top traditional economic journals, and she has published in other top journals, including *The Journal of Political Economy, The Journal of Labor Economics*, and *The Review of Economic Statistics*. She is also one of founders of the field of feminist economics. Julie understands the dangers of trying to pass muster with both the pearl clutchers and the granolas, the mainstream and the feminists.

She knows that even if one tries to be both, the field can still be quick to punish. According to Julie, women can get "punish[ed] for the feminist stuff, even if [their] mainstream stuff is good."[30] In an experience that is not unusual for women in the profession, Julie was denied tenure when she moved to a new institution, even though she moved from a university where she already had tenure. She believes that her feminist work is what caused her to be denied tenure at the new institution. She has moved on from these setbacks, but I found her experience deeply relatable.

I wanted to understand more about how female economists who are authentically themselves have thrived in the profession, so I interviewed the person who tipped me off about Julie: Kate Bahn, chief economist and senior vice president for research at the Institute for Women's Policy Research. I first came across Kate on social media, where her handle is @LipstickEcon. Kate has pink hair and is unabashedly economist-while-female. I loved everything about her persona and needed to know more about who bubble-wrapped her and protected her from Economic Man as she grew up in the field. (Spoiler: It may just have been her mother.)

Kate's first reaction when asked how she remains so authentic to her preferences was to highlight how the sea of traditional male economist attire, ill-fitting gray suits or button-down shirts with khakis and New Balance sneakers, at the annual economics meetings always felt blah to her. She recognized quickly that her personality would not always be accepted in economics, pointing to an anonymous website where other economists criticized her hair color.

Kate's mom is a scientist who always worked in STEM fields and was the family's primary breadwinner. Kate, like me, grew up seeing the female caregivers around her working for pay outside the home. The fact that Kate's mom was a scientist gave her the impression that it was normal for women to be active in STEM jobs and to have advanced degrees.

Growing up, Kate was interested in social justice and politics. She took her first economics class at age nineteen and never looked back. She describes it as love at first sight. The logical and systemic way that economics described the world resonated with her. For Kate, economics is the language of power and, if she wanted to work in policymaking and politics, economics seemed like a natural fit.

Kate was passionate about labor and women. Her goal was to be a chief economist for a labor union, and her undergraduate senior thesis was on how Hurricane Katrina impacted women from differing classes and racial groups in New Orleans. After working for a few years, she knew she wanted to go to graduate school for a PhD in economics.

From the beginning, Kate felt like she did not fit in at her PhD program. Only around 20 to 30 percent of those enrolled in the program were women, and there were only one or two women faculty members. She did not feel like her quantitative math skills were as good as those of other students, and she was interested in studying gender, something that was seen as less serious or less rigorous. To top it all off, she wanted to do applied work.

Kate's perception, backed by data, is that women were more interested in doing labor and applied policy work, areas which have historically held less prestige in economics. This contributed to women being taken less seriously and to views that they contribute less to the profession. Kate also thinks this influenced her experience, as the program she was in offered fewer resources for her and her research, and she was not privy to the word-of-mouth tips some of the teaching assistants and more senior graduate students were sharing with each other. Additionally, she was not invited to social events like poker night, hosted by graduate teaching assistants for lower-level graduate students, because of her gender. She talked about this in a 2018 *New York Times* article on biases against women in economics.[31] She was told at the time, "We want to talk about things that we don't want to talk about in front of women."[32]

THIS IS WHY WE CAN'T HAVE NICE THINGS

Kate's experiences are evergreen. When I made the leap back into academia from the federal government in 2022, I landed in a research institute. The position was anchored as a tenured faculty position and, as such, needed a home department. With a PhD in applied economics and more than twelve years as a research economist in the federal government (nine of which were as a senior or principal economist and a senior advisor), the economics department seemed an ideal fit, except for the fact that some men in that department did not want me. My record did not look like theirs, and they voted against my joining their team. Instead, I landed across the street in a school of public affairs. It ended up being a good fit for me, but it was a disservice to the female students in the economics department, who could have benefitted from my mentorship and guidance.

These issues are not specific to academia. In the 2000s, the federal government shed administrative assistant and secretarial jobs (mostly held by women) in what was declared a "cost savings" endeavor.[33] It was argued that technological advancements in calendar scheduling made those positions superfluous and that as budgets decreased, it was better to lose those who planned and organized than those designing and developing the work. How did this shift play out for PhD research economists and other highly skilled employees? In statistical agencies, where I spent most of my time in government, women PhD researchers took over the administrative burden of scheduling and organizing—making them less efficient at their craft and less productive in their research. It also affected the men who picked up some of those tasks, but to a lesser degree. When the administrative assistants were not around to handle critical tasks, many men and women scientists defaulted to unconscious gender normative expectations of who would do the grunt work to keep the organization running.

As for Kate, she made it through her PhD program by finding her crew—a small group of other eclectic women who studied in her program. They liked ballet, Burning Man, yoga, and meditation. They formed an all-women study group. Kate started an informal club called Econo-Misses, where female students would get together to share battlefield stories and the bruises they endured while surviving in their programs. They found community and shared the relatable stresses and frustration of unequal domestic workloads and childcare obligations. And Kate eventually started a blog, *Lady Economist*, with a grad school friend.

Although she followed an uncharted path, Kate went on to a successful career doing work that she loved. Kate is clear that both men and women have played critical roles in helping women advance in the profession. Kate also leaned into non-academic groups that were working on topics she was passionate about, groups that appreciated having an economist's perspective. After consulting for the WNBA players' association, she took a job at the Center for American Progress with the support of a male professor from her graduate program. Today, she is chief economist and senior vice president at the Institute for Women's Policy Research, a position that makes the most of her training and talents.

Even in Economic Man's world, bold, unruly women find their way and influence the field. They often indirectly or directly advocate for an environment where other women can thrive, even as they themselves experience challenges and setbacks. This is true not only in economics, but throughout many other male-dominated professions, whether space exploration, engineering, or security services. The point is, just like Taylor Swift, we keep going, showing up, and reinventing ourselves in male-dominated professions. Whether he likes it or not, Miss Americana is forever tethered to her Heartbreak Prince.

In 2023, Harvard economist Claudia Goldin won the Sveriges Riksbank Prize in Economic Sciences in Memory of Alfred Nobel, usually referred to as the Nobel Prize in Economics. She was the first woman to win it independently, as opposed to alongside male economists.[34] A total of ninety-three individuals have won this recognition across fifty-five prizes since 1969, when it was first awarded; only three of them have been women. Elinor Ostrom and Ester Duflo are the other two female economists who have received the prize.[35] While women make up about half of the total population, only about 20 percent of full and associate professor positions in economics and business in the US are held by women.[36] They make up only 3 percent of all individuals who have ever won this award.

Claudia earned her PhD in 1972, which also happened to be the first full year that the American Economic Association (AEA) Committee on the Status of Women in the Economics Profession (CSWEP) was in existence and the year it produced a report on the status of women in the economics profession. The report highlighted the fact that women made up 68 percent of special lecturers but only 21 percent of instructors. They occupied 9 percent of assistant professor positions and a measly 2 percent of full professorships.[37] Perhaps the most hopeful note we can garner from these statistics is to recognize how far the profession has come in creating space for women since the birth of Claudia's PhD. Today, women make up slightly more than one-third of university economics majors and graduates. They make up 32 percent of all PhDs granted, 37 percent of non-tenure track professors, 34 percent of assistant professors, and 18 percent of full professors.[38] There is still a lot of work to be done, but progress has been made.

I remember waking up on October 9, 2023, to the news of Claudia's Nobel prize, which spread like wildfire on my social media feeds.[39] The announcement brought elation to many female (and male) economists around the world.[40] We had waited so long for a woman to win on her own independent laurels, for the Nobel Prize committee to demonstrate women's value instead of continually doubting or ignoring it. It tears at a person's soul when the talent, ingenuity, and hard work of one's demographic class is continually dismissed and undervalued.

Claudia won, and it seemed like she won along with the rest of us—perhaps even for the rest of us.[41] We were so proud. To top it off, Claudia won for advancing knowledge, research, and stories about the historic arc of women's paid work and how women show up in the economy outside the family home. The day after she won the prize, Claudia went right back to work meetings and mentoring the next generation. There is, after all, no rest for women determined to move the dial.

NEW ROMANTICS

Women have been pivotal in advancing the field of economics, even when they do not always get their flowers. Nancy Folbre has repeatedly brought caregiving and the care economy to the forefront of economic theory as a necessary household and societal activity that uses limited resources. She has uncovered and brought attention to women's unpaid work. She did this even as early on, academic advisors told her it would be the death of her career.[42] Claudia helped us uncover the rich history of women's paid labor and has highlighted major policy trends that changed the direction of our lives.[43] Julie Nelson has helped advance feminist economics, advanced the study of risk and gender within the field, and tried to help the field see the benefits of Miss Americana & The Heartbreak Prince by arguing that either perspective alone is only "playing with a half deck."[44]

Shelly Lundberg fell into household economics and economic demography when she faced barriers erected by dominant men in the field that prevented her from advancing in her first area of research. We could not have been better off for it. Shelly and a small handful of scholars have advanced more realistic (read: smarter and wiser) models of family behavior focused on intrahousehold bargaining (read: the fights you have after a holiday dinner over who is going to do all the dishes). These models align more closely with the female experience than the model of a benevolent dictator. Thanks to the efforts of these mostly female economists, we can move beyond Gary's benevolent dictator. Gary's version was a man's vision of the household. The vision of Shelly and her colleagues is ours.

The field of economics would be so much richer and more balanced if it did a better job of applying women's perspectives to advancing our knowledge, understanding, and perspective of the economic lives of the other half. We need to prioritize the voices of female leaders and figure out how to strategically keep the fight alive and lean in even when facing backlash to our ideas—even when dominant economists tell us that discrimination is rational and will disappear on its own.

Other female economists who have carved paths and opened gates for us include Lisa Cook, a member of the US Federal Reserve Board of Governors who has been steadfastly dedicated to the experiences of women and minoritized persons in economics. Janet Yellen served as chair of the Board of Governors and, after an incoming president replaced her with a less qualified man (although awesome in his own right), she later served as US Treasury Secretary, showing women a direct path and method of influencing economic policy. Marianne Bertrand from the University of Chicago identified gendered responses on income in surveys that influence how we think about and understand gender gaps.

Heather Boushey's books have explained to many how economic policies have created challenges for the middle class and highlighted the plight of women as they are crunched for time. Emily Oster has enlightened an entire class of parents on data-driven parenting decisions. Janet Currie and Marta Bailey, among others, have expanded our knowledge of the role of policies on women and children's economic advancement and well-being. Claudia Sahm gave us the Sahm Rule, which helps predict future recessions. Jenn Doleac has fought hard in an #EconMeToo era with other women in her cohort against sexual harassment and misogynistic behavior in the profession and in academic departments, even while she experienced her own case of Economic Man exclusion, which drove her into a non-academic job—one that she appears to love and be thriving in and that lets her control the purse strings that advance the next layer of economic research in her area of expertise. Using my best Patrick Swayze voice, I would argue that she successfully showed the profession that "no one puts baby in the corner."

The point is, there are many women doing amazing things against all odds. If you look around in your own profession, you will most likely find women doing amazing work that highlights their lived realities. But we must look for them. Keep your eyes open.

This is what Taylor Swift has done within her own craft and in her own male-dominated profession. She has elevated other female musicians, like Ice Spice, Gracey, and Sabrina Carpenter. She has shone a spotlight on bold and brave women with her songs and lyrics—women like "the Bolter" Idina Sackville, Clara Bow, Stevie Nicks, Rebeka Harkness, and many others. She has supported female artists by including their music in playlists she makes and distributes.

The most successful method of keeping women down or in their place is to pit them against each other. But whether it is the ability to uncover this truth or recognize our shared challenges, we all have some level of power. Just as Taylor and other leading women in the field of economics and elsewhere have done, we can move past the rhetoric from yesteryear that has kept women in the corner for generations. We might just be done with 1950s *Mad Men* propaganda delineating how we should treat each other, even in manly circles like economics and the music industry.

THREE

Misogyny

YOU HAVE THE RIGHT TO PROVE THEM WRONG

There is no career path that comes free of negativity.... There might be times when you put your whole heart and soul into something, and you're met with cynicism or skepticism, but you can't let that crush you. You have to let that fuel you.... We live in a world where anyone can say anything that they want about you at any time. But just please remember that you have the right to prove them wrong.

TAYLOR SWIFT,
2021 BRIT Awards Global Icon Speech

IN 2013, TAYLOR SWIFT was at a meet-and-greet event in Colorado. She stood to take a picture with a DJ from a local radio station when he unexpectedly reached under her skirt and grabbed her butt.[1] Her team told the radio station, and they fired the DJ. The DJ then sued Taylor in 2015 for losing his job. Taylor countersued for one dollar, and the case went to court.

On cross-examination in 2017, a lawyer representing the DJ asked Taylor if she felt bad the DJ had lost his job because of her accusations. She responded, "I am not going to allow your client to make me feel like it is anyway my fault because it isn't. I'm being blamed for the unfortunate events of his life that are a product of his decisions. Not mine."[2]

The DJ lost his case, and Taylor won her countersuit. It was not about the money; she wanted justice and to prove a point. Her legal team argued that the countersuit served "as an example to other women who may resist publicly reliving similar outrageous and humiliating acts."[3]

Inappropriate sexual behavior can happen to anyone. Even the biggest music icons in the world are often exposed to this behavior as they maneuver through their careers. Taylor wanted to show other women an alternative way to counter victim shaming. They could choose to show up against perpetrators, to not live in silence with the shame and guilt that often comes with violations of privacy. They could insist the blame fall where it rightly belongs, on a society often led by misogynistic tendencies and assumptions.

FOOLISH ONE

Taylor won the BRIT Awards' Global Icon honor in 2021, one year into the pandemic. The award had been given almost annually since 1977. Taylor was the youngest musician ever to win. She was only the second solo woman winner, after P!nk, who won in 2019.[4] Her iconic acceptance speech reminded the audience that most of us cannot control what others think, their criticisms, or how they react. We can only control our own actions, thoughts, and beliefs. Taylor reminded us that while others may see us in a certain unfavorable or "less than" light, we have the right to prove them wrong.

The freedoms we enjoy today exist in large part thanks to those who came before us. When women want change, they know that living in a world built for men means that it is often ineffective to loudly ask for it. Instead, they work behind closed doors and through whisper networks. For example, the suffragists' movement for the right to vote in 1920 was nudged quietly into existence partially by Febb E. Burn, the mother of twenty-four-year-old conservative Tennessee legislator Harry T. Burn.

On the day of the Congressional vote, she told her son to "be a good boy" and vote in favor of the Nineteenth Amendment. He did just that. Harry stated, "I knew that a mother's advice is always safest for a boy to follow, and my mother wanted me to vote for ratification. I appreciate the fact that an opportunity such as seldom comes to a mortal man to free 17 million women from political slavery was mine."[5] Febb, as Burn's mother, had influence over his conservative vote.

Harry had something in common with Adam Smith in terms of their mothers' heavy-handed influence over their daily lives. Yet Harry decided to use his mother's encouragement to improve the plight of half of humanity, while Smith, by all accounts, did not. All this has led me to wonder: What will we plan for the women who come after us in the 2120s? What will the world look like for them, and who will they have to prove wrong? Will there still be sexual assault and violence driven by power imbalances?

This chapter covers the sensitive topics of sexual assault and misogyny: how they are manifested in male-dominated environments, how silence lets them breed, and how exposing them helps not only those who experience violence or assault, but also others around them. The wide reach of social media has helped improve awareness of the challenges involved in addressing these topics. To readers sensitive to issues of sexual assault, please consider this your warning that this chapter discusses examples of sexual assault, including my own.

INNOCENT

For centuries, women have been vilified, our sexuality used to coerce us into submission or dismiss our truth. Women are deemed too sexual or not sexual enough. It feels like we can never win. However, if the past decade has taught us anything, it is that when we are united in speaking our truth to the world, we can improve the environment for the women (and men) around us and those to come.

Women today are refusing to be ignored, not believed, or told to deal with the bad behavior of others silently. The #MeToo movement has exerted a commanding influence around the globe. In many parts of the world, women and society in general are no longer tolerating questionable behavior toward them. They are refusing to let it go unchecked.

These churning tides mean that movements like #MeToo include scores of baby-boom women standing up to their abusers or assailants later in life. And while women still face harassment and abuse when they come forward, as in the case of a recent Supreme Court nominee who at best mistreated and at worst assaulted a colleague in college, a stronger vibe of believing women's stories has taken hold. Look at the way vast swaths of society now believe the victims of famous men like the elder actor from *The Cosby Show*, the entertainment industry mogul, the industry giant at Fox media, and a recent US president.[6]

Women's stories and experiences, even when they involve powerful men, are finally being believed, their voices leading to actionable consequences. That belief, and the ability to reinvent or reframe the larger societal storyline toward survivor truths, helps protect the women who come after us by reducing the knee-jerk reaction of shame. It reinforces that bad actors will be held accountable for their actions, which can in turn mitigate their behavior.

Changes brought about by the #MeToo movement demonstrate both power in numbers and that women today have support when exposing inappropriate behavior. They are reclaiming control when wronged. Yet even with these advancements, backlash occurs, and as with recent national elections and related events, we see extreme bro-ism gain traction, if not in society as a whole, then on social media, in elections, and among people in positions of power and influence.

SPEAK NOW

Economics has its own version of #MeToo. It seems that every few years, a media story breaks large enough to cause tremors in the halls of academia, and economics departments are no exception.[7] The power dynamics of academia are heavy and perverse. The stories that surface usually involve male professors abusing their power of authority with female students or colleagues. Over time, many of us have become exhausted by this repetitive behavior, carried out by a small minority of those in power. As institutions try to maintain silence in order to protect the privacy of those involved and to avoid legal actions, a younger generation of fed-up women economists has begun speaking out on social media to support each other and to help curb the behavior.[8]

I wanted to support them. My own story of sexual assault while studying abroad is so familiar that it has lost any flavor for me, but I tell it here because it is such a regular occurrence for women that it deserves space in print. Even today, at least one in five college students experiences sexual violence abroad.[9]

I was sexually assaulted as a sophomore in college, not by a professor, but by an acquaintance while I was on a study abroad program. My story started with a group of friends out dancing and drinking in a foreign country where the legal drinking age was eighteen. After being served too many drinks, I left with three male friends, one of them the boyfriend of one of my roommates, who was not out with us that night.

Even though this story is from 1997, it is still embarrassing enough that, as I write it, I automatically begin to think through all the ways in which I could have avoided the situation. I was too naïve, too trusting, too gullible.

The most important thing I can say is that sexual assault is not our fault. It was not my fault for being too trusting and too naïve. It was the fault of those who took advantage of my trust. It was and is the fault of a society built around normalizing this type of male behavior and training men to think it is acceptable.

After we all left the bar together, we drove to the boyfriend's house, where he lived with his parents. He brought me into the house and sexually assaulted me while his friends were waiting outside in their car. They then drove me back to my house. The next morning, I felt physically ill when I shared with my other roommate what had happened. A piece of my spirit shrank that day, the day I lost my ability to decide when and what I chose to do with others, the day I realized that consent is not an automatic given and authenticity is a farce for some.

The effect of that experience lives deep in my soul, and I carry it with me everywhere. It has affected all subsequent intimate relationships I have had and hides in the corners of my marriage, popping out at inopportune times. Anger builds inside me when I think about why we raise boys (in particular) to detach feelings and respect from the physical act of sex, and why we sometimes raise them to see women as objects instead of intellectually deep humans with feelings, wit, and desires.

So when young women in economics started getting agitated at having to deal repeatedly with the bad behavior of a few greedy men, I was at the front of the line to support them. Experience had shown that we could not naïvely count on university departments and professional associations to have our backs; in the past, that had proven to be a relatively hopeless exercise. There were, however, easy actions we could take to visually and verbally show dissent.

Every year, the American Economic Association (AEA) has an annual meeting in January. In 2023, a few of us women economists leading the charge on social media against bad behavior in the profession toward our more vulnerable colleagues came prepared. As the discussions escalated on social media around an anonymous jobs website for economists, inappropriate derogatory discussions on said website, and the collection of stories of women who had experienced inappropriate or unwanted behavior, I became antsy. To me, this issue was not difficult to act on or improve. I knew from experience that silence only allows the behavior to continue and the rot to grow. Yet the power dynamics within the profession are stacked against young women coming forward alone. They needed support and action. A handful of us decided to act.

I looked up the cost for making buttons and found a local printer for posters. I crafted a design for #EconTwitter #MeToo buttons and put in an order. I started a petition online titled "Stop Predatory Behavior in the Economics Profession," which garnered around 700 signatures.[10] I was not the only one outraged. Our community was acting and vocalizing dissent and frustration loudly on social media.

Early in January 2023, I arrived at the airport with my carry-on, which included my clothes and everything I needed to participate in the meetings, and a suitcase I checked onto the airplane that contained around fifty pink cardboard yard signs saying "#MeToo." At the meeting, attended by around 6,000 economists that year, we distributed the signs to individuals wanting to silently protest and buttons to information tables and events across the venue.

Even the president of the AEA at the time, Christina Romer from the University of California Berkeley, wore a button. It was a silent but powerful gesture that as a community, we would no longer tolerate the bad behavior. We were acknowledging it as an issue.

The entirety of these actions was not time consuming, easy to implement, and let people know we were watching. The profession continues to struggle with how to handle issues of abuse, but our peaceful protest mattered and had sent a message.

JUMP THEN FALL

If you experience any type of sexual harassment, assault, or inappropriate behavior, know you have options. You can choose to tell someone. While victim shaming and blaming is less common today, it still exists, and the person you confide in might not believe you. If they do not believe you, you can choose to tell someone else. You could tell someone and they might not act on the information, or they might try to hide it. If that happens, you can keep on telling people until you find that one person who believes you. Finding support is important, not only to your own healing, but also for helping change the system for the better. It takes courage, and each person needs to do it on her own timeline, when she feels ready. Nothing else matters.

I know how scary and embarrassing it can be to talk about sexual harassment or assault, but the impacts of keeping it secret, for you and the community around you, are scarier. Continue telling people until you find someone who has your back, someone who believes you and will act in your defense and on your behalf. Try not to talk yourself out of sharing your pain even if it means you share your feelings of shame. It does not matter if your assailant has an alternative version of events. The only version that matters is yours.

I know from experience that over time, the more we tell our stories, the less painful, shameful, and embarrassing they become. Talking to others can ease the burden. By sharing our experiences and believing those who share theirs, we let the events and actions blow across the plains, breaking up in meaning and power as they travel, until landing in the soil of our mixed experiences to become the foundation for the next generation.

I can only hope that we have moved the dial ever so slightly in the direction of justice and the freedom to be naïve and safe. Although we live in a world created for the ease of someone else, we should stop letting that be the driver of how comfortable we feel stepping forward into society to let our voices be heard.

BETTER THAN REVENGE

As a group, women have been carving out space to play by their own rules, in their own ways. They create their own environments to thrive despite barriers and actions that hold them back, even when it includes something as brash and undeniable as an unwanted kiss on an international stage. When unwanted behavior found its way into the limelight at the 2023 Women's World Cup, it seemed women were poised to demand accountability.

On August 20, 2023, Spain's team won the Women's World Cup. The joy of a hard-fought win was drowned out by anger at Spanish football federation president Luis Rubiales, who, after the victory, kissed Spanish player Jenni Hermoso on the lips without her consent while on stage and live on television.[11] With all the drama of a raging toddler, Luis subsequently refused to acknowledge any wrongdoing.

The world watched the story unfold. Four days after the World Cup final, the International Federation of Association Football's disciplinary committee opened hearings.[12] Five days after that, the entire Spanish team refused to play again until Luis was removed from his post.[13] After ten days, and in a palace intrigue twist, Luis's mother was taken to a local hospital due to fatigue and stress related to a two-day hunger strike in support of her son, reminding me of the lyrics in Taylor Swift's "mad woman" highlighting how often women support men's bad behavior.[14]

On September 5, amid the kiss controversy, the team fired head coach Jorge Vilda, replacing him with a woman, Montse Tomé, a former assistant coach.[15]

By September 10, about three weeks after the infamous unwanted kiss, Luis finally quit as Spain's soccer chief.[16] While it didn't happen immediately, intense pressure to apply consequences for his inappropriate behavior finally led to his ousting. The rights of women to be fantastic and respected even among those in power won that day. Almost two years later, on February 20, 2025, Luis would finally be found guilty of sexual assault by Spain's high court.[17]

The summer after the World Cup, on July 29, 2024, a seasoned BBC reporter commented when the Australian women's swim team, which had just won gold at the Paris Olympics, was taking a long time to exit the pool deck. He said it was because the women were taking too long to do their makeup. The reaction this time was much swifter; he was immediately fired from his job reporting on the first Olympics to have an equal number of female and male athletes.[18]

The world does not always move fast, but it is evolving. Behavior that was tolerated even a decade ago is no longer accepted.[19] Some of these changes come from leaders at the top. In that regard, the Olympic organization has inspired some hope: in March 2025, the International Olympic Committee elected its first woman president, Kirsty Coventry of South Africa.[20] She beat out six male candidates in an organization whose leadership has historically been dominated by European men. Change is happening.

BREATHE

In 2024, Kamala Harris's campaign released an ad reminding married women that their vote was private and would not be known to their spouses.[21] The ad showed male spouses voting for the Republican candidate and reassuring each other that their wives would do the same. The camera then pans to their wives, who nod and mouth the name Kamala to each other.

A whisper campaign also started in women's bathroom stalls across the country: sticky notes were placed on the back of stall doors reminding women that their vote was private, theirs alone, and that their partners did not have to know how they voted.[22] Even in 2024, women continued to nudge and influence in ways that lean into their understanding of power imbalances. These ads brought the influence women know they have in informal and shadow spaces into the mainstream. Although Kamala lost, the campaign supporting her showed that we continue to move forward, even if sometimes it does not feel like we are. The campaign also highlighted the ways in which women communicate to each other through whisper networks in a society often controlled by men.

If we continue to have hope and act, gender and economic equity can and will occur. Examples and statistics inspire hope, giving us the long view of how far we have come in advancing the female agenda. Women everywhere, and their male allies, continue to push, prod, collude, and negotiate for fair economic and human rights for women.

In the United States in 2021, 53.1 percent of individuals aged twenty-five and older with a bachelor's degree or higher were women.[23] Women now make up more than half (50.7 percent) of the college-educated workforce.[24] For the first time, women run more than 10 percent of all Fortune 500 companies, a statistic that could use improvement but that is almost five times greater than in 2004 (1.6 percent).[25] In 2021, when Kamala Harris was sworn into office as the first female vice president, women made up almost one-third of the US House of Representatives. In 2022, seventeen countries were led by women, compared to only six in 1992 and three in 1972. Women and girls are on the move, refusing to be held back.

Young women should be inspired by what we have accomplished and how far we have come despite recent setbacks. When at a crossroads between not believing and going for it, choose to go for it. Drown out the negative noise, the banter, and the whispers of "she can't, she shouldn't, she won't" and replace them with "I can, I should, and I will." If we women see opportunity in our experiences, one moment at a time, we can create micro improvements in our own lives and those of the women who come after us. This advances women's quality of life and economic lives.

The advent of social media and rapid global communications can be used to nudge even more women toward self-determination and awareness. Women should not have to fit into an economy constructed primarily by and for men, no matter where we live. If we continually compare ourselves to men, we continually fail, because the current economy was built for men. Care advantage and care privilege are universal and real, as is the vulnerability women experience when sexually exploited, but we do not need to stay in this status quo.

CHAMPAGNE PROBLEMS

A quote attributed to Queen Marie Antoinette during the French Revolution has come to symbolize an ignorance to the plight of those with less. "Let them eat cake!" might just be the perfect metaphor for the silent stance of policymakers when it comes to women's needs and priorities and to understanding how we keep them safe. Perhaps instead we could "let women and caregivers control the policy purse strings!"

Policies matter. They can help women gain equity and live in a society more justly built to support their lives. Research has shown that letting women control the family purse leads to higher household investments in childcare, school supplies, children's education, and food and clothing for kids.[26] Let women control the household finances and, on average, households spend less on private goods for pleasure, like alcohol and tobacco. Giving women economic power has shown, on average, time and again to be wise fiscal policy for economic growth.

Not only is it good for society, it is also good for the women themselves. Greater economic independence in relationships leads to less domestic violence, healthier intimate partner relationships, stronger financial support in retirement, and lower poverty throughout the lifespan.[27] As girls grow up, the best advice their parents can give them is not to find a great man, but rather an excellent education and a well-paid job.

The best chance we have as individuals to nudge society toward those goals is to use our vote to its fullest capacity. We can harness the power our grandmothers and their grandmothers gave us to vote into power people who support a world that lets us shine and advance while also being mothers and caregivers and without feeling exhausted and like we have failed because we struggle to compete with the care-privileged among us.

We can craft our own new realities within the domains that we control. We can invite men and others to meet us there. We can stop putting up with a status of lesser, a status where we struggle to fit into a system not designed to favor us. We can stop trying to conform to a system not meant to benefit us.

Let's invite everyone to meet us in this new space, a space in which we are not held back and neither are they, but one in which we have equal opportunities at equity and safety. In this space, misogyny is not tolerated, and we formally honor those who engage in care activities by valuing their contributions through policies and programs that lift them up.

We can prove the patriarchy wrong, and we should. Any movement toward a more equitable and just society needs to start with a meaningful redistribution of resources that support the critical elements of family life and human capital investments like education.

All along the Eras Tour, in city after city, Taylor Swift led by example, reinvesting in the communities in which she performed. She donated millions of dollars to local food banks and other community centers.[28] In the city of Liverpool in the United Kingdom, her donation was expected to provide meals for the community for an entire year.[29] During Beyoncé's Renaissance Tour in 2023, she donated more than $2 million to programs supporting students and small business owners.[30] The overly cynical might claim that artists donate to maintain an image, and in some instances, that might be true. But these women are donating to critical programs helping families and individuals thrive and get ahead. They see the vision, most likely because they themselves are surrounded by caregiving women and men who know the value of investing in and caring for society and communities.

CHANGE

Violence against women is driven by misogynistic beliefs, and it is not just limited to physical violence. Misogynistic behavior holds women back and diminishes their contributions. It often silos control among those with power, but it is time we took back our power.

In an act of defiance, Taylor rejected the notion that her master albums could or should be owned by anyone other than herself. When her record label sold her first six masters, Taylor decided to rerecord them under a new label. Radio stations and fans rallied around Taylor and began playing and listening to *(Taylor's Version)* albums, which included previously unreleased songs that she identified with "[From The Vault]" at the end of the song title.

Rereleasing the albums meant that an entire new generation of youth were exposed to Taylor's earlier work. Kids could sing along to songs that their parents already knew and had experienced growing up. This also influenced the Eras Tour, as many young kids wanted to see the concert, as did their parents. Both had been influenced by Taylor's music at different points in their lives. But the rerecordings meant that young girls could find Taylor's earlier music relatable at a time in their lives when they were experiencing feelings, situations, and emotions like those evoked by her earlier albums. All the while, their parents relived the memories of their youth.

By rerecording, Taylor found a path around a "scootered" misogynistic roadblock that was holding her back. Her strength and determination had ripple effects throughout the music industry. It changed how industry executives and musicians enter into agreements. Taylor singlehandedly shifted the landscape for entertainers by showing the strength of her star power and autonomy in a rigid industry controlled by a few moguls. She demonstrated that even under the weight of a domineering industry and profession, finding supporters and staying determined to live your truth under your terms, with a little bit of strategic planning, can be impactful.

FOUR

Care Work

INVISIBLE

> My most vivid memory of growing up was my mom and dad tell-
> ing me I was different and unique and special and that I could do
> whatever I wanted with my life.
>
> TAYLOR SWIFT,
> 2016 iHeartRadio Music Awards Speech

MARKETING FOR THE *BARBIE* MOVIE infiltrated public spaces. There
were collaborations across multiple dimensions, including a fuchsia Xbox
console, Barbie Crocs, and crossover commercials with Flo from Progressive
Insurance.[1] One aspect of the marketing campaign showed real people with
the pink Barbie emblem behind them and a tag describing who they were or
the role they played in the economy. Fans began creating symbols of Taylor
Swift with the title "This Barbie Is the Music Industry."[2] It was spot-on but
made me wonder, who are all the people behind Taylor that do the grueling
care work so she can focus entirely on her craft? Today she has staff to take
care of those tasks, but that was not always the case.

THIS BARBIE IS THE MUSIC INDUSTRY

When Taylor was younger and making her start in the world of music, it was
her parents, especially her mother, who took care of her daily needs. A
younger Andrea Swift went to college at the University of Houston, married,
and worked as a mutual fund marketing executive before switching careers
to work as a stay-at-home mom.[3] Andrea devoted herself to caring for and
raising her children, helping them pursue their dreams. She is known for
traveling with Taylor at the beginning of her career, waiting in the car with
Taylor's brother while a young Taylor knocked on Nashville music executives'
doors looking for a record deal.[4]

Andrea's path was common for many white, middle-class women of her generation, many of whom got educated and worked for pay until children arrived at which point, if they were married and the family could make it on one income, they shifted their focus to the home and the unpaid care work required to raise the next generation. Andrea invested her education and talents into her children. Taylor is quick to acknowledge and thank her mother for the roles she has played in her success. And let's be clear, Taylor's success has also paid off for Andrea. It was always a solid investment and one that she most likely could not have been prouder to support.

But Taylor's success does not just come from the countless hours of unpaid effort invested by herself and her family members, or her time spent training with a professional songwriter; it is also due to the legions of fans who have supported her work and talent. The demographics of her fans are universal and representative.[5] These fans have helped propel Taylor to the top and are equally responsible for her status as "This Barbie Is the Music Industry." They are drawn to Taylor's talent and see themselves represented in her lyrics. The recognition that Taylor gives her fans and her mother is something from which we could all learn. The time has come for us to officially recognize unpaid care and effort as work and worthy of being acknowledged for what it is—a formal aspect of a functioning economy and a critical component of economic growth and development.

In this chapter, we walk through what women's work is, which is so much more than just paid labor in the formal labor market. It includes all the care work we do in our homes for our families like washing clothes, cooking meals, transporting our little ones to daycare or soccer practice or summer camp. Once we comprehensively define work done by women and caregivers, we envision an economy where policymakers make the necessary policy decisions for women to thrive, we acknowledge the role of caregiving within that space, and we cover how women economists have been advancing theories that describe the complete arc of economic activity done predominantly by women. Last, this chapter touches on gendered topics of dire importance like fertility rates and social policies that support women's economic freedoms and ability to thrive in our economy.

I CAN DO IT WITH A BROKEN HEART

Women's work occurs in the boardroom and the shadows of rustic pantries. We do it in dimly lit bathrooms, sitting on toilets next to small sticky children taking baths, or at folding tables where we volunteer to sell concessions at our children's high school games, in community organizations, and with parent-teacher associations. Women engage in all kinds of economic activity not recognized in the data we collect and report because it is work that we do on behalf of our families, usually without direct monetary compensation.

This fact manifests itself in several ways. Thousands of hours of women's unpaid work go unaccounted for in official measures of our economy like gross domestic product (GDP) and labor force participation (LFP). Official government statistics ignore unpaid work done in the home in every country in the world, yet in 2020, as the pandemic raged on, nonpaid economic activities done in our homes for our families accounted for an equivalent of 25 percent of GDP in the US.[6]

If economic statistics included both paid and unpaid work, we would know that women are more economically active than men. For example, women working full-time year-round in paid jobs spend up to one extra hour a day on domestic tasks in the home relative to their male counterparts.[7] One hour a day may not seem like much. It can include mundane tasks like preparing dinner or folding clothes. But one extra hour a day adds up to one extra month of economic activity each year, implying that men have one extra month of leisure every year relative to their female counterparts who also work full-time year-round.[8]

The richness of women's work is rarely fully studied in dominant university economics departments or among economic research groups at prominent Ivy League schools. It is hardly considered within most legislative halls or in executive meetings at national statistical agencies. Women's economic stories are observed and told through a male lens of the economy by those who often have the privilege of receiving care from someone else, often a woman. This care work, therefore, is commonly ignored, making it invisible.

Work in a restaurant as a cook and you get paid a wage from an employer, and you show up in numbers used to calculate essential economic statistics like the monthly jobs statistics or unemployment rates from the US Bureau of Labor Statistics.[9] Work at home cooking meals for your family and maybe you get a hug or kiss from your spouse or child, perhaps the right to use some discretionary household resources, but you are excluded from jobs statistics and unemployment rates even though you are doing the same activity.

Women have always been economically active, but the totality of our effort is largely invisible in society's accounting of work when we do it inside our homes and for our families. Society might know, consciously or subconsciously, that it is there, that caregivers in households across the country spend one to two hours a night engaged in prepping, cooking, and cleaning up after evening family dinners, but there is no official outside-the-home economic value assigned to this care work. It is invisible labor.

This has immediate implications for family care providers. When we do not measure it, we cannot see how much more stressed mothers are today as they are increasingly crunched between holding paid jobs outside of their homes and engaging in family care work within their homes. How has the average day changed for mothers over the decades? Do they have any leisure time, and what about sleep or time for self-care, like exercise? When official statistics do not track this data and its change over time, both women and entire societies lose out. Policies and legislators remain mostly blind and hindered in their ability to create systems that balance the burden and ease the financial and emotional stress.

MY BOY ONLY BREAKS HIS FAVORITE TOYS

The record-breaking movie *Barbie* imagined an economy run by women. It was an artistic vision of what the economy might look like if ruled by girl dolls. We can only imagine Barbie's economy started with initial endowments controlled by women, as it represents, after all, the imaginative minds of girl play and starts with the Barbies in control of most, if not all, endowments and resources.

Grossing over $162 million its opening weekend, in July 2023 the movie brought the economic power of women and girls out in full force.[10] In terms of sales, it beat lots of male-centric films like *Oppenheimer*, *Avengers: End Game*, *The Super Mario Bros. Movie*, and *The Dark Knight*.[11] It sustained success by passing the $1 billion box office mark in three weeks, making it one of the first movies to generate a billion dollars so quickly and solidifying Greta Gerwig's place as the first female director to claim this success.[12]

Surprisingly, or maybe not, *Barbie* hit during a summer when female artists and entertainers of the world dominated.[13] The market power of women and girls hungry for content made for women by women was so overwhelming[14] that it begged the question of why had it taken this long to connect female producers and innovators to those who enjoy content that speaks profoundly to the female experience?

The movie *Barbie* presented us with two distinct economies: one run by women, called Barbie Land, the other run by men, labeled the Real World. In the make-believe economy of Barbie Land, girls' imaginations ruled the script, storyline, activities, and actions of all the dolls—including Ken and Alan. Barbie controlled everything—the parliament, emergency services, construction, all real estate, even the beach. Barbie could do anything outside her Dream House, be anyone in the Barbie Land labor market—a doctor, an astronaut, even the president. Barbie oozed confidence; she owned her power. She controlled everything . . . until she didn't.

Ken traveled with Barbie to the Real World and discovered the power men had there. With his newfound enlightenment, he went back to Barbie Land and took control. He converted Barbie's Dream House into Ken's Mojo Dojo Casa House. He convinced the other Kens to follow his leadership instead of Barbie's. All this behavior, however, did not stop the Barbies from quickly figuring out how to regain their power—an advantage easily provided to those who have controlled endowments and resources for so long.

Persistence and reinvention reign in the Barbie Land economy. Ken reinvented himself after experiencing the Real World, forcing Barbie into her own form of reinvention. What we might learn from this fictitious example is that the theme of reinvention can be used to unstick unequal endowments and motivate change within an economy. The more challenging question, however, is how, when, and where to do this in a way that brings about a more equitable society.

This leads to more questions than answers. How can this Barbie economy inform our economic theories, models, and beliefs? Does it help us answer questions around initial endowments, and how we might consider incorporating them into modern economic models? More importantly, does it say anything about how initial endowments might shift, either at the onset or as an economy advances, to increase equity and maximize social welfare among us all?

At the end of the day, while Ken focused on ruining his favorite toy to gain power, Barbie was more than prepared with a mastermind-level plan to regain her strength. There might just be something for the rest of us in the actual real world to learn after all about the power of sparkly pink toy dolls to stand up for themselves and control their domain even when it is under attack by a group of chest-pounding Kens.

As with the historical economic theories of Adam Smith, economic productivity inside the Barbie dream home magically appeared. Prepared food literally jumped out of the toaster and onto Barbie's plate. Clean, crisply ironed clothes appeared in her closet with a magic sparkle. No time needed to be dedicated to cooking the food or ironing the clothes. Barbie's support system, like Adam's mother, was invisible. This Barbie Land economy, while driven by little girls' imaginations, is nothing more than the "real" economy with a reversal of binary gendered expectations.

The Barbie Land economy mimics how those in power have the privilege to ignore support and care work and take it for granted. It also sheds light on why the struggle to see care work is so real. If the work is invisible, how can we expect positive change that rebalances care responsibilities within our homes and society? Even in a feminist role-reversal Barbie economy, it is easy to ignore, undervalue, or take for granted activities done by others to support and care for those who thrive in the markets outside of our homes. Care work is stubbornly invisible.

In the movie, worlds collide, and a more nuanced interactive presentation takes place that pushes beyond gender into individual identity. It aspires for the audience to move beyond reduced gendered expectations or, at a minimum, accept with a more clarifying vision the ways in which gender influences the world, markets, and economy around us yet does not define us.

The movie makes one think: What if economies across the globe were re-envisioned, rather than by men, by mothers and caregivers. Not by the young women who are told they can be anything, do anything, but by the older, more mature, seasoned women raising them. The women who tell us we can do anything because they want, need us to believe it. They know the road will be challenging, and if we are to fight for change, we need to believe it is possible. If these older, more mature women re-envisioned economies, the effort to toast Barbie's bread and iron her clothes might just not be invisible after all.

SHAKE IT OFF

America Ferrera's character, Gloria, gives a moving speech in *Barbie* describing what it is often like to be a woman. She demonstrates the competing, impossible demands on women today: "It is literally impossible to be a woman. . . . You have to be thin, but not too thin. . . . You have to have money, but you can't ask for money because that's crass. You have to be a boss, but you can't be mean. You have to lead, but you can't squash other people's ideas. You're supposed to love being a mother, but don't talk about your kids all the damn time."[15] The full speech highlights the complex tightrope women walk in an economy and society built for and around men.[16] Walking on a thin line is often exhausting.

Gloria's speech was so relatable that news reports appeared of women crying during that part of the movie or choosing to stay with or leave a boyfriend based on how he reacted to the speech.[17] I remembered hearing a similar speech in the Netflix Taylor Swift documentary *Miss Americana*. Taylor says, "There is always some standard of beauty that you're not meeting. Because if you're thin enough, then you don't have that ass that everybody wants. But if you have enough weight on you to have an ass, then your stomach isn't flat enough. It's all just . . . impossible."[18]

These speeches are relatable because women walk a virtual tightrope every day trying to balance all their roles and personas, all the expectations imposed on them by others and by themselves. We are so hard on women, and that is what America's character and Taylor get right. While it is not impossible to be a woman, it is exhausting to be a woman in a man's economy where we are expected to live by rules built for privileged men to thrive—many of them with huge amounts of care provided for them. If we take back our power, reclaim our identities, and prioritize a world that helps us thrive, perhaps it could become easier.

What would that look like? First and foremost, the characteristics that tend to hold women back in a man's economy would make us shine on our own. Balancing parenthood with work life would be the norm. Limited resources would be prioritized so that caregivers get paid for raising healthy, well-functioning children, and infrastructure would be prioritized around the needs of the microeconomies of families and households. Parents would have access to high-quality, affordable healthcare and childcare. Children would have safe transportation to and from school. Breakfast and lunch would be provided during school hours, and the three-month free-for-all summer vacation would be replaced with varied breaks throughout the school year that align with employer work breaks. Employees would be encouraged to discuss the balancing of work and family, and employers would work to accommodate that balancing without judgment, because the entire society would have the expectation that karma is real and what goes around comes around—that at various points in our lives we all either need care or give it, because care is critical for survival and a healthy economy and society.

In this world, women wouldn't struggle for equality and caregivers wouldn't struggle with exhaustion. In this world, it is possible to be a woman and caregiver without the shame, exhaustion, and tightrope walk of pleasing everyone. This world can and, in fact, does exist on some level in some places. We see crumbs of this in Scandinavian countries, societies that recognize, fund, and invest in the next generation of adults and workers at much higher levels than we do in the US. Parental leave policies normalize workers' need to care for infants and children, and some even formally recognize the role extended family play in child rearing.[19] Childcare is amply available, affordable, and of high quality, as are schools.

Those in countries held back by or struggling to balance demanding household work with paid work perhaps wonder why more countries cannot be or are not structured in a way that more formally distributes the burden of care by recognizing the amount and level of effort required to keep households and communities healthy, safe, and happy. The short answer is that many of us assume the responsibility of care is a personal endeavor, not something we should formally plan for or redistribute resources to within our communities. This is especially true in the United States.

LONG STORY SHORT

Do you recall the women in your communities who solved the care crisis driven by the pandemic so that the rest of us could return to some sort of normalcy? Maybe you were one of them. Think back to September 2020, when politicians were saving the airline industry and writing public health policies that kept liquor stores open:[20] a group of children in Silicon Valley sat in a neighborhood soccer mom's backyard with a teacher hired through connections at their private school. They spent the day engaged in distance learning via Zoom portals while their moms worked, volunteered, or even took some much-needed respite. Pandemic educational pods varied in design from region to region, but they all had a similar effect.[21] They saved working mothers when no one else would.*

---

* Working mothers are all mothers. Whether working for pay in the labor market or engaged in economic activities that support their families and children in the home, all mothers work.

The government supported families through tax credits and rebates but did not have solutions for exhausted family caregivers whose children were not physically returning to school in the fall.

Mothers across the country stepped up to solve the childcare crisis. Children sat in basements, garages, backyards, and community gyms while privately contracted teachers, rotating parents, and other caregivers took turns supervising their remote learning environments.[22] As the country stretched toward recovery and grasped at normalcy, pods sprouted up everywhere, developed in a vacuum that only mothers who have always struggled to get their needs met would understand. In Minnesota, mothers formed pods of six, pooling funds from five of the families to hire a local college student or neighborhood high schooler to supervise garage-pod school. These families included a space at the table for a child whose family could not afford to chip in for a private supervisor.[23]

In the Washington, DC, area, parents corralled the neighborhood children into damp, musty basements or garages and each parent, many of them career federal staffers, took one day of leave a week to supervise the group.[24] In Boston and New York, YMCAs offered limited spots in their staff-supervised educational pods so parents could work.[25] Across the country, mothers understood the task. They were, once again, being nudged by invisible expectations of their roles and responsibilities as caregivers. They created these educational pods out of need: the need for their children to start socializing in person again, and their own need to work and rebalance their lives.

On the other hand, many paid caregivers faced increasing requests to accommodate learning pods and unique care demands. These individuals, many of them teachers and childcare and eldercare providers, sacrificed their family's health by going into other people's homes during COVID to provide care. They were modern-day warriors.

Caregivers live in a society that requires them to come to the rescue, not only for others but also to save their own family or their personal economic independence.[26] But the way women and caregivers do this differs depending on the cultural and societal expectations where they live. We saw this play out in real time with pandemic educational pods.

Many women have lived economically brave lives and contributed substantially to their communities. These women deserve recognition. As a society, highlighting their stories and recognizing how their actions, work, and efforts impact the economy and society over time is an essential endeavor—especially if we aim to encourage the younger women around us to be courageous as they embark on their own adult-life journeys driven by their unique passions and desires.

INVISIBLE STRING

The field of economics is flush with macroeconomic models predicting how labor markets and prices will react to policies and structural changes in the economy. Even though the field in modern times has been dominated by men who love math, and, in historical times, by men who ignore the economic activities happening right under their noses within households, there have been economists in the past and there are economists today who care deeply about creating and adapting models to incorporate structural realities driven by social norms and unequal endowments.[27]

There are entire buckets of economic literature devoted to how increasing women's economic activity outside the home and their given resources at birth or marriage can increase their power over household resources and decision-making.[28] These resources can shift negotiating power over the household budget and can influence whether the budget is used to pay for cleaning, meal preparation services, schooling, or extracurricular programs for children. Policies focused on equalizing gendered control over resources have improved women's ability to thrive and succeed outside and inside the home.

Shelly Lundberg is known for developing theories with colleagues about how individuals within a household bargain with each other over limited resources to decide how much to spend on clothing, food, or education for children.[29] Studies in low-income countries have focused on assessing the very basic nature of this type of bargaining and have come up with empirical evidence suggesting that women are more likely to spend resources on household goods like clothing for children, education, or food than men are.[30] These studies also find that when men are in control of household resources, they spend a larger portion of them on personal or private goods like tobacco or alcohol.[31]

When I discuss this research with my colleagues from middle- and high-income countries, the rebuttal (mostly from male economists) is swift and sharp. Those living in high-income countries tend to think their behavior is not linked to the type of sexist behavior often observed in lower-income countries. They argue that dads in high-income countries would spend the same amount on the education of their children as women would. However, that is disproven when we look at the research conducted in middle- and high-income countries. There, mothers are still more likely to invest in others rather than themselves—or in themselves through purchasing goods and services that reduce their domestic care load.[32]

I see this reverberate in my own family. My spouse cares deeply about gender equity and engaging in decision-making as equals, yet our preferences are different. My tolerance for purchasing cleaning services or meal prep boxes is much higher than his—mostly because I value my time, a scarce resource, in a different light than he does. Meanwhile, my spouse has owned up to three triathlon bikes at one time. His triathlon bikes, a private good, are the equivalent of the cigarettes and alcohol seen in the economic studies of low-income countries.

Gendered preferences in prioritizing resource allocation and spending within households is a legitimate issue across the globe. While there is variation in individual preferences within genders, on average, gendered trends exist. Because of this, policies like divorce laws dictating who gets control of resources when families split have influence in determining the allocation of resources in intact families.[33] A sudden change in divorce policies that shifts control of family resources upon separation can have profound effects on intact marriages, overall social welfare, and community well-being.

Divorce laws are not the only policies that can shift a family's economic investments and outcomes.[34] The same is true for policies and social norms that make it easier or more feasible to get a high-quality education. Increases in women's education and more family-friendly policies in the workplace often correlate with increases in women's labor force participation.[35]

Policies that make it possible for family members who provide care to work for pay outside the home increase household investments in the next generation by putting more direct economic resources in the hands of family members who provide primary care. Over time, we have seen this play out both in the increasing educational attainment of women, making them more sought-after in the labor market, and in investment in things that are important to family members providing care who work for pay outside the home, such as policies that support the childcare and eldercare industries. Still, there is much to be done.

Often what is lacking in the argument for public supports or public-private partnerships in markets that help caregivers thrive, like childcare, is data: continuous data highlighting the return on investment in high-quality early childhood education as it relates to economic outcomes for caregivers, like lifetime and household earnings; or data linking individuals who provide family care and work outside their home for pay to macroeconomic indicators such as economic growth. These statistics connecting investments in care to economic outcomes are lacking or ignored today because we live in a society and culture that takes care for granted.* This is the challenge of the twenty-first century, and it won't be solved unless we all speak up and demand better of ourselves, our friends, families, communities, and those who represent us politically.

We will know when we succeed. When we do, the childcare industry will be equally prioritized in hard economic times. Bailout scenarios for businesses considered "too big to fail" will include childcare in the discussion, and threats to the childcare industry will be as easily resolved as they have been for the airline or automobile industries in the past.[36] We will know because childcare will be accessible and affordable for all. Parents will have more choice in how they want to live their best life given the resources available to them. Economic growth will flourish. There will be less crime. And, if we are lucky, our family members who provide care work for us will be happier, or at least more content, less stressed, and living better balanced lives, which will inherently increase well-being for all.

EVERMORE

Some claim that the modern-day school calendar was developed to help farmers who needed their children home and working in the fields when planting and harvesting was at its most intense.[37] Others find that the calendar was based on urban elite desires to vacation in cooler places during the hot summer months.[38] Neither of these reasons had anything to do with the best intentions for children or their daily care providers. Our roads, train routes, and flight patterns were developed to facilitate trade between cities, states, and nations, not to help children get safely to school or care providers safely to parks and daycare facilities.[39] In the same light, the labor market was not built with family care providers in mind.

Modern economies were designed with the expectation that workers get to and from work with ease. There was little consideration for employees with

---

* My project, The Care Board, is an attempt to begin fixing this glaring gap in economic statistics. For more information, see https://thecareboard.org.

childcare or schooling needs for their children. The typical workday was designed by the employer, who was usually care-privileged. Care privilege belongs to those of us who have someone else taking care of our basic needs, and individuals with care privilege have historically been men.[40] In addition, once in a job, individuals without care privilege struggle because the systems to advance at work were built to keep those with power and privilege on top.

What happens to women and caregivers when they interact with an economy originally built for men and those with care privilege? They hide their caregiving roles from employers for fear of not being taken seriously.[41] They worry and stress.[42] They accept less leisure and sleep relative to their care-privileged counterparts.[43] They work harder and are usually rewarded for it with less pay and slower paths to promotions.[44] Maybe this is your reality. If it is, you are not alone. This is the reality of most caregivers today who work in the formal labor market.

An average 1950s *Mad Men* workday was from 9:00 a.m. to 5:00 p.m. (or later). Similarly, in the 1980s, films like *9 to 5* made waves, highlighting how women in paid office jobs often struggled to meet their 9:00 a.m. to 5:00 p.m. work schedules while balancing their nonpaid work lives.[45] Today's work schedules are slightly more flexible but generally follow an eight-hour cycle. Before the workday begins, caregivers often have already worked anywhere from forty-five minutes to an hour getting their loved ones ready for the day. Parents of children under age six spend a total of 910 hours annually, around twenty-three weeks (more than five months) of full-time work, caring for and helping other household members.[46] This includes waking up, clothing, feeding, and transporting small children to daycare or school. It often also includes preparing lunchboxes with rice, chicken, fruit, and a juice, milk, or water.

The care provider does not have the luxury of heading straight into their workplace from home. They make at least one pit stop, often multiple, to drop off small children at their chosen destination for the day. Dropping off almost always requires getting out of the car, metro, or bus with said child, their lunchbox, and bag of necessary items for the day (often a backpack if they are of school age). The caregiver then walks the child into said daycare or school, signs them in, talks with the staff, helps the child take off their coat and put their things in a cubby, leaves—sometimes with a stressed child crying about being left—and gets back to their mode of transportation, and finally heads to work.

By the time they get to work, their care-privileged colleagues, many of whom woke up, showered, (worked out?), dressed themselves, ate breakfast, and went straight to work, are fresh and ready to start their day. The family care provider, on the other hand, is already tired, their hair in disarray. Maybe they had to drive across town to drop their child at daycare. Maybe they did not sleep through the night. The care provider is often the first woken up during the night by small children who cannot sleep, or for whom the only way back to sleep is next to the care provider—which disrupts the even flow of deep sleep they need to feel fully rested and to function well the next day.

At any point in the workday, a family care provider may be randomly interrupted by a phone call from their child's daycare or school, calling to explain a situation related to biting or a fall from schoolyard equipment. By mid-afternoon, the care provider may be juggling transportation from school to an after-school program or, in some cases, may need to take time off to pick up a child from school and transport them back home. As the close of the workday approaches, they may be rushing to get out and make it to daycare or the after-school program to pick up their child before it closes. Care providers arriving late for pickup can experience penalties up to $2 per minute they are late, increasing their stress as they attempt to leave work on time and cross their fingers there are no traffic jams or buses running late.[47]

At this point in the day, the care provider's third shift starts. Unlike the care-privileged, who may leave work and head to a happy hour or home to kick off their shoes and crack open a beer and watch sports or the news until their dinner magically appears, the family care provider usually arrives home to the madness of finding snacks for tired and cranky children while simultaneously changing out of work clothes and prepping dinner. After dinner there is dinner clean up, baths for children, and some sort of bedtime routine. By the time the care provider crawls into bed, she (or he) often has had minimal personal free time to recharge and energize. The cycle starts all over again a few hours later, when she (or he) is woken up by a small child who has just had a nightmare and wants to snuggle their way back to sleep.

It is difficult to find any sector of our formal economy that was developed with the family care provider in mind. Since women disproportionately carry the load of direct care in many societies, most economies were developed without consideration for women's needs. As women's educational attainment continues to increase and their role in paid employment becomes critical for family well-being,[48] an economy built for the care-privileged has become ever more glaring. Post-pandemic labor force participation of mothers has accelerated, making the issue even more visible.[49]

Care providers engaged in invisible labor are exhausted. But just how exhausted? Nations do not regularly report statistics on the number of hours engaged in unpaid family work in our homes, hours that include washing dishes, making meals, and cleaning. In fact, the US did not even start collecting data on how people use their time until 2003.[50]

Not developing and reporting these statistics means we do not fully understand how mothers' increased labor force participation and time spent caring for their family post-pandemic has impacted their mental health and that of their family members. There are, after all, only twenty-four hours in a day, and something usually has got to give for family care providers when labor force participation increases—it's usually their mental health.

LOOK WHAT YOU MADE US DO

Today, women think twice about having children. Many are choosing not to have them. In 2022, 17.6 percent of women in their twenties had children under age five, compared to 46.3 percent in 1970.[51] Young women have done the math and some have calculated that children are too expensive or too disrupting to their lifestyle and career goals.[52] Women are also delaying births due to advancements in educational attainment and reproductive health, as well as increased economic independence. Average age at first birth has increased to 27.3 years, up from 25.6 years in 2011. In addition, women are having fewer total children in their lifetime compared to previous generations.[53]

According to an opinion piece written by economist Dean Spears and published in the *New York Times* on September 18, 2023, children born today are likely to see global population peak before it begins a potentially steep descent.[54] That is because, as Dean argues, families across the globe are choosing to have fewer children. And, as Dean is quick to point out, very few, if any, countries have ever recovered to a population rate above the replacement rate of 2.1 once they go below it.

Economists place the cause of this fertility decrease on long-run changes in educational attainment and improvements in health and longevity primarily driven by technological innovations like the pill, intrauterine devices (IUDs), pacemakers, and vaccines. Because higher education leads to higher incomes and a focus on a career rather than a job, and because parents will continue to struggle to balance career with the needs of family, Dean argues that the replacement rate is not likely to increase.

When it comes to living in an economy built by men, Dean and I agree that population rates are not likely to increase given the current state of expectations around how we work and how we live. But there is a way to increase the number of children families have that does not involve taking away the reproductive health rights of women. We could re-envision our economy, priorities, and expectations around how we do work and family.

We could create a Barbie Land–style society, call it Fertility Land, that encouraged a strong and healthy balance between career expectations and family life. This economy would provide a bold set of care policies. Instead of it being cost prohibitive to have and raise children, policies would strengthen families' ability to have multiple children, should they wish, and stay engaged in their careers and jobs. In this economy, childcare would be affordable, and, for those who choose to supervise and raise their small children in the home, stipends would be available to compensate for the otherwise unpaid work involved in raising the next generation. In Fertility Land, men would increase their activity and engagement in childcare and domestic work. Their career advancement would slow and that of women would accelerate, leading to more equality and reductions in the gender wage gap.

Still, Dean's predictions may not come true. They remind me of the fallacy of population decline that circulated among demographers and economists at the turn of the nineteenth century. In 1798, Thomas Robert Malthus published *An Essay on the Principle of Population*. In it, Thomas argued that increasing food production through innovative technologies improved the well-being of the population but also led to exponential population growth and a continued risk of a lack of sufficient food for this ever-expanding populace, which would eventually lead to starvation. This model (driven by math!) proved wrong on a global level. There is still enough food in the world to feed everyone, should our policies allow it.

Thomas's theories, however, led to the identification of something called the demographic transition, which has been observed in most countries across the globe. It starts in a population with high fertility and high mortality. Technological innovations and growth lead to decreases in mortality rates through improved health. This leads to a natural increase in the population, as birth rates are still high and individuals are living longer. Eventually, the technological advancements and decreased death rates lead to increased economic growth and productivity, making having children more costly (because of the loss of earnings from moving away from paid work to care for children), which then drives a decrease in birth rates. Eventually populations end up in a stage of low fertility and low mortality—which is where many countries are today.

Neither Thomas's theories of population growth nor Dean's warnings of population decline considered where a society led by women and caregivers might take us. Like Adam's, Thomas's and Dean's theories were driven by the modern economic concept that markets, with their invisible hands, are efficient. None of these theories speaks to the roles community, government, and policy infrastructure can play in the care, health, and well-being of a society and the workers and care providers driving its economy.

I THINK HE KNOWS

Similar opinion pieces and theories on population decline are, in many respects, evergreen. An article like Dean's showed up two years earlier, in May 2021, also in *The New York Times*, highlighting the impending global population bust as global fertility was on the decline.[55]

This article highlighted two opposing demographic phenomena spurred by the pandemic. First, older people had died in disproportionate numbers.[56] Second, they were less likely to be replaced by births, as the pandemic lowered the total number of pregnancies and births. Births plummeted partly because there was very little risky fornication going on across households during the pandemic, resulting in a reduction in unexpected pregnancies. In addition, those making intentional decisions to procreate were hesitant to bring a new baby into a pandemic-ridden world. Going to the hospital during a once-in-a-century pandemic was risky, and our individual (and collective) economic stability seemed, well, shaky. Intentional pregnancies are more likely to happen when people believe they are on solid footing economically (and otherwise) and able to raise a child. Last, international migration came to a grinding halt. Fewer immigrants meant there were fewer non-citizens and new citizens having children in the US.

Even with overall rates decreasing, there were birthing bubbles among subpopulations. For example, births among US citizen women in high-skilled jobs or with higher levels of education increased. The acceleration of telework during the pandemic made white-collar work from home with an infant more manageable and less costly than when infants required daycare.[57]

What did all this mean for gender equity post-pandemic? The last half of the twentieth century had slowly moved the dial on gender equality in the workplace by attacking low-hanging fruit like overt sexism. Women's educational attainment increased during that same period, and women slowly moved into more traditionally male (and higher paid) jobs, including leadership positions. But by the mid-1980s we had stalled. Even today, women still make only eighty-three cents to each dollar made by men, a statistic that has remained relatively flat for decades.[58]

This was the rut we were stuck in until the pandemic started making work life increasingly feasible for more women and care providers in white-collar office jobs and some other jobs that transitioned to remote capabilities (e.g., teaching). The pandemic also exposed the heavy burden of unpaid domestic labor at home, reduced commute times, and made telework more acceptable. When flexible work got easier, more women (and men) with higher levels of education chose to have children and raise a family.

So, we are left with this. If we care about the extinction of humans, then perhaps we had better care about the gender inequities in our lives. During baby busts or when a global emergency calls for a lifestyle that allows care providers a different kind of balance, women and care providers gain power, and that power can increase their economic well-being. It allows them to push for policies and programs that invest wisely in quality childcare programs and allow mothers to better balance work with family—the kinds of programs that are needed if we want women (and men) with children to work and want childless working women (and men) to have babies.

The women of Taylor's generation and younger are economically independent and just fine on their own. I am willing to bet that if society does not offer more social investments to help families (and women) succeed outside the home, it would provide these investments to ensure the survival of humanity, and I think the patriarchy knows.

OUT OF THE WOODS

Policies driven by traditional social norms focused on the family often stifle individual independence. They tend to create environments in which women rely on men's actions, money, or decisions for survival. Throughout history, policies have either restricted or accelerated women's economic freedom.

For example, the right to vote was granted to women in 1920 in the United States with the ratification of the Nineteenth Amendment.[59] This had a dramatic effect on the development of family and social policies. It accelerated women's ability to influence policies and resource allocation and advance women's rights and equality.

Other rights, like the right to independently open a bank account, were not given to women until the latter half of the twentieth century. In the 1960s, banks began to allow women to open bank accounts with the co-signature of a father or husband.[60] The Equal Credit Opportunity Act of 1974 finally gave women the right to open a bank account and sign up for a credit card without a male co-signer.[61] Not having the right to independently manage a bank account and one's own resources restricted women's economic independence for centuries and gave them less bargaining power within relationships and marriages.

We see the effects of this still today. Women are less likely to be involved in investments.[62] Women hold 11 percent of leadership roles in hedge funds and private debt firms, and only 12 percent of global fund managers are women.[63] Women seem more comfortable managing daily household finances, perhaps because they are more likely to be making the primary decisions on how to distribute resources within the home.[64] For various reasons, women accrue less savings for retirement, and it is common for women from my mother's generation* or earlier to feel unexpectedly overwhelmed or surprised by the state of family finances when a spouse dies.[65]

Marriage and divorce laws alter economic autonomy and the income or wealth generation of those who marry. Dowries, once universally common and still common today in some parts of the world, provide the spouse of a daughter with economic resources that pass to him upon marriage, often to help support a daughter's transition into her new family.

Today, in the United States and other high-income countries, couples decide whether to sign prenuptial agreements to protect the economic gains acquired by each individually before marriage. As women have increased their levels of education and leaned toward entering careers instead of jobs,[66] women's economic rights entering marriage have changed.

Research shows that once they are married, women often make larger financial and economic sacrifices than men to stay in the marriage.[67] They are more likely than men to leave work temporarily or permanently after children are added to the family.[68] They are also more likely than men to move to lower-paying jobs when a spouse is offered a better job in a different location.[69] As adults, daughters take leave or time off from work to help an aging parent

* Those born on or around 1950.

more often than their brothers do.[70] Men also experience temporary setbacks due to the birth of a child, the need to care for a parent, or a spouse's job relocation, but on average the large proportion of marital partners who sacrifice economic gains in support of their family's well-being are women who engage in disproportionate amounts of unpaid domestic housework. This fact rings true across the globe. When family policies direct resources to care providers who are engaged in unpaid care work in the home, women and families often benefit.

FRESH OUT THE SLAMMER

What if we started again from scratch and developed version 2.0 of the Barbie economy, only this time we acknowledged all the invisible labor that goes into making Barbie successful, including the grandmother or grandfather who dispensed sage advice and maybe took care of her when she was young so her mother could work? We would see the mother or father, who makes her breakfast and dinner every day, pass her the toast instead of it flying from the toaster onto her plate. We would see someone wash and iron her clothes instead of them magically appearing, wrinkle free, in her closet. If her family were lucky enough to have enough resources to hire outside help, we would see those domestic helpers front and center, and they would receive fair pay with health benefits instead of a minimum wage with no benefits.

In Barbie 2.0, invisible care becomes visible. We can see how unpaid and paid care work allow Barbie the time and freedom to become president, host thrilling dance parties, and explore any career she wants. But in the real world, for Barbie to be as free as men have been in this exploration, someone needs to pick up the slack of the essential unpaid care work that makes the world go 'round. This is the piece that we, as a larger society, have yet to figure out.

We have gotten good at telling girls they can be or do anything, just like boys. We tell them that all the way through college. We tell them that at holiday family dinners that all the women in the family have organized, prepared, cooked for, and cleaned up after—the older men helping only when asked or directed.

I remember the feeling I had in college of how awkward it was to be told that I could do anything in life and to be treated relatively equally in college, only to return home to traditional gendered behavior when my family got together for the holidays. How could I be anything if the women in my family did all the work to prepare for these family events that we all loved so much? Where would I find the time?

This is the conundrum women find themselves in today, and it is why we cannot have it all. We have yet to break up the workload of the household beyond gendered norms. We have yet to figure out how to have men do more and women do less in the home. Until we figure that out, women who are excelling in the world outside their homes will continue to feel exhausted and will continue to question their ability to make it all work. We need a Barbie Land economy 2.0 that recognizes and pays for the invisible labor and work done within our homes and formally recognizes its contributions to families and the larger society. One that equalizes the domestic work of the home across genders.

HITS DIFFERENT

In 1880, around one in seventeen women between the ages of twenty-five and fifty-four (5.9 percent) living with their own children under age five worked in the formal labor market, compared to 99 percent of fathers of the same age (figure 1, panel A). The differences were also stark among women from different backgrounds. One-third of all Black mothers worked in the formal labor market, compared to two percent of white mothers (figure 1, panel B). Women who could not read or write were more likely to work outside of the home for pay than women who could read and write (figure 1, panel C). By the 1980s, women with some education beyond elementary school were more likely to be working than those with an elementary school education or no schooling, driven by women with college degrees or higher.

Measured by various characteristics, the employment of mothers of small children has shifted over the past century and a half, and gaps have been closed. In 2021, 69 percent of mothers of children under age five worked outside the home. Mothers used to work for pay much less frequently than fathers; the gap between mothers and fathers working for pay shrank by 67 percentage points between 1860 and 2021 (figure 1, panel A). More Black than white mothers worked for pay (figure 1, panel B); the gap between Black and white mothers has shrunk from around 30 percentage points to around 5 percentage points.

Mothers with less education or no spouse have higher rates of paid labor (figure 1, panels C and D). The gap in paid labor between mothers and fathers—and Black and white mothers—has narrowed. Today, mothers with a spouse in the home are more likely to be working for pay than in previous

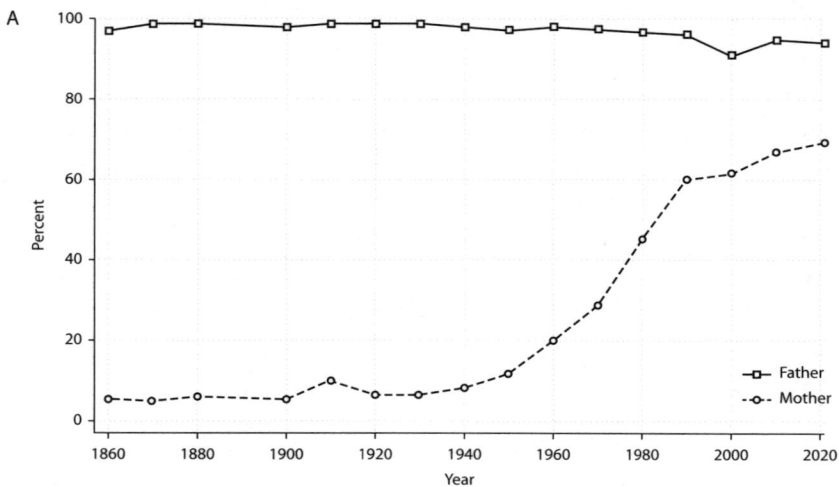

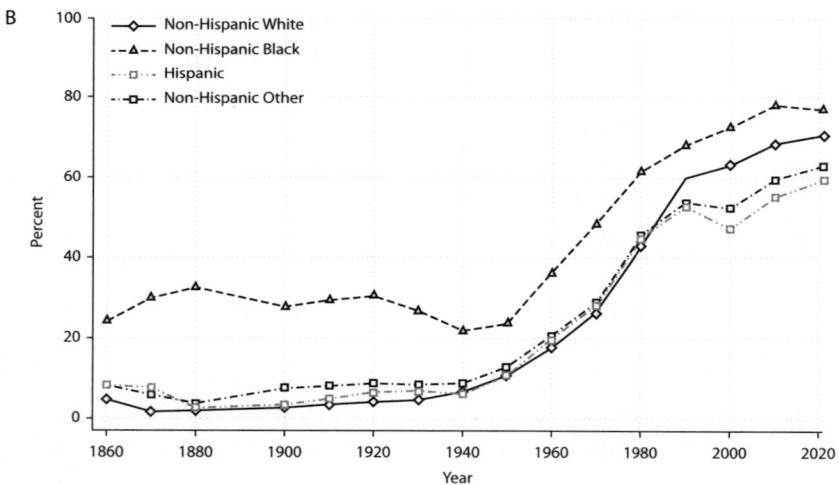

FIGURE 1. Traditional labor force participation of prime-age adults (ages 25–54) living with children under age five, 1860–2021. Panel A: Fathers and mothers. Panel B: Mothers by race.

C

Legend:
- ○ - Literate
- □ - Not Literate

Percent (y-axis: 0 to 100)
Year (x-axis: 1860 to 2020)

D

Legend:
- ○ - Lives with Spouse
- □ - No Spouse in Home

Percent (y-axis: 0 to 100)
Year (x-axis: 1860 to 2020)

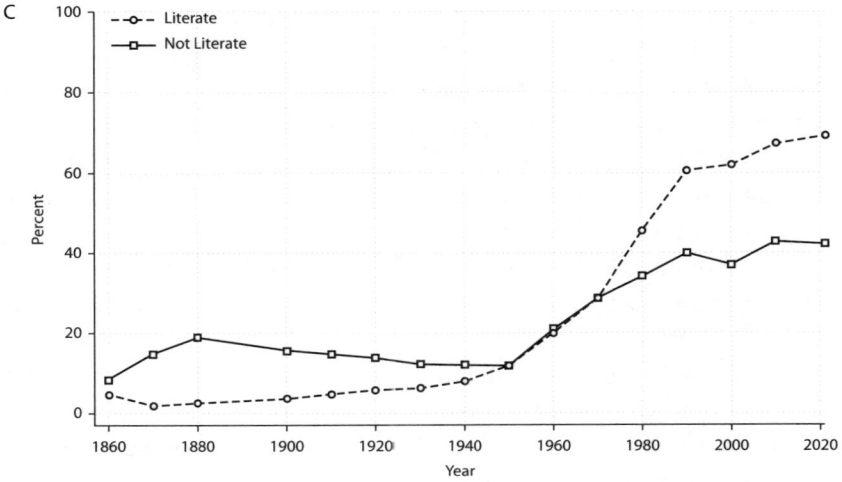

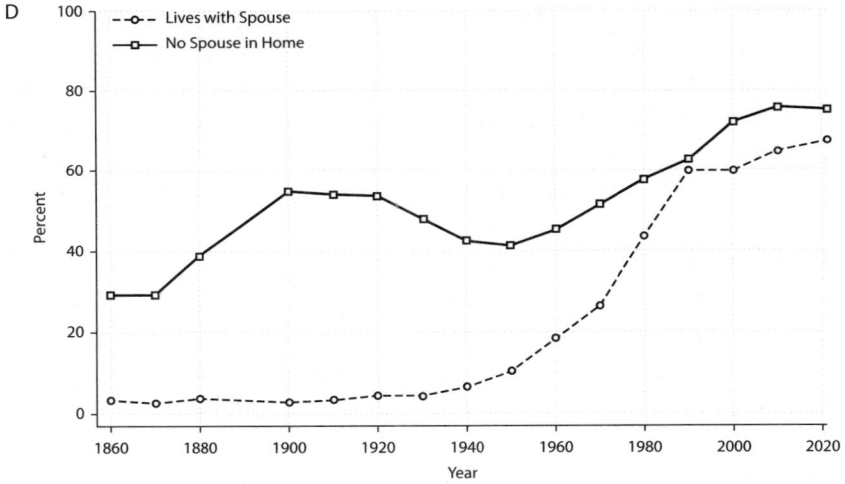

FIGURE 1. Panel C: Mothers by literacy. Panel D: Mothers with/without spouse in the home. Source: Author's calculations using decennial census data and current population surveys, US Census Bureau / Bureau of Labor Statistics, ipums.org. Note: Up to and including 1930, literate includes individuals who stated *Yes, literate (reads and writes)* and after 1930 includes individuals who have achieved a fifth-grade education or higher.

decades, but still less likely than mothers with no spouse (figure 1, panel D). We need to dig deep into the data to find these stories. But they exist, and they should encourage us not to underestimate the economic contributions of women of the past in propelling us forward.

These statistics demonstrate that society desperately needs to update its assumptions with regard to the roles women play both in the home and in paid work outside the home. Given that so many mothers are now engaged in paid labor outside the home, why hasn't society placed more priority on structures that balance caregiver needs and priorities with well-being—structures like affordable and reliable childcare? The labor of care for our small children, families, and households is invisible in figure 1. If it were there, 100 percent of mothers presented would be working over the entire time span.

The women of our past advocated for a better life for their daughters and sons, a just society where we could all flourish more equally. And, contrary to popular belief, women have always engaged in civic and work-related duties and always contributed to our economy. We might just not realize to what degree, because their stories were either not told or were under-told in *his*tory books.

Yet even in domains as masculine as the military, women made significant contributions. Clara Barton, a nurse and founder of the Red Cross, was given a special pass onto the battlefields during the Civil War, and during that same period, Dorthea Dix was given the job of superintendent of the US Army nurses. During World War I, about 3,000 nurses were deployed to Europe; even though women did not yet have the right to vote, they were allowed to enlist, with up to 12,000 serving in the US Navy as telephone and radio operators and translators. Up to 350,000 women (about half the population of Vermont today) served in uniform during World War II.[71]

Stories of the women who came before us are nothing if not economic stories about our foremothers, women who worked every day either within their households, for employers, or for themselves through small business and entrepreneurial endeavors. They were strong, active, organized, smart, curious, and determined to sustain or improve the lives of their families, communities, and society at large.

THE MANUSCRIPT

It is relatively easy to find trailblazing women in any city across the globe. In the US, regional stories highlight variations and the unique contributions of

TABLE 1 Prime-Age (25–54) Mothers and Work by Region of the US, 1950

Region	Total population of prime-age mothers	Total working (paid and unpaid)	As % of all mothers	Total in unpaid family work	As % of all working mothers
West North Central	1,830,934	367,555	20%	70,327	19%
East South Central	1,477,179	327,632	22%	34,121	10%
West South Central	1,932,682	414,937	21%	36,882	9%
Mountain	682,489	146,439	21%	12,813	9%
East North Central	4,141,880	898,429	22%	63,670	7%
South Atlantic	2,798,202	761,252	27%	55,614	7%
Pacific	1,954,337	472,951	24%	22,411	5%
Mid Atlantic	4,287,914	854,612	20%	22,654	3%
New England	1,275,674	298,354	23%	4,252	1%
Total	20,381,291	4,542,161	22%	322,744	7%
Total central regions	9,382,675	2,008,553		205,000	
Central regions as percentage of total	**46%**	**44%**		**64%**	

SOURCE: Author's calculations using the 1950 Census, US Census Bureau (ipums.org).

NOTE: West North Central includes North Dakota, South Dakota, Nebraska, Kansas, Minnesota, Iowa, and Missouri. East South Central includes Alabama, Kentucky, Mississippi, and Tennessee. West South Central includes Arkansas, Louisiana, Oklahoma, and Texas. East North Central includes Illinois, Michigan, Ohio, and Wisconsin. Total working includes those working in paid jobs and those who identified their occupation as an "unpaid family worker."

a diverse set of women. Even in the middle of the twentieth century, women's work varied by region. Table 1 shows 1950 rates of engagement in paid work and unpaid family work of prime-age mothers with children under age five.

Transformative innovation has taken place in the agricultural sector and rural farming communities over the past century. Farms have historically been economic drivers of societies. If you have ever worked on a small family farm, you know that the work often requires all hands on deck, regardless of gender. The agricultural sector provides our food. Women needed to actively participate on the farm and engage in work for survival. Without farmers and modern agribusiness, we could not survive. This history influenced farm families and their children even as younger generations moved to cities.

These historical roots of paid and unpaid labor on family farms live on in us today. As table 1 shows, almost half (46 percent) of all prime-age mothers in the United States in 1950 lived in the central regions of the country, and

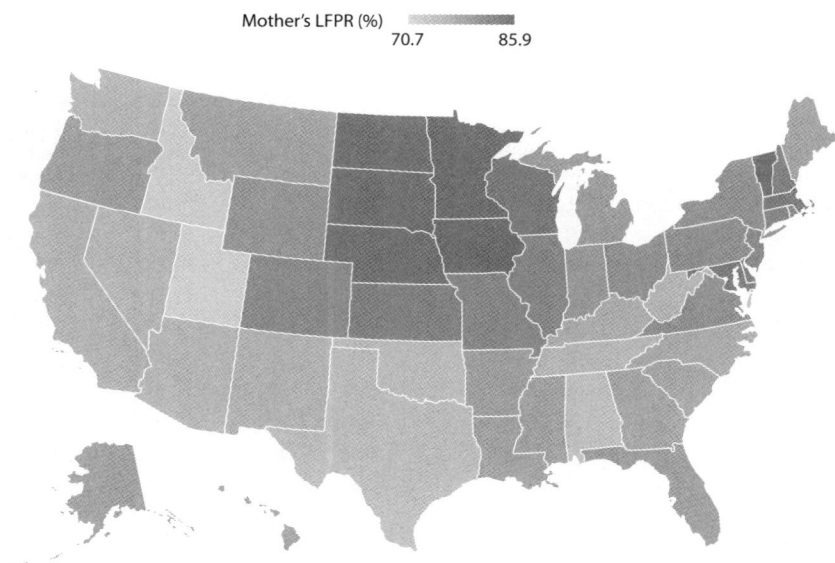

Mother's LFPR (%)
70.7   85.9

FIGURE 2. Labor force participation rates of prime-age mothers (25–54) with minor children, 2023. Source: Author's calculations based on the 2023 American Community Survey, US Census Bureau, ipums.org

they made up almost half (44 percent) of all mothers who worked, whether their work was paid labor or unpaid family labor. The center of the country was, in fact, different in the ways that mothers experienced work. About two-thirds (64 percent) of mothers in the central regions identified themselves as working in unpaid family work.

By the 1950s, multiple generations had tilled the land of family farms and instilled a solid work ethic in the baby-boom children of the time. Even though the farm crisis forcing sales to big agriculture held off until the 1980s, the mid-nineteenth century was a time when young people started leaving farms in pursuit of work in cities.[72] As young women left the farm for city life, they brought with them a belief that work was, or at least could be, less gendered.

In 2023, prime-age mothers living in farming states had the highest labor force participation rates (figure 2). In Minnesota and New Hampshire, for example, up to 86 percent of mothers were working for pay outside the home. These regional variations, if anything, tell us that the gender paradigm of work and parenthood is not predetermined or set in stone.

There once was a girl named Rosie. In 1938, she became a riveter. She may have had children, or not—either way, it did not hinder her ability to rivet. The 1940 Defense Housing and Community Facilities and Services Act (also known as the Lanham Act)[73] provided around $52 million in federal funding for child-care services across the nation between August 1943 and February 1946. In 1940, 8.2 percent of prime-age mothers living with children under age five were working for pay outside their home; by 1960 that number more than doubled and around 20 percent worked for pay (figure 1, panel A). The World War II period coincided with an important shift in the composition of working mothers. Prior to 1940, it was predominately mothers with low levels of education who worked outside the home (figure 1, panel C). But once Rosie was given her chance to shine—an innovation of war—women with higher levels of education eventually surpassed their counterparts in labor force participation.

The primary goal of the program was not to benefit mothers and their children but rather to supply labor: the military was in dire need of workers who could build bombs and other wartime matériel for World War II. This formal arrangement, however, had benefits for both the military and for women. Sending men to war and asking women to fill in manufacturing jobs had a ripple effect on benefits to their children's future employment opportunities.[74]

Once the children of Rosie were all grown up and working adults themselves, her daughters were still constrained by childcare needs. But in the late 1960s they held out hope for a formal childcare system that would provide support so that mothers could work. By 1970, 29 percent of mothers living with children under age five were working in the formal labor market (figure 1, panel A). In 1971, the US Congress passed the wildly popular Comprehensive Child Development Act (CCDA).[75] Sponsored by Senator Walter Mondale of Minnesota, the act had support on both sides of the aisle, as it was generally agreed that providing daycare benefits, especially to working single mothers living with children under age five (just over 50 percent of whom were working in 1970 [figure 1, panel D]), would help Americans thrive. Unfortunately, the CCDA never actually became law; President Richard Nixon, after originally showing support for it, vetoed the bill.[76]

There are two overlapping explanations to why the bill failed. The first is that shortly after he vetoed the bill, the president visited communist

China—a first for a US president in over twenty-five years. Richard, anxious about political backlash for establishing relations with a reigning communist party, feared that some might view the fight for a more comprehensive child-care program as being aligned with communist ideals. Pat Buchanan, the president's chief of staff at the time, had seen children's centers in the Soviet Union where children around the age of five or six chanted Leninist slogans, creating a visual impression of centers for children as being communist or socialist.[77] To save face for the upcoming visit to China, the president's advisors, principally Pat, encouraged him to veto the CCDA so as not to appear to be supporting socialist issues. Since he was up for reelection, Richard struck down the bill.

It did not take Pat much effort to come up with a rationale for vetoing the bill. He recommended vetoing it entirely. His argument was that family values were at risk if children spent their days in a childcare center rather than with their mothers. He wrote the veto speech Richard gave, in which he argued that committing "the vast moral authority of the national Government to the side of communal approaches to childrearing," versus taking a family-centered approach, was wrong.[78]

The second explanation comes from academic Deborah Dinner,[79] who has argued that the feminist arguments in favor of childcare that were linked to the broader push for the bill gave Richard an additional argument to veto it because they promoted women's economic independence from the family. Other scholars and policy experts agree. Both international geopolitical issues and family values considerations doomed the passage of the CCDA.[80]

Neither Richard nor Pat had individual women and children's best interests at heart. Rather, they used women and children in a game of politics that was meant to maintain power and the status quo. It was a setback and a disappointment, but it did not stall mothers' desires and need to become economic stewards for their families.

Neither Richard nor Pat could not stop what Rosie had unleashed. Between 1970 and 1980, the labor force participation of prime-age mothers living with children under age five increased 17 percentage points—46 percent of all mothers ages twenty-five to fifty-four living with children under age five were working for pay by 1980 (figure 1, panel A). Most of those mothers were working out of economic need within their households.[81] Between 1980 and 2000, prime-age mothers' labor force participation increased another 16 percentage points—62 percent were working in the formal labor market. According to the US Bureau of Labor Statistics, by 2024, labor force participation was 65.4 percent for mothers with children under three years old, and the gap between married mothers and other mothers was less than one percent.[82]

Revenge is a dish best served cold. No White House staffer was going to keep mothers from gainful employment if they wanted it. Once society let Rosie out of the home, there was no one and nothing that could put her back in. Partially due to the economic environment of World War II, women started making decisions about their economic lives based on a broader set of preferences.[83]

Can we take comfort in the idea that the care-privileged arrogance of 1970s politicians is a long-gone trend? In November 2021, the US House of Representatives passed the $1.75 trillion Build Back Better Bill. Lauded for its focus on making lives better for children, parents, the elderly, and workers, and assessed by the Congressional Budget Office as not increasing the US debt, it included support for comprehensive, affordable childcare programs.[84] A comprehensive childcare plan was once again active in the US Congress. And once again, it was close to becoming law.

This time, though, it wasn't a presidential staffer who would tank the bill, but rather a US senator. The vote for the Build Back Better Bill failed in the Senate by one vote. The senator whose vote tanked support for working mothers across the country was, again, a traditional older white man, this time from coal country.[85] Joe Manchin was the new Pat. Joe most likely never struggled to provide informal care for his family while he worked. Ignorance is bliss for those care-privileged enough to have others carry the weight of invisible labor.

SUPERSTAR

Living in an economy built around the lives of the care-privileged is not easy. It is constructed in a way that benefits some and provides additional challenges for others. Sometimes those providing care internalize it: we think it is our fault we did not get the promotion because we took maternity leave. Sometimes we fantasize what it would be like if we fit that world like a glove. We daydream about what our privileged colleagues do after work, because their choice set is often broader than ours. Being female and, especially, being a caregiver in an economy built for the care-privileged means we hustle and are constantly tired. Yet many of us find our way. We strive and thrive for balance. We engage in a multitude of economic activities and find holes, slits, and slivers of light toward a path of survival. Around 90 percent of us find ways to reinvent our path. We do it to survive.[86]

Women are as active as ever in the labor markets outside their home, and this has to do with more than just educational attainment, although that is a major driver. The prime-age women of today have high levels of educational attainment precisely because policies were adapted that encouraged their participation in education, and parents valued education for both their boys and their girls. Baby boomers, an often maligned, or, alternatively, over-celebrated generation, may have given us more than bra burning, civil rights, and war protests.

They left their externally rebellious college years and turned to the world inside their home. They continued their protests and fight for equality within their families. They raised their daughters to become doctors, lawyers, teachers, and leaders. They told them that they could do anything, be anything, if they only put their minds to it.

And so we did. But no one prepared us for the challenges we would face trying to manage big careers, demanding full-time jobs, and on-call caregiving inside our homes. We were crushed when we started families after settling in on a career instead of a job. Childcare was prohibitively expensive. Even when it was available, the hours rarely meshed adequately with the demands of a full-time job. We are now at a crossroads.

Advancements in gender equity move in waves or steps, two steps forward, one step back. Our parents and grandparents got us here. They reduced overt sexism in the workplace. They encouraged us to educate ourselves. They dreamed big for us so that we would believe we could. Now it is our turn.

Today we must make the implicit assumptions about women, care, and domestic tasks in the home explicit. We must ask why the social structures in our homes exist and actively challenge those norms. We should directly ask for gender equity in the workplace and in earnings, even though it can no longer be our sole focus. Instead, we should also be pushing for gender equity in the home.

We should no longer tell women to lean in more to get ahead at work, although they can if they want to. Rather, men should lean in more at home. It is not absolutely necessary that women's earnings increase, but men's earnings will go down to meet women's earnings as men take on more shared care work, because this unpaid labor will disrupt their ability to engage in unlimited work outside the home.

And, lucky for us, there are so many women and allies fighting for these rights. This is the future of gender equality and equity. It is part acting "as if" and part using the resources we have accrued to date to dream up and pursue the life we want. It is remembering nobody owns us but us. We must foster more conversations within our homes and workplaces to encourage change. We can reframe and rethink community goals, push the invisible into the visible, and create work environments that allow us to better balance paid work and care work in order to help ourselves and the next generation move ahead. We must make invisible labor visible so we can all thrive.

FIVE

Generations

MARJORIE / THE BEST DAY

> One of the hardest forms of regret is the regret of being so young
> when you lost someone, that you didn't have the perspective to
> learn and appreciate who they were. I'd open up my grandmoth-
> er's closet and she had beautiful dresses from the 60s, and I wish
> I'd asked her where she wore every single one of them.
>
> TAYLOR SWIFT on writing "marjorie"

TAYLOR SWIFT IS KNOWN FOR WRITING SONGS about women,
including the women from her own family tree. Her song "Timeless" from
Speak Now (Taylor's Version) is rumored to have been inspired by her maternal grandmother.[1] The song "marjorie," on the album *Evermore*, is more
directly about her relationship with her grandmother Marjorie Finlay, a
soprano opera singer and TV talent in Puerto Rico.[2] The song talks about
being clever and kind, powerful and polite, characteristics Taylor probably
learned from her grandmother. She is bolstered by her grandmother's endear-
ing support and has acknowledged how this relationship has influenced the
artist and person she is today.

Taylor wrote "The Best Day" from *Fearless* about her childhood relationship with her mother. And the song "Soon You'll Get Better" from *Lover* is
about dealing with her mother Andrea's battle with cancer.[3] Taylor mashed
these two songs together on night one of her Eras Tour in Vancouver,
Canada. Her lyrics directly tell the story of how she relies on her mother for
guidance and support.

We are the result of the women and individuals who came before us. The
decisions they made, or did not make, influence our opportunities and economic choices. Like waves in an expansive ocean, we move and sway over
generations. We live in the today and the future influenced by our ancestors.
If we want to more deeply understand how far women have come, we need to
understand the path to how we got here.

Just like chapter 4, this chapter builds on how the women before us influence our current economic state. Just like Marjorie and Andrea did for Taylor, the women before you in your family influence how you see the world and what opportunities and paths you choose to follow. Increases in educational attainment, paid work opportunities, and social policies have also interacted with who we are and the options we see as available to us. The women of the past have pushed to help us get to this moment, and even if there are temporary setbacks, that does not change strength of the accomplishments they achieved on our behalf.

THE BOLTER

When we rediscover critical pieces of the past, we have an opportunity to reclaim our abandoned history. We can share untold stories or tell them from a previously unheard perspective. Economists can do this, as I have attempted in earlier chapters, but so can everyone else. Frances Osborne did when writing about her great grandmother, Idina Sackville, nicknamed "the bolter." And Taylor did when creating the song "The Bolter," which appeared on *The Tortured Poets Department (TTPD)*.

Frances is the great-granddaughter of Idina Sackville and came to learn of Idina's existence when, at the age of thirteen, she saw her picture in the London *Sunday Times*.[4] The *Times* was covering a book written about white Londoners in Kenya in the early twentieth century. Idina was adventurous and determined. Her picture was in the *Times* because she was one of those settlers.

Idina's reputation was said to be well known in early twentieth-century England. She was independent and nonconformist. Idina's nickname came about because of the many marriages she entered and then bolted from. This included divorcing her first husband and leaving their two small children with him. She married a second husband and moved to Kenya.

In England in her day, these choices were frowned upon. Negative rumors about Idina made it into a book being reviewed decades later by the *Sunday Times*. Rumors considered so scandalous that Frances's mother claimed she hadn't told Frances and her sibling about Idina because she did not want them to be known as the Bolter's great-granddaughters. She didn't want them to carry that shame.

But Frances was intrigued in the same way I was intrigued to find out that my many-times-great-grandmother, Lisbet Nypan, was the second-to-last woman burned at the stake in Norway after she was accused of witchery.[5] While news of this rebellious woman passed through generations in whispers and hushes, I was enthralled, mesmerized by her, and honored to have such a bold woman in my lineage. So much so that I was determined to name my first-born daughter after her. I lost that battle with my spouse, but my admiration for and my pride in Lisbet Nypan remain unwavering.

Idina was a woman who aspired to intense love and would not be bound by the confines of societal expectations. She loved deeply and often. The hidden stories of "bad women" that make it into family lore and historical legend can generate intense curiosity. Frances, years later, decided to rewrite the lore and legend of her great-grandmother, stripping the story of its misogynistic, woman-blaming tones and simply telling Idina's truth. Idina was a woman trying to survive in a society in which women were meant to be seen, not heard, and in which they were not meant to have feelings or aspirations beyond those society dictated.

Taylor Swift is known to write lyrics inspired by people and events in her life and from books she reads. On *TTPD*, "The Bolter" tells the story of a woman who loved hard but often felt trapped by societal norms and the confines of relationships once the love had vanished. In Taylor's version, we hear a different story of the tortured lore spread about Idina. This version speaks with the eyes, mind, and spirit of Idina herself. It is the lighthearted story of a woman's struggle to come to terms with the loss of a relationship and her continued pursuit of love. Finally, Idina's story breaks with tradition and those driven to uphold it. Taylor has done this for various famous women of the past. We would all benefit from more of these stories being told from women's perspective.

THE LAST GREAT AMERICAN DYNASTY

On July 7, 2023, Taylor Swift posted a photo on social media with the caption, "Happy belated Independence Day from your local neighborhood independent girlies."[6] The photo was of Taylor and a group of friends at the house Taylor owns in Rhode Island, which was known as "Holiday House" when it was purchased by Rebekah Harkness's spouse in 1948.

Rebekah was born in 1915 to a well-to-do family in St. Louis, Missouri. Like Idina, Rebekah married multiple times. Her second husband was an oil company heir who left his riches to her upon his death. Rebekah dabbled in developing a ballet company and funded the development of a medical research building and subsequent research projects in New York. She was known to spend time with the likes of yogi B. K. S. Iyengar and painter Salvador Dalí.[7] Like Idina, Rebekah was followed by rumors of her personal eccentricities, including stories that she cleaned her pool with Dom Pérignon champagne and dyed her neighbor's pet key-lime green following an argument.[8]

Taylor Swift wrote about Rebekah's life in a song on the *Folklore* album called "the last great american dynasty." It was accompanied by a skit in the 2023 US Eras Tour. Taylor's version tells the story of Rebekah's life from the outside looking in. It is a tale of how neighbors and society saw Rebekah's untraditional behavior. The song then flips and tells the story of Taylor buying the house, at which point she became the disruptor and the subject of community gossip. Taylor rewrites a story told from society's perspective to one told from Rebekah's, as well as her own, reclaiming the joy and freedom of independent women who break the rules of societal expectations.

CLARA BOW

TTPD includes a song titled "Clara Bow," with lyrics that describe what traditional music industry leaders tend to say to talented young women who come through their office doors. Taylor wrote this song because of her own experiences with industry leaders who would compare her to Clara Bow, Stevie Nicks, or other female entertainers and then tell her what she had that they did not.[9] Taylor's critique of the industry focuses on its leaders' quick ability to criticize amazingly talented, established musicians and entertainers in order to explain how an up-and-coming one might be additionally special, and the cycle that ensues when women are compared to other women iteratively over time.

Clara Bow was born into poverty in 1905 to a mother who was not interested in marriage or children and a father who did not think she would survive.[10] In her youth, Clara fell into acting by being in the right place at the right time and having natural talent. Her natural talent, she would argue, was to just be herself, but Clara was "The It Girl," based on her starring role in the popular movie *It*. Her fame was unmatched at the time.

Clara had multiple boyfriends throughout her acting career, and her reputation eventually suffered for it, but what was more interesting about her was her strategy for negotiation with production companies. After receiving a low salary in her first contract, she hired a lawyer and negotiated a much higher salary. She was the first actor to receive a contract without a behavior clause, which would terminate her contract if her reputation were tarnished during its duration.[11] Clara might have been born to few resources, but as her fame increased, her economic agency and acknowledgment of her fame created powerful opportunities for her of which she was able to take advantage. Even though she was always tied to industry leaders through contracts with production companies, she exhibited the same kind of agency and independence that Taylor Swift has shown.

These women (Taylor's version) all have commonalities. They pursued love and did not shy away from it. They were independent and true to themselves. They did not back down from their own preferences when society balked at them. They became famous, and if their reputations became tarnished, it was because they choose to be themselves and true to who they were while female. The field of economics and other male-dominated professions would benefit if we told more stories of the women in them from their perspectives, just as Taylor has done and continues to do.

I FORGOT THAT YOU EXISTED

Following World War II, English economists James Meade and Richard Stone set out to quantify the economic activity and growth happening in the country.[12] Until the 1940s, no standardized methods for identifying whether an economy was flourishing or faltering existed. James and Richard focused on developing metrics to measure the growth of England's economy.

They looked to quantifiable changes in productivity, like an increase or decrease in the number of boats built by boat-building companies. By adding the dollar value of an increase or decrease in the production of items like boats, and economic activity like the value of output from meals made and sold in restaurants, they could assess the total value of the economy every year.

When it came to businesses and individuals who charged for an object or service, it was easy enough to look at receipts or prices and thereby, without much doubt, determine the worth of the object or service in society and markets. Adding everything up was the easy part—collecting the data for all businesses and industries across the entire country was the challenge.

There was, perhaps, another tiny irritant that would manifest itself in their methodology—a woman by the name of Phyllis Deane. Phyllis was younger than James and Richard. At the time they were developing their macroeconomic measures of the economy, she was working as a research officer in the National Institute of Economic Research in London, where she was assigned to their project.[13]

Phyllis had previously travelled to Nigeria for fieldwork. There she observed the heavy physical labor of women and children in Malawi families within their homes, labor like carrying water from a ravine to their house every day. She was aware of and interested in the economic value of time women spent on household production activities like fetching water from a well or building a fire to cook meals.[14]

Back in England and working with James and Richard, Phyllis brought this up as a missing link in estimates of the country's changing economy. She believed the value of time spent on the production of household and family well-being should also be measured. Workers needed to thrive in their homes before they could thrive in the world outside of them. If workers were under-nourished in the home, they would not be as productive in their work building boats, for example, and fewer boats would get made.

James and Richard agreed it was a valid point. But how would they assess the value of economic activity done within the home if there was no price tag on it, no one purchasing it? There were, in fact, various options for measuring this type of household productivity. Some options that have been considered in recent history include assigning a minimum wage value to domestic work; calculating the value of the service if purchased outside the home; or estimating the value of the family worker's time if they had been engaged in paid work outside the home. But all of this proved too confusing and overwhelming for the likes of care-privileged James and Richard. In the end, they did what society often chooses to do with women's work: they decided to ignore household production in measures of economic growth and vitality of the nation. They ignored women's work, ensuring its invisibility within the economy and society's perceptions of economic activity.

This had ramifications not just for England but for the entire world. Around the time of World War II, James and Richard had developed a measure of national accounting for England's economy, and they called it the gross domestic product (GDP). Richard was subsequently asked to consult with the United Nations and help develop tools that other countries could use to measure their economies. Almost a century later, this is the measure still in use today to determine the economic health and well-being of economies across the globe.

Phyllis died in 2012 at the age of 93.[15] Even though she wasn't successful at convincing James and Richard to incorporate household production into GDP measures, she did alright for herself. In 1965, Phyllis authored *The First Industrial Revolution*, a key textbook for students of economic history. It would be the first of many books she would write.

She went on to become one of the most respected economic historians in England and in 2010 was named a distinguished fellow of the History of Economics Society in the United States.[16] While the men she worked for may have stifled her voice early on, she did not let that stop her from making an impact on the profession and having a successful and meaningful career. Unfortunately we have yet to figure out how to get policymakers to change official GDP estimates to include household production.[17]

THE PROPHECY

Academic Joanna Rostek, a junior professor of English Literature at the University of Giessen in Germany, recently did the grueling work of uncovering a subset of women who, while less well-known as economists, had been writing about economic thought during the time that Adam Smith developed the invisible hand.[18] If Adam Smith was the father of modern economic theory, then these women were the mothers of modern economic thought. Joanna discovered seven female writers who, like Adam Smith, wrote about economic theory around the same period, except they wrote about how humans behave within their relationships and families given individual preferences and limited resources within the home.

Not surprisingly, you may not have heard of some of these women in your ECON101 class, since their writings have not been folded into the traditional history of Economic Man. Some you have heard of but would think of as writers of literature, not economists. To help solidify their place in history as economists, I name them here: Sarah Chapone, Mary Wollstonecraft, Mary Hays, Mary Robinson, Priscilla Wakefield, Mary Ann Radcliffe, and . . . Jane Austen.[19] You heard me right, Jane Austen. [20] It turns out that economic history graduate courses should have been reading Jane Austen's *Pride and Prejudice* next to Adam Smith's *The Wealth of Nations* all along.

Joanna argues that the writings of these women are deeply economic in nature. They cover three prominent overarching themes: marriage, paid work, and what she terms "moral economics."[21] She includes in her analysis a published historical piece arguing that women should be paid the same as men for their efforts in the labor market. The piece was published around the 1800s—even then, gender inequities in pay were on women's radar.

The male economists of that period were extremely successful at ignoring and undervaluing women's theories, ideas, and work in the home. Lucky for us, the Sarahs and Marys and Priscillas and Janes were bold enough to speak their economic thought through their writing so that we could rediscover it today. Their footprints should give us courage to forage ahead knowing that they have always existed.

WHO'S AFRAID OF LITTLE OLD ME?

One spring day in 1880 a girl was born to a middle-class couple in a small town. Her name was Frances Perkins. Her parents believed in the value of a good education and sent her off to study at Mount Holyoke College. Upon finishing her studies she moved back to her parents' home and worked at several random jobs, but college had broadened her horizons and she felt restless. She soon landed a full-time job teaching science at an all-girls school in Lake Forest, Illinois, and volunteered at Hull House in Chicago. She then headed to Philadelphia, where she investigated claims of sexual assault against vulnerable immigrant women while studying at the Wharton School. After that, she moved to New York for a fellowship at Columbia University and became involved in women's rights, equality, and social justice.[22]

Her life and work were always intertwined. In New York, she married and got pregnant just as she was about to separate from her spouse. The role of wife and partner felt limiting to her professionally. While she ended up having a miscarriage, she decided to rededicate herself to her relationship. She got pregnant again and had a stillbirth. Finally, after a third pregnancy, she gave birth to a baby girl.[23] Two years later, she volunteered to lead an organization dedicated to improving birthing conditions for impoverished women.

When her spouse became mentally ill and could not work, she took a paid job as an industrial commissioner for the State of New York. Two years later, she moved on to a position on a council for immigrant education; after that she landed a stable job in government leading labor policies on the state industrial commission and overseeing the health and welfare of workers in the state. She stayed in that job for six years, as the sole breadwinner for her family.[24]

At one point her mother, who had worsening dementia, moved in with Frances and her husband and daughter, and Frances became a member of the sandwich generation—people who care for both their minor children and elder parents at the same time (and, in Frances's case, a spouse as well). Frances was eventually promoted to run the state industrial commission. By this point she had reinvented herself multiple times, just as many women do over the course of their lives.

She reinvented herself not only with respect to job titles and occupation, but in other ways. She changed her name, religion, appearance, and age for paid work. She did not think it prudent to be older than her boss, so she lied about her age. In other instances, she altered her appearance to look older, so that the men around her would treat her like they would their mothers, rather than as someone to flirt with or to whom they might be sexually attracted. She eventually became known as "Mother Perkins" at the youthful age of thirty-three.

Five years after she took a leadership role running the state industrial commission, she was asked to become the US Secretary of Labor. She had yet a second tug-of-war between her life outside the home and the one within it when her daughter became a teenager and needed more complex care, guidance, and oversight. This became a critical moment in her life trajectory because she had to figure out how to both take a demanding leadership role while also managing the growing needs of her teenage daughter.[25]

Frances Perkins blazed these trails for the rest of us over a hundred years ago. She is perhaps best known as the Labor Secretary of President Franklin D. Roosevelt and an architect of the New Deal. Her grit, persistence, and ability to manipulate male-dominated power in her favor are true characteristics of many women of her time and ours.

Frances's grandmother had made a big impression on her. Frances indicated that she chose to take the Labor Secretary position during one of the most stressful times of her life because of her grandmother, who told her that "whenever a door opened to you, you had no choice but to walk through it."[26] Frances chose to walk through the door and became a driving force of US labor policy. The policies she created under the New Deal still exist, policies like unemployment insurance, social security, and minimum wage.[27] Imagine what our lives would be like today if Frances had not persisted.

Frances realized early on that acting as a mother figure was the best way to use her power of persuasion to move public policy in the direction of creating safety and wellness for workers. Frances learned that "the way men were able to accept women in politics was to associate them with motherhood. 'They know and respect their mothers—ninety-nine percent of them do,' she said."[28]

Like so many other female economists throughout history, Frances was considered both a social worker and an economic policy influencer. She cared deeply about labor, unions, and workers. As an economist, she remained relatively invisible to academic circles. But in terms of assertiveness and determination to push forward economic agendas she believed in, she was not as much of an outlier as one might think. Other powerful women from our past have used their strength and vision to fight for the rights of others, even if it made them anti-heroes.

ANTI-HERO

There is an old saying that "behind every great man is a great woman." But perhaps it should be "beside," not behind. Beside Cesar Chavez, the powerful face of the United Farm Workers (UFW), was an equally determined, smart, compelling leader fighting for the rights of farmworkers across rural America. Her name is Dolores Huerta, and she was born in New Mexico in 1930. That was the same year President Herbert Hoover used erroneous data to declare the Great Depression over, only to have Frances Perkins, who at the time worked for the State of New York, campaign for Franklin D. Roosevelt by highlighting the error to any reporter who would listen and, in doing so, solidifying her position as a labor leader, which would propel her into the Secretary of Labor position a few years later.[29]

Dolores was an infant at that time, a child of the Great Depression. When she was five years old, her parents divorced. Dolores's father eventually became a state legislator in New Mexico, but Dolores would move with her mother into her grandfather's home in Stockton, California. Dolores was raised primarily by her grandfather, as her mother worked around the clock to provide for her and her siblings. She has acknowledged that "her mother played an influential role in how and why she became a strong and outspoken woman." And "this reversal of traditional gendered caretaker roles allowed [Dolores] to see that independent and assertive women could succeed in the U.S. American workforce and society."[30]

Growing up during the Great Depression and World War II eras gave her a strong sense of the need to fight the injustice faced by workers, particularly farmworkers. The influence of her grandfather and mother as hard workers focused on equal opportunity for their children drove her passion for social justice. Dolores finished high school and went on to college. She married, had kids, and became a teacher. Dolores had two children when she divorced her husband and quit her teaching job to reinvent herself by advocating for improving the lives of farmworkers.

Dolores believed in herself and knew her authentic path was not teaching. She wanted to have more of an impact on increasing awareness of the rights and the plight of farmworkers, a group that had been largely overlooked during the efforts of Frances Perkins when she was Secretary of Labor. Dolores remarried, had five more children, and became involved in grassroots advocacy with the Stockton branch of the Community Service Organization (CSO), which worked to protect the rights of people in poverty, help them acquire public services, and register to vote. At the CSO, Dolores became heavily involved in farmworker issues.

Dolores Huerta met Cesar Chavez and in 1962 they cofounded the Farm Workers Association, which would eventually become the UFW. The UFW lobbied for farmworker rights and eventually succeeded with the passage of the Agricultural Labor Relations Act of 1975. Like Frances, Dolores used motherhood, family, and her gender role to reach the ears of powerful men and the community by acting like a mother figure.[31] Her ability to organize and lead brought protections for workers and awareness of the dangerous work in farm fields.

Dolores's determination and grit, learned from her mother, translated into an ability to stand up for the rights of a large constituency of workers who until that time had been invisible to many. She stood up for their health and safety, but also for their economic well-being. She, like Frances, contributed to the larger economic story of the United States by making positive changes for large swaths of workers—and both women did it while raising children and caring for aging parents.

BEJEWELED

Listen to the Radiolab podcast titled *Dolly Parton's America*,[32] and you come away with a particular awe for the boldly lived economic experience of a savvy businesswoman born into poverty in the Tennessee Smokey Hills (the Great Smoky Mountains), who leaned intensely into her femininity throughout her entire career.

Born in 1946 as one of twelve children of sharecroppers, Dolly grew up in a one-room cabin with her parents and siblings. Dolly belongs to the largest US cohort of children born in a single generation, the baby boomers. While feminists of her generation rarely saw the singer as being one of them, this perspective has turned out to be shortsighted. Today Dolly is a force with which to be reckoned.

She credits her musically leaning uncle for bringing her to Nashville at the young age of eighteen, where she joined the circuit with hundreds of other amateur musicians trying to make a break.[33] She got her break in 1967 by joining the *Porter Wagoner Show*. She worked as a sidekick for Porter Wagoner, and while the job seemed ideal initially, it evolved into a situation that limited Dolly's success and hampered her career goals.

Dolly's career came at a time when women's rights and autonomy in decision-making around their professional paths were confined by rigid expectations of the role of women. It became clear over time that Dolly was holding the *Porter Wagoner Show* together, yet she wasn't given a role that accurately reflected her value and talent. She was never seen as an equal to Porter and was expected to stay in her lane as a supportive sidekick. She could have chosen to agree with this view of her place in the entertainment business, but she knew her worth and was willing to stand up and challenge the status quo and the misogynistic expectations she experienced. She used self-agency to fight for what she wanted.

Dolly decided that she needed to leave the show if she was ever going to build her own brand and pathway. She wrote the song "I Will Always Love You," walked into Porter's office, declared that the time had come for her to step out on her own, and sang the song to him. He agreed to let her leave if she let him produce the song, and Dolly agreed. Like Frances and Dolores, Dolly understood that to advance in a man's world, she needed to act not as if she were their equal, but as if she were their mother or caregiver. Dolly's actions were seen as nothing short of defiant by those around her who relied on her charisma and talent for the overall success of the show. Yet Dolly trusted her gut feeling that to accomplish her goals, she needed to expand. She would never again play the role of sidekick.

In 1979, Porter sued Dolly for $3 million for breach of contract, arguing he lost revenue on cancelled shows once Dolly left and that he deserved a portion of her earnings because he was still her manager.[34] Dolly's experience was not too different from Taylor Swift's experience when the executives around her sold her master recordings. It was also not that different from the experience of Clara Bow in fighting for an improved contract that excluded a clause saying the studio could drop her if negative publicity made its way into the headlines. Dolly and Porter eventually settled out of court and rebuilt their friendship. When strong-willed women go against the preferences and desires of a male-dominated industry, there is often blowback. Women who succeed often resolve the blowback through reinvention and masterminding.

One might argue that Dolly's bold career decisions came from internal grit and determination. She knew what she wanted and was willing to take risks and reinvent herself to reach a bigger goal. She also recognized her value and didn't minimize it because of her gender, as others might have. She chose a career path that tightly aligned with her own passions and was not willing to let men who dominated the industry take the reins. But she did it in a way that demonstrated she knew how to use her gender and that of those around her to smooth her path forward. Dolly made it in the world of music because she believed she deserved a front seat and was willing to act like a man—or a man's caregiver, if you will—to get it.

KARMA

On March 9, 2016, at the age of fifty-seven, a confident, wise, vibrant-as-hell Madonna gave a ten-minute acceptance speech at the *Billboard* Women in Music ceremony. She had won the Woman of the Year award. In her speech, Madonna said, "People say that I'm so controversial, but I think the most controversial thing I have ever done is to stick around. . . . To everyone who gave me hell and said I could not, that I would not, that I must not: Your resistance made me stronger."[35]

Madonna grew up in an ordinary family. Born Madonna Louise Ciccone in 1958 in Bay City, Michigan, to religious parents of Italian descent, she was the oldest girl in a large family of six siblings.[36] She lost her mother at age five, which left a lasting impression and made her the female leader in the household until her dad remarried. At the age of eighteen, she left her family home to study dance on a scholarship to the University of Michigan. Inspired by a dance instructor and defying her father's wishes, she left Michigan after only two years and headed to New York to pursue her dreams.

Life in New York was not easy for Madonna in the beginning. Sometimes homeless, couch surfing, and experiencing at least one sexual assault, a common experience for young women then and now, Madonna remained focused on her goal of being famous and sharing her art with the world. She had something to say, something to contribute, and was determined to be heard.

Her lyrics were authentic, her voice something young women at the time needed. They were the first fans to uplift Madonna's music and artistry.[37] They heard themselves represented in Madonna's voice. They gravitated toward it, rocketing Madonna to stardom, where her talent would carry her throughout her adulthood.

This phenomenon, in which fans strongly identify with the authentic lyrics of young female artists, would be replicated a few decades later with artists like Beyoncé and Taylor Swift. Swifties, if we define them more broadly as those who gravitate hard toward art and talent that speaks to them, have always existed, if only we cared to look for them.

In an interview, U2's Bono discussed how he met Madonna through Sean Penn, saying, "I don't think people realized she was as smart as she is. I'm not sure I did."[38] This instinctual, culturally embedded underestimation of the intelligence and talent of young women persists today. We have seen it play out in the media as Taylor Swift's fame has increased. Perhaps one thing that has changed is that we see prominent male celebrities coming to the defense of these female stars, men like Flavor Flav, Ryan Gosling, the Kelce brothers, ESPN commentator Stephan A. Smith, and NFL Commissioner Roger Goodell.[39]

Just think about the "dads, Brads, and Chads"[40] who criticized Taylor when she began attending Kansas City Chiefs games to watch her boyfriend play. Many resented the hype surrounding the singer (never mind that she was a mega pop star hauling in millions of dollars through Super Bowl–like events each weekend in cities across the country) and were annoyed that the NFL, ESPN, and other networks were zooming in on her during the games. This sort of chauvinistic complaining was nonexistent when Travis Kelce repeatedly showed up at Eras Tour shows throughout 2023 and the summer of 2024 in Europe; Taylor fans were excited that he was at the concerts to support her.

Taylor is similar to Madonna. Madonna oversees her music, writes her own lyrics, and has tied her experiences growing up female into the type of artist she has become. She championed young women's voices and advocated for the LGBTQ+ community. Madonna's Blond Ambition Tour of the 1990s was in many respects the original Eras Tour. It focused on the various eras or "worlds" of Madonna's music career. It became not only a concert, but an immersive theatrical experience—one that opened doors for other artists to think big and challenge the music industry to create the kind of concerts we experience today, spectacles featuring Beyoncé, P!nk, Taylor, and so many others. In 1990, Madonna bumped the Beatles out of their spot for most consecutive top-five singles,[41] a feat Taylor Swift would accomplish three decades later, when she also surpassed Elvis Presley for most weeks at number one on the *Billboard* charts among soloists.[42]

Throughout Madonna's career, she surrounded herself with individuals who cared about creating meaning in art, who believed in the power of reinvention as a tool for success, and who would not undermine her talent and skill because she was a woman. She worked with director Susan Seidelman on the reinvention-story movie *Desperately Seeking Susan*, and she began learning to lean into reinvention by working with people like Steven Meisel, a photographer whom Madonna credits with first introducing her to the idea of reinvention.[43] Madonna has thrived throughout her career by leaning into continual change and adaptation to stay relevant and tell stories that, in that moment of time, needed to be told.

Madonna reinvented herself perpetually throughout her career, and continues to do so today. She has done it through defiance—not caring what others thought or said about her artistry. She rebelled against her father's preferences and opinions of her in her youth. She defied the music industry by sticking tightly to her own vision of how she wanted to create music, art, and entertainment. She disobeyed society's unspoken and spoken rules by pushing against norms regarding sexuality and female pleasure. Madonna's reinventive nature is tightly entwined with defiant actions that pushed against expectations of how women are supposed to behave. Like the other women discussed in this chapter, she has used reinvention, persistence, and a clear reading of those with dominant societal power to become her true self.

WILDEST DREAMS

On the same day Claudia Goldin's Nobel award was announced in 2023, she published a working paper titled "Why Women Won."[44] It seemed somewhat controversial to argue that women had won during a time when reproductive rights were being attacked via the reversal of *Roe v. Wade*, but Claudia's paper encouraged us to take the long view. She highlighted more than 150 critical moments in history that had advanced women's rights in the home and workplace, including the implementatior of policies that affected voting, marriage, divorce, education, reproductive rights, paid work, retirement, and investments in financial markets.

The road to women's economic freedom has been rocky, for sure. It has developed over more than a hundred-year span with input from varying constituent groups. Some groups argued for gender equality in the workplace while others argued for an acknowledgment of differences in the sexes in terms of fertility, childbearing, and household roles. Male politicians were often not influenced by either argument but rather driven by a fear of the power of the female vote.[45]

During the civil rights era, the right to vote gave women the political power to help pass policies that women cared about through federal and state legislation, executive orders, and critical court cases. These policies supported economic advancement and independent prosperity for women across the country. State extensions of unilateral divorce laws in the 1970s made it easier for women to leave a marriage if they so chose and made it easier to escape domestic violence. Title IX increased access to sports and educational opportunities for women and girls. *Roe v. Wade* ensured access to abortion services, which increased access to reproductive health services. Women gained the right to independent financial services like banking and credit. Claudia highlights that close to half of these critical policies and laws (45 percent) were implemented between 1963 and 1973 (see figure 3).[46]

EVERYTHING HAS CHANGED

Claudia was right that the twentieth century proved kind to women in terms of policies and laws supporting women's economic autonomy and equity. Two critical policies bolstering future advancements included the Nineteenth Amendment, ratified in 1920, which gave women the right to vote in federal and state elections, and the Lanham Act, which in 1943 provided workers with universal childcare. While the Lanham Act was temporarily enacted during wartime, it gave an entire generation of mothers a taste of economic independence through paid work, which likely changed forever how they chose to raise their daughters and sons.[47] Women born around the time of the 1920 legislation ratifying women's right to vote became the mothers

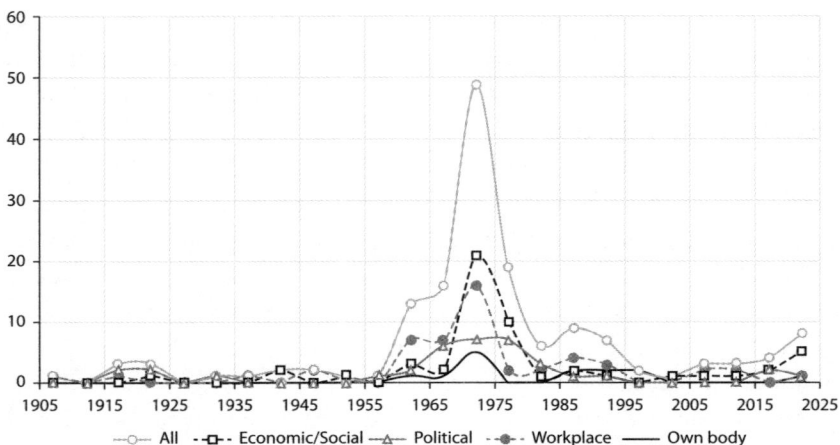

FIGURE 3. New policies and laws benefitting women's rights in the US, 1908 to 2023. Source: Reprinted with the permission of Claudia Goldin from Goldin, "Why Women Won," Working Paper No. 31762, National Bureau of Economic Research, October 2023, https://doi.org/10.3386/w31762.

who used the Lanham Act's childcare centers so they could work, and they raised children who fought as young adults for civil rights in the 1960s and 1970s.

Armed with the right to vote and a taste of economic independence gained through paid work, the mothers and daughters of Lanham were prepared to advocate for themselves, creating an environment ripe for improving rights and equality for women in the 1960s. The Equal Pay Act of 1963 crafted federal policies for pay equality, and the 1964 Civil Rights Act included a provision that prohibited sex discrimination. Marriage bars became illegal in 1964, which meant that employers could no longer fire women from certain jobs when they married. In 1965, the Supreme Court ruled in *Griswold v. Connecticut* that married couples had a right to birth control, giving married women more control and autonomy over their fertility and family planning. Single women would have to wait another decade for the right to birth control.[48] In 1967, affirmative action was extended to women by President Johnson through Executive Order Number 11375.

By 1968, the Internal Revenue Service (IRS) had developed policies allowing single and divorced women older than thirty-five to receive head of household status for tax deductions. In 1973, only twelve states had no-fault divorce, which grants divorce when only one partner wants it, instead of requiring both partners to agree to it. By the end of the 1970s, all states had shifted to no-fault divorce.

Making divorce easier through laws like unilateral divorce was not a favored policy among those who place traditional family values high on their list of priorities. But the ease of a divorce process and the redistribution rules of divorce can have rather large positive effects on women and children, who often have less bargaining power within intact families and households. Divorce laws can increase married women's agency and bargaining power.[49] As mentioned, this has been shown to increase household investments in items that women tend to prioritize.[50] When a marriage is easier to dissolve, married women's labor force participation increases because they are less able to rely on the future earnings of their current spouse.[51] This has a ripple effect of improving their overall lifetime earnings trajectory because working more during marriage leads to higher overall individual lifetime earnings. This, in turn, provides more individual financial stability.

As unilateral divorce expanded across states in the 1970s, some worried it was the beginning of the end of family life, and a spike in divorces during the subsequent two decades gave conservative policymakers lots of angst. But recent studies have shown divorce did not ruin the family or family values.[52] It has, in fact, led to more equitable bargaining within households, less domestic violence, and better marriage matches, which most of us would argue is a good thing.[53] This easing of the divorce process took place around the same time that women gained independent access to credit. As mentioned in chapter 4, women have only had the right to open a bank account independently in their own name for the past fifty years (since 1974).

My mother divorced my father in 1978. She found herself a small two-bedroom basement apartment in the less desirable but more affordable part of town. But because of the 1968 IRS policy change and the 1974 Equal Credit Opportunity Act, she could live independently with financial freedom. Had she married, become a mother, and divorced two decades earlier, her economic fate would have looked much different. If it were not for these policies, developed to advance women's economic agency, my own life would also have looked very different because of economic restrictions that would have been imposed on my mother. Women are closer to an equitable society today than they have ever been. Now is the time to keep fighting for rights that directly influence our economic power and prosperity.

Bold women who have exerted economic and emotional sass have existed throughout history, as demonstrated in these stories. They are, at a minimum, impressive, and at most, awe-inspiring. These women used their economic prowess to push back on stereotypical gender norms or to lean into them to get what they needed, and they persisted in the face of adversity. But were these economically viable paths unique to them or a mark of the women of their time—the women from my family or your family who perhaps were not well-known?

It might seem like the icons discussed above are unique, that they do not represent the rest of us. But looking at data from women of their generations or cohorts might allow us to identify how unique or common the experiences of these icons were. Figure 4 depicts general trends in marital status, education, children, and work for women in the age cohorts of Frances, Dolores, Dolly, Madonna, and Taylor.

The women's experiences often trend similarly to those of their cohort group. While we like to think of these famous women as rare and their talent might be, their life stories are more like those of the rest of us. Generational marriage trends track with these women. Dolly was like most of her cohort in that she married, had less than a college degree, and worked for pay. Madonna married later in life, divorced, remarried, and had children later in life. Frances married in her early thirties.[54] By age thirty, almost 80 percent of her counterparts were married (figure 4, panel A). Her daughter, Susanna, was born three years later;[55] almost two-thirds had at least one child of their own (figure 4, panel C). While Frances had an advanced degree, less than 10 percent of her peers ever had a bachelor's degree or higher (figure 4, panel B). Women tended to work until marriage, and few worked once they had children in the home.[56] Frances represented a minority in her cohort as far as education and work were concerned.

The largest shift in living as a single, never-married woman in early adulthood happened between Madonna's and Taylor's generations, where the rate for women age twenty increased by about 30 percentage points (figure 4, panel E). Taylor represents a cohort of millennials who are staying single longer. This corresponds with a similar decrease in marriage rates at the same age. Divorce was higher for the Dolly and Madonna cohorts as unilateral divorce laws became the norm across the country in the 1970s. Those in their thirties, for example, were twice as likely to be divorced, separated, or widowed compared the women in the Frances and Dolores generations. Divorce rates for the Taylor

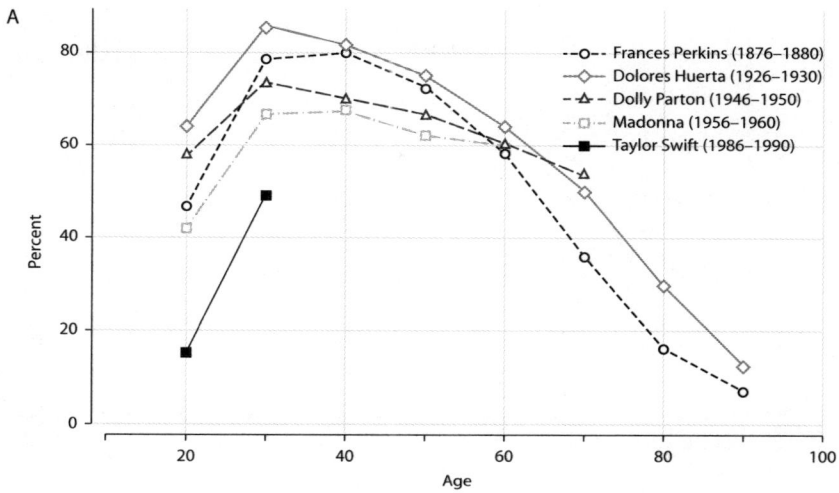

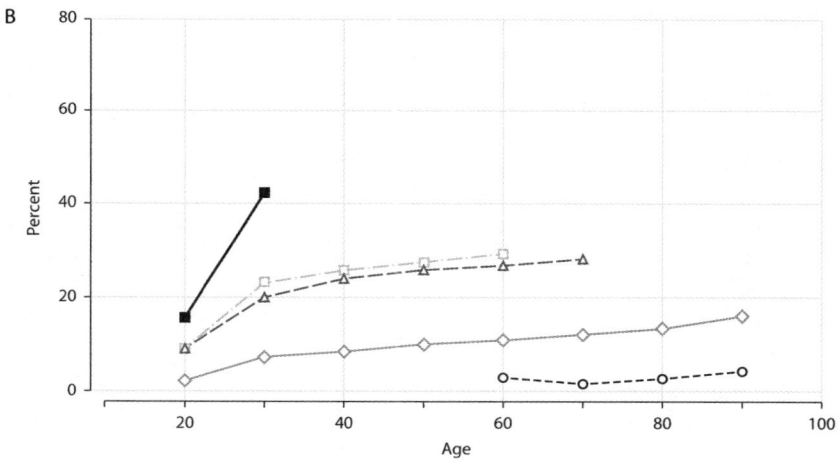

FIGURE 4. Generational trends for women by age and birth group. Panel A: Currently married. Panel B: Bachelor's degree or higher. (No educational attainment data was collected prior to 1940.)

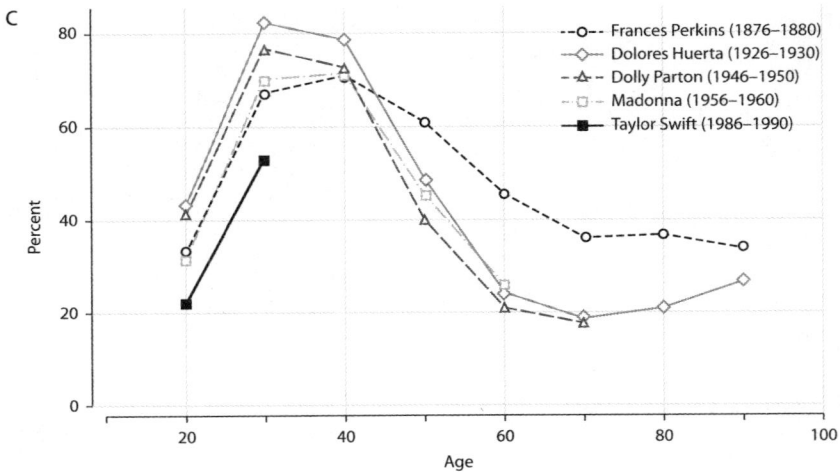

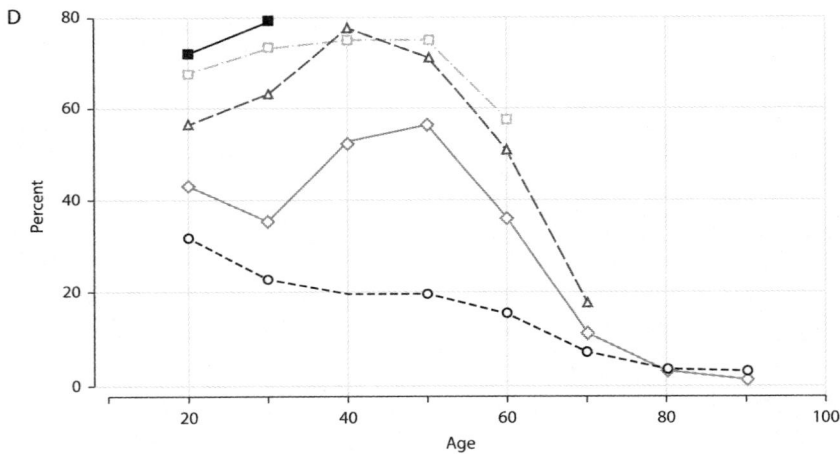

FIGURE 4. Panel C: Living with own children under age eighteen. Panel D: Labor force participation.

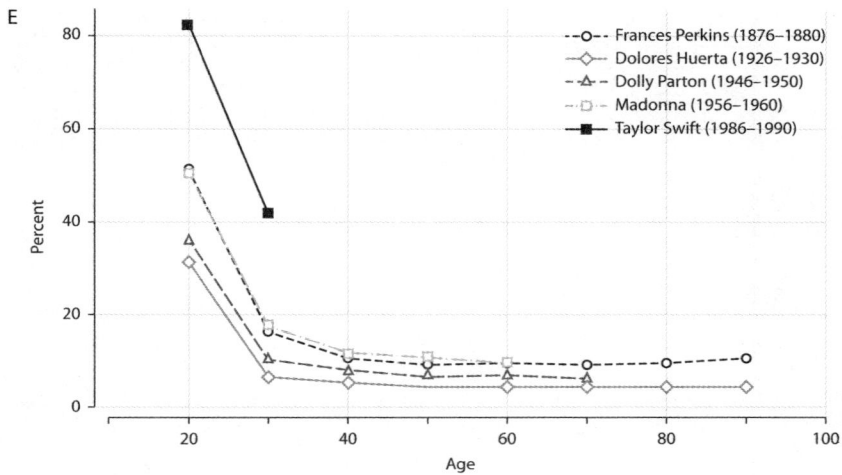

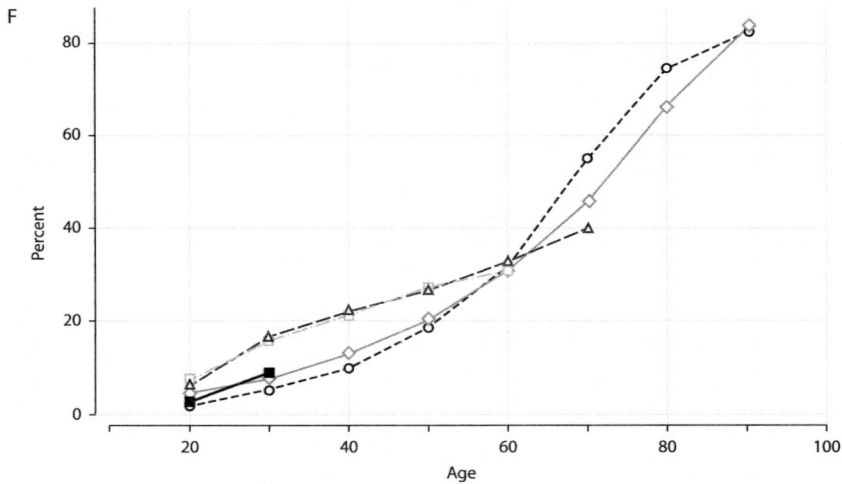

FIGURE 4. Panel E: Single, never married. Panel F: Divorced, separated, or widowed.

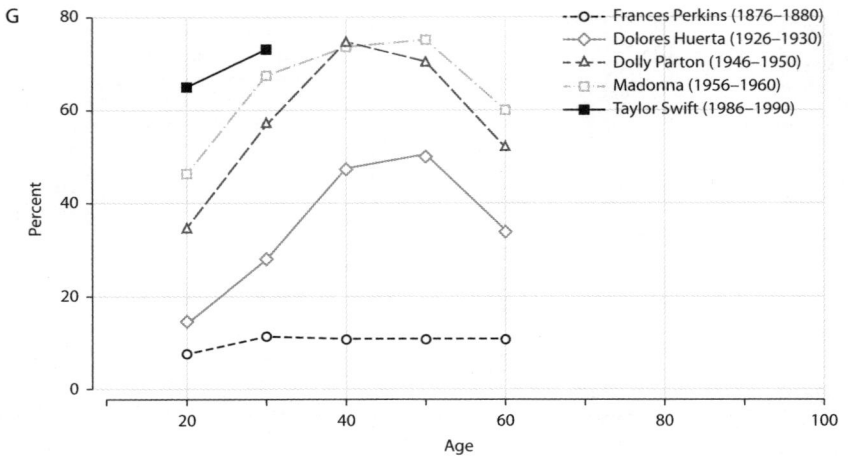

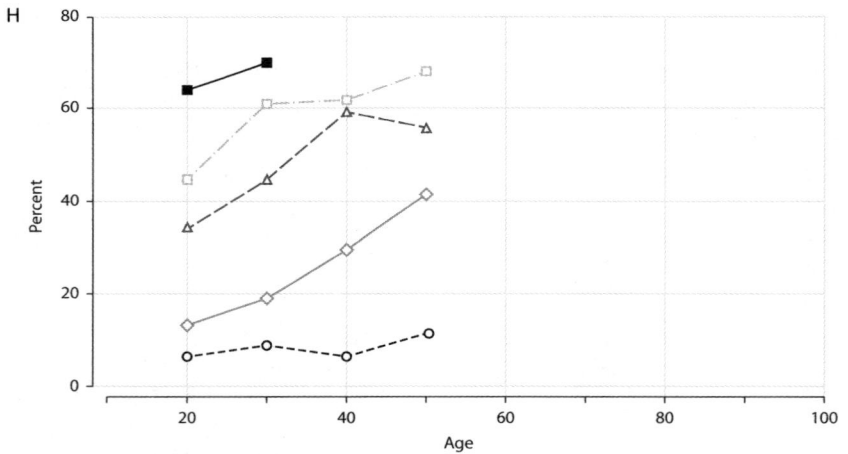

FIGURE 4. Panel G: Labor force participation rate of women living with children under age eighteen. Panel H: Labor force participation rate of women living with children under age five. Source: Author's calculations using decennial census data and current population surveys, US Census Bureau / Bureau of Labor Statistics, ipums.org. Notes: Each line depicts women in the birth group of the woman indicated in the key. Dates in parentheses show the range of birth years for each group.

generation in their twenties have returned to a pre-Dolly level partly because members of Taylor's generation cohabitate more and marry less.[57]

Increases in women's educational attainment—particularly college attendance and completion—have driven up age at first marriage and given women more economic power and control over who and when to marry.[58] Still, by age thirty at least half of women in all cohorts were married. The increase in education corresponds with a reduction or delay in living with own children (i.e., a delay in childbirth and adoption).

We see these delays play out within the Madonna and Taylor cohorts, for example— women who take full advantage of their twenties to advance career goals and step into marriage and motherhood later in life. While Dolly never had children, Frances and Dolores had children and continued working with the support of family members and paid caregivers—Dolores's grandfather took on a large role in caring for her children when they were younger, and Frances hired helpers to care for her daughter while she worked.[59] Even so, Frances's and Dolores's paths to work and motherhood were not as common within their cohorts.

Panels G and H of figure 4 show this. But perhaps even more striking is the large gap in women who work while living with their young minor children in the home between their generations and later generations. In some sense, Frances and Dolores were trailblazers. In the Taylor generation, of those who have children under age five in the home, almost three out of four work for pay. Just as Frances and Dolores found ways to make it work, so too do the women of today. Female entertainers who are mothers, like P!nk, Beyoncé, and Madonna, tour with their families and in some cases incorporate their children into portions of their performances. Recent advancements in flexible work driven by the pandemic increased mothers' labor force participation, although the return-to-office trend risks lowering that again.

Women across generations have shown that they will not be held back. Many women search for creative solutions that allow them to incorporate work with family. Frances, Dolores, Dolly, Madonna, and Taylor are not that different from the rest of us when it comes to figuring out how to balance the personal with the professional. Like others of us, their successes and achievements have come with the support of family, friends, and colleagues. Once we start understanding these commonalities, it becomes easier to see ourselves in their successes, and we become more willing to challenge the status quo and policies and programs that hold us back from becoming our best selves.

SIX

Motherhood

BIGGER THAN THE WHOLE SKY

For many years . . . I witnessed a young girl with very few friends
become one with many, learning to stand up for herself and the
things she believes in. Being brave enough to explore her musical
curiosity, having a voice against those who hate, and giving of
herself to those in need . . . I am a very proud mom.

ANDREA SWIFT,
2015 American Country Music Awards Speech

MOTHERHOOD IS SPECIAL. It consumes us, gives us hope, overwhelms
us. It is one way we pass down generational knowledge. It is also often our
biggest reinvention. Making room for a plus-one in life is never easy, but it is
required for those who choose to have children.

On the flip side, as daughters, to know where we are going we must know
those from whom we came. For most of us, our mothers, grandmothers,
aunts, teachers, sisters, and girlfriends taught us our swagger and grit. From
Brooke Shields and Drew Barrymore to Taylor Swift and even the
Kardashians, momagers and mothers more generally play a major role in our
success.

The power of mothers is so strong that in 2024, *Glamour* magazine made
them Women of the Year.[1] Tina Knowles (mom to Beyoncé) ended up on
Glamour's "Women of the Year" cover along with Maggie Baird (mom to
Billie Eilish), Donna Kelce (mom to Travis and Jason Kelce), and Mandy
Teefey (mom to Selena Gomez).[2] The moms had made it, their invisible labor
finally acknowledged. Interviewed by journalist Samantha Barry for the
magazine, they talked about their proudest moments and the significance of
their role and what it had meant to them. They reflected with Samantha on
a quote from the *Barbie* movie: "We mothers stand still so our daughters can
look back to see how far they've come." Tina stated, "That's kind of what we
do, right? We stand in a gap for our kids."[3]

Mothers sometimes help their kids shine and reach their goals and, in some instances, protect them from the misogyny baked into the world and society in which we live. The women before us often protect us, look out for us, and help us figure out how to get from point A to point B when we are young. Sometimes this role is filled by another close relative. It is usually someone who sees beyond your gender, who supports your raw talent and steadfast determination. Someone who helps you break down barriers and build confidence.

This chapter describes how mothers, parental figures, mentors, and sponsors support our ability to advance into our best selves. It discusses the economic value of the contributions caregivers make for us, the economy, and society by investing in the next generation and highlights how mothers today often try to "have it all" by incorporating their role as mother into their career paths. Whether you lean in or lean out professionally, as you grow your family, your path is uniquely yours for the making. I highlight how mothers adapted during the pandemic and focus on what we know about policies that make it easier or more difficult for mothers to thrive.

THIS IS ME TRYING

My favorite made-for-TV mother is not June Cleaver from *Leave It To Beaver*, but rather the role played by Jamie Lee Curtis in the FX on Hulu streaming series *The Bear*. She made her first cameo appearance in season two. Jamie Lee played an addict mother who was unstable, vengeful, and angry. As the matriarch, she led the production of the family holiday dinner because it was what was expected of her, even if those assumptions varied among family members. It was tradition. In trying to fulfill that role, she created discomfort for the entire family. She struggled with the role of caretaker, free laborer, and memory maker for the family. Jamie Lee dug deep into the conflicts that can appear as people assume caretaker roles by gender and parenthood status when those expectations do not align with their preferences or personalities.

Just when I thought her role could not get any better, she reappeared in season three. By then we are aware of her faults and sympathize when her daughter, the Bear's sister, who is pregnant and does not want her mother around, goes into labor when nobody else is available. Her desire for a mother figure in that precise moment spurs her to call her mother—a woman who has caused her pain and frustration throughout her life.

What happens next describes the human fabric of family, gender, and care in the complicated world we live in. The two women settle into their differences and find shared meaning. They create space for each other to be who they are while also being vulnerable about their disappointments in each other.

I love this storyline because it is authentic. The writers and actor Jamie Lee strive and succeed at portraying a complicated yet realistic mother and show us how complicated the role of mother can be, and how devastating it can be for others, including our children. They remind us that parents have faults. The storyline reminds us that we are not all lucky enough to be born into a family where the role of caregiver blends easily with gendered expectations.

There is value in recognizing the powerful role mentors and sponsors play in our lives. The person who plays a critical role in supporting your path to fulfillment might not be a female family member like your mother. They might be your dad, uncle, grandfather, professor, boss, or colleague. Whatever form your support system takes, having these people in your life helps you succeed. And, for a subset of us, our mothers play that critical role.

DANCING WITH OUR HANDS TIED

Some women with influence in the entertainment and sports industries have blended their career with the dynamics and needs of family life. During the 2023 Super Bowl halftime show, Rihanna gave what could easily be described as the performance of her life. She lit up the stage with song and dance that was both visually beautiful and musically appealing. But perhaps the most surprising news from her performance was that the show unintentionally became an announcement to the world that she was pregnant with her second child.[4]

Twitter (now X) was on fire with fans asking "Wait Rihanna is pregnant again?"[5] While her publicist did confirm her pregnancy after the show, she made no actual mention of it herself. She was just out there doing her job. Rihanna treated the pregnancy as just a fact of her life in that moment, like wearing a gold bracelet or Nike shoes. It later came out that Rihanna's costume suit did not fit on the day of the performance, so she had no option but to show her belly with the suit partially zipped up.[6] She decided to be ok with that.

Rihanna is not the only woman entertainer keeping up with her career while growing and raising a family. In the 2021 Amazon documentary *P!nk:*

All I Know So Far, P!nk documented her demanding tour schedule and her experiences traveling on tour with her spouse and children.[7] But touring with her family in tow was not where it ended. At the 2021 *Billboard* Music Awards, P!nk performed a new song, "Cover Me in Sunshine," a duet she sang with her nine-year-old daughter Willow while the two performed acrobatic stunts together. In addition, P!nk gave Willow a minimum-wage job during her Carnival tour in 2023.[8]

Beyoncé shared the stage with her eleven-year-old daughter Blue Ivy during the Renaissance World Tour 2023.[9] I attended the last concert of the tour in Kansas City, Missouri, that May. The audience screamed as Blue Ivy popped up from the stage floor and danced, leading a group of professional dancers. Blue ended her experience to a standing ovation and a football stadium full of Beyoncé fans chanting, "Blue, Blue, Blue."[10] Beyoncé, standing on a Range Rover–like stage prop, looked down on her daughter with the sparkling eyes and gigantic smile of a proud mother.

The 2024 Paris Olympics had something unique in the athlete village. The year women final reached parity relative to men at the Olympics, Allyson Felix, an eleven-time Olympic medalist and mother of two who knew the challenges of pursuing an athletic career while mothering, partnered with Pampers to offer the first-ever temporary nursery for athlete parents in the Olympic village.[11] Along the same lines as Sheryl Sandberg, who noticed the need for a parking spot closer to Facebook's headquarters office and then asked for it,[12] Allyson knew the challenges of caring for little ones while trying to compete in the Olympics and was determined to do something about it.

These mothers are learning from their own experiences and taking action so that those who follow will not be hindered by the same roadblocks. In this way, today's mothers are driving the successes of future generations of women. We need more of this, and we need concrete policies that help mothers with less privilege and fewer resources blend work and motherhood.

One might question the pros and cons of blending children with paid work and careers, especially in the entertainment industry, but the facts are these: Women have children. Women have careers. When women have careers and then children, the ways in which we blend these two essential life activities should not be judged by anyone—especially in a world and economy that does little to help us balance paid work with family caregiving. There is no infrastructure to support a balanced life for caregivers who work. This makes it difficult to lean in at work.

Even so, I did. Not because it was easy, but because, as an economist, I understood the long-term cost to my career, bank account, and longer-term economic agency if I did not lean in. It was far from easy and at times took a toll on my mental health and well-being, but these are the normal, common, and frequent choices women are faced with today.

LEANING IN

Women today do what they can to not get stuck in their careers when they start a family, but they are on their own. I was studying for my PhD when my spouse and I started our family. I gave birth to my daughter within twenty-four hours of presenting my thesis ideas to my dissertation committee in my preliminary oral defense. I remember going to the restroom minutes before I was about to present. I was nervous and exhausted. Being pregnant with my first child, I did not know all the ins and outs of childbirth. But I knew I needed to finish this presentation before the birth of my daughter to stay on track with my program. In the bathroom, I lost my mucus plug. I returned to the conference room and, unconventionally, sat down in a chair at the front of the seminar room to give my presentation. Less than twenty-four hours later, I was in the hospital giving birth.

My son was born less than two years later and less than a month after I presented my final defense to my committee (also sitting down). I can lay claim to having produced one PhD, two kids, and two peer-reviewed academic publications with advisors during my PhD studies—more than most economics students at the time. I did it because it was the way for me to create a family while advancing my career—which, for me, the daughter of divorced parents and the person most impacted by their economic struggles, was critical to my identity.

I went on job interviews while five months pregnant and started my first post-doctoral job with the US Department of Labor while eight months pregnant with my second child. I went on leave one month into my job. The year was 2010 and paid parental leave for federal employees did not yet exist. The United States is one of just a few countries that do not have a national law for paid maternity and parental leave. I had no sick leave built up in my new job, but I was lucky enough to have generous colleagues who gifted me leave days from their own leave bank accounts. I was able to take about four weeks off with pay and then work from home for another few weeks as

I transitioned myself back to work and my son into the care of my mother-in-law and his grandmother, Teresa.

The reality is that most women and mothers work for pay. In 2023, around 78 percent of women aged twenty-five to fifty-four without dependent children worked for pay; the rate goes down to about 73 percent for similar women with children.[13] There is only a five-percentage-point gap today. Some women stop working for pay when they have children because their household can survive on the earnings of others in the home and they prefer to stay home. But it is more common for women to quit work and stay home to take care of small children because the cost of childcare is more than or equal to the wages that they themselves would make if they kept working. Even so, the majority of women keep working because their households need the income, so, under duress, they patch together solutions for childcare. It may not feel worth it to essentially work for no pay, or for the overall household finances to be worse than they were before the family had children.

But there is a strong economic rationale to keep working for pay even when all your earnings go to childcare. Stepping out of the paid workforce, for however short a period, has significant and long-lasting impacts on your future earnings. Research has shown that mothers do not regain their pre-birth earning level until their children reach the age of nine or ten, and mothers' earnings never return to the lifetime earnings trajectory their incomes were on before having children. They remain permanently below the level of fathers.[14] Even if the cost of childcare is equal to the mother's or father's wages during the first years of a child's life, parents benefit in the long run in terms of their total lifetime earnings if they keep working. Stepping away from work creates challenges in terms of both seniority and wages.

It is challenging to get back into the workforce, and one often returns to similar or lower earnings, having lost out on potential raises implemented during one's time out of the labor force and any potential raises linked to accumulated months of experience. In fact, a caregiver's best weapon for making positive improvements for women everywhere, and for the next generation of women, is to stay engaged in paid work. It is also the best economic option for each individual woman, as the individualized benefits are real. It benefits the mother and the future of her children—the youth of tomorrow. But leaning in comes at a serious cost as well.

Society makes it amazingly difficult for mothers to work outside the home. Yet mothers persist. They often find a way to lean in both at work and at home (or they don't). But leaning in often comes with sacrifices to health and well-being. Women are left to their own determination, fight, and wit in the struggle to overcome the barriers in a society built for the ease of men and the care-privileged. They often do that through reinvention.

SO IT GOES . . .

All this leaves us in an unanticipated trap. Our baby-boom mothers focused on making sure we had opportunities outside the home. Encouraging us to get an education, they prioritized the paid-work world. They were so focused on giving us opportunities outside the home that there was not enough time to focus on creating awareness in society as a whole of the inequalities within the home.

Wars are won one battle at a time. Exposing gender inequality in the home while fighting for equality in the workplace ran the risk of losing the entire war. Our mothers and grandmothers focused on the biggest battle at hand— the one outside the four walls of our homes. The one that was most likely to guarantee our economic independence and freedom to choose the life we wanted to live inside our homes. To gain freedom of choice and decision-making within the home, we first needed the freedom to independently access economic resources from outside.

Our mothers and grandmothers achieved their goals for us, yet here we are, still struggling.[15] Women have landed in an exhaustion trap, and many have been forced to reinvent themselves to find balance. Prime-age mothers of kids under age five spend about only one hour a day engaged in leisure activity that does not involve simultaneously supervising a child.[16] Dads spend two hours per day in leisure activities, compared to four hours for women without minor children and six hours for men not living with minor children.[17]

Moms have little time for themselves. They have little to no care privilege compared to the rest of us. You can see this play out on social media on mommy blogs like *Scary Mommy*, or in movies like the 2016 film *Bad Moms*.[18] The more successful we are outside of our homes, the more we risk becoming exhausted and damaging our mental and physical health. We reinvent ourselves to continue advancing or run the risk of systemic constructs pushing us down. All the while, we are exhausted from burning both ends of the candle. Something has got to give, and maybe that thing is what we pass down to the next generation.

I had a boss from a slightly older generation, a generation in which rules, expectations, and gender were often not discussed but driven by rigid unspoken social and cultural norms. She once told me that earlier in her career, while working at a hospital, she noticed that female doctors would sneak out a side door to attend their child's sports games, keeping their white doctor coats on until they got to their cars and then putting them back on in the car before heading back into the hospital. They did not want to appear as though they were out doing something non-job-related—something (gasp) related to their family life.

We would hope that by now things had gotten better, but for many of us they have not. Talking about the dynamics of family at work is risky. Once, during a staff meeting about travel for conferences, when I was a supervisor in the federal government, someone commented that we should not use work travel as family travel by vacationing at conference locations with family members who toured while employees conferenced. I was a mom of two young children at the time and constantly exhausted. I made a snarky comment asking why anyone would use conference travel for family travel, stating firmly that conference travel for me was a break from the non-stop demands on me as the go-to caregiver of a young family.

I was told later by my female boss that male leadership was taken aback by my comment, believing that I would only schedule conference travel to get away from family, instead of for work-related purposes. How absurd, I snorted, and then rolled my eyes. Clearly, any talk of the real pressures on working mothers and their families as it related to work travel was controversial. The unwritten rule was "Do not ever talk about the realities of family life at work, or about work travel as it relates to your family life, especially as a mother."

LEANING OUT

Sometimes we get so exhausted that we need a moment to recover, and that can mean stepping back from a career either temporarily or permanently. We saw this with the former prime minister of New Zealand, Jacinda Ardern, who stepped down in the middle of her second term to spend more time with family, and Serena Williams, who retired from professional tennis in 2022 to grow her family.[19] Before Jacinda and Serena, Anne-Marie Slaughter stepped down from a high-powered executive policy position in the Obama administration because it was too challenging to balance the needs of her job with the needs of her family, which included a teenager. She wrote a scathing piece in *The Atlantic* in 2012 reminding us how we women still couldn't have it all.[20]

Leaning out is completely fine if you have the financial resources to make it work, but it comes at a personal and financial cost in the short and long term—a sacrifice that may be necessary to safeguard mental health and physical and emotional well-being. Women are always faced with these decisions because we live in a society built for the ease of men.

The truth is that the only correct path is the one that feels good for you, and that looks different for all of us. All we can do in a society that gives us little wiggle room for success outside of our homes when we begin families is to be strong and cheer each other on—no matter which path we choose. There is, after all, no right or wrong way to woman.

Maybe this is what we have been getting wrong all along. There is only the path that feels best for you. The path that speaks best to you. The path that, as *New York Times* bestselling author and Harvard-trained lawyer Eve Rodsky said when I interviewed her, should make you feel like "Oh, I can't believe I JUST DID that!" instead of "Oh, I can't believe I just did THAT."[21]

THE ALCHEMY

It is not only moms who are getting themselves unstuck from barriers to advancement today. Just look at women like Megan Rapinoe, whose determination, grit, and dedication helped lead to equal pay for women in professional soccer.[22] Look at Margot Robbie, who executive-produced the blockbuster *Barbie* while starring in it and pushing, along with director Greta Gerwig and filmmakers, to get Mattel executives to give them budgetary control and creative ownership of the movie.[23]

According to the *New York Times*, "It was women who, especially early on, pushed *Barbie* ahead in the face of skepticism. 'If ever there was an example of why Hollywood needs more women in positions of power, this was it,' according to author Ana-Christina Ramón."[24] Those who championed *Barbie* included Mattel Films chief Robbie Brenner, "who rescued *Barbie* from development hell," and Warner's former head of production, Courtenay

Valenti, who "has been credited with seeing promise in *Barbie* from the earliest stage—recognizing that it was not (just) a commercial for a polarizing toy, but an idea that could reverberate through the culture. Ms. Valenti fought for Ms. Gerwig to have a budget big enough to execute on her vision."[25]

Over the past decade, the entertainment and sports industries have been on fire in terms of female leaders giving women space to thrive, create, and produce content by and for women. The results have been a resounding success. Look at Taylor Swift, who steadfastly refuses to be stuck in anyone's stereotypically gendered sludge. On a continuous loop of reinvention, side-stepping almost as quickly as her Kansas City Chiefs tight end love affair blossomed, she remains on top of her game, reinventing industry standards in the production of concerts, albums, music, and even movies and books.[26]

GETAWAY CAR

If we are not stuck, where has an all-consuming once-in-a-century pandemic followed by a bejeweled 2023 and a loud 2025 Mojo Dojo Casa White House left us? To answer that question, I spoke with an expert communicator on the topic, Claire Cain Miller, a reporter at the *New York Times*. Claire writes data-driven stories for the section "The Upshot" and during the pandemic, she struggled (like most moms) to balance paid work with caring for the school-age children in her family.

February 3, 2021, was the first time I spoke to Claire about parents' labor force participation and the impact of virtual schooling on their ability to work. Claire had been one of the first journalists to follow the data and pull away from stereotypical assumptions and declarations that the pandemic was leading to an implosion of women's paid work. She said she kept hearing that the pandemic was pushing women out of the workforce, but she was struggling to find women, especially minoritized women, who had stopped working, with many mothers saying they could not afford to.

It had been one year since the onset of the pandemic, and Clair was seeing on the ground what I had been seeing in the data. The labor force participation of mothers of school-age children had been on the rise. They were the first to return to their pre-pandemic labor force participation rates, months before retirement-aged women, college-aged women, and prime-aged women without children.[27]

In the months that followed, I received requests from the *Wall Street Journal*, *Washington Post*, *MarketWatch*, *Axios*, and others to provide data telling a more accurate and comprehensive story of how women, mothers in particular, were interacting with the paid workforce. Many journalists were concerned about setbacks for women and, specifically, about mothers' independence and economic power. Almost all of these journalists were women with small children. Ironically, they had not left the workplace (and neither had I).

Once we were able to disentangle broad statistics on women and work and dig specifically into mothers who worked outside the home, things became clearer. Mothers returned to their pre-pandemic labor force participation rates one year after the onset of the pandemic (by March 2021), but college-age women and women of retirement age would take an additional year to return to pre-pandemic levels. By using data to tell the actual story of women's lived experiences during the pandemic, we were able to shift the dialogue away from traditional tropes of women and work into something more meaningful that more accurately defined the role women play in the economy today.

When I reached out to Claire for this book, we went all the way back to the start of the pandemic. Claire remembered a vivid conversation she had in 2020, early in the pandemic, while standing on her lawn and talking to a good friend who was at a distance down the sidewalk. Her friend had three little kids and said to her, "I'm going to have to quit [my paid job]." That is when Claire came to a panicked realization that mothers were probably going to have to quit their jobs. There was no way they would be able to continue working while providing 24/7 care to their children. Despite her own intense feelings of being overwhelmed by her own transition into pandemic life, Claire knew that she had to begin writing and documenting the pandemic stories of mothers.

In some sense, her story was like my own. I had been commuting between Minneapolis, Minnesota, and Washington, DC, for work in early 2020. The pandemic forced my entire family into our home near Washington, and I was paralyzed from advancing my research as my family and I adjusted to our new life. In my new remote work life, I was reduced to engaging in strictly administrative tasks. The only research I could force myself to focus on in earnest, with all the daily pandemic distractions, was to study the impact of the closures on mothers like me.[28] I think a lot of us who work at the crossroads of understanding women, motherhood, and work had similar reactions during that time.

Claire reminded me that at the onset of the pandemic there were many layoffs, especially in service sectors, where lots of women work. This made it hard to get an accurate perspective of the situation because it was unclear if mothers stopped working because their employer laid them off along with everyone else, or because they decided to stop working to care for children. She recalled that about 1.5 million mothers left the workforce—a statistic she had gotten from me at the time.[29] Less reported were the number of fathers and those without children who also left, similarly in the millions.

Most of us know how this story ended. Moms did not leave the paid labor force in a mass exodus.[30] There are theories as to why moms returned to work more quickly than others did. The one that makes the most sense to me is economic. Claire argued that moms would never give up on their kids: it is "the one responsibility that you can't change." You can quit your job, divorce your spouse, move out of your house, but you cannot quit your kids. But what we all got wrong was that in today's economy, not quitting your kids means getting back to work as quickly as you can, so you can to put food on the table and keep a roof over their heads.

Moms went into overdrive to solve the caregiving crisis the pandemic had created for them while continuing to work for pay because their families needed the financial resources their jobs were bringing into the home. In the book *Finding Time*, Heather Boushey highlights that most families need two incomes—a reality since the 1980s. Mothers contribute economically to the household by working outside the home, and more than ever, households depend on women's earnings for survival.[31] A household with only one income earner is a luxury afforded only to those at the very top of the earnings distribution. Today, around 65 percent of married-couple families with children have both parents employed in the labor force.[32]

One income is usually no longer sufficient to cover the increasing costs associated with food, housing, childcare, transportation, utilities, and the extracurricular activities of children. More and more families are finding that a second income is critical to maintaining the middle-class lifestyle their parents raised them in. It is their getaway car for survival. And women with higher levels of education are finding the resources they contribute to their household from outside the home to be a meaningful and significant contribution to the household budget. This continues to be the reality for most women today.

Shaken by the pandemic, women's engagement with the labor force accelerated as they found new alternative ways to engage in paid work. More flexibility in terms of hours and scheduling provided women with the ability to generate economic independence while supporting their families financially. This might be, to the surprise of many, why the fractured childcare market did not disproportionately hold women back post-pandemic.[33] Caregivers should not have to bear alone the heavy burden of creative solutions to care or the increased burden of working while caring for their families. Failed childcare markets have been a crisis for the economy for decades, if not longer. Policymakers have largely ignored it. We need better systems.

In 2007, I was living in Minneapolis, Minnesota, less than five blocks from the I-35 bridge along the Mississippi River when it collapsed, killing thirteen people.[34] I walked that bridge every day on my way to classes at the University of Minnesota. I was shocked. How could something so firm and dependable, a foundation that I relied on every day for my own safety, just crumble with no advance warning?

This tragic event made policymakers start taking road and bridge infrastructure more seriously. Nancy Daubenberger, a bridge engineer for the Minnesota Department of Transportation, told NPR that "the state immediately inspected gusset plates on every single truss bridge in the state . . . [and] the Minnesota state legislature raised the gas tax and funded a $2.5 billion bridge improvement program."[35] Commuters in Minneapolis took roundabout detours as the bridge was under reconstruction. It took fourteen months to build a new bridge.[36] While commuters who relied on that bridge had detours available to them, the detours were grossly inconvenient.

This episode proved to me that we can fix bottleneck and infrastructure problems quickly when we want to. The urgency to create better solutions was clear when we look at the speed and determination used to rebuild the I-35 bridge. The same is not true of our broken childcare system and policies that would make the lives of women more manageable in today's economy. Resources are limited, so we invest them in items prioritized by those in power. I have now lived through a banking financial bailout, one automaker bailout, and a handful of airline bailouts by the federal government. I have yet to see us come to the rescue of time- and resource-constrained mothers. We should push our elected officials to make conscious policy decisions to prioritize childcare and related policies that help ensure equity in labor markets. Our votes and voices matter.

But in the meantime, parents use work-around "detour" childcare solutions, asking grandparents, friends, or neighborhood high schoolers to babysit. They bring their children to work with them or shift-share with parents of their kids' schoolmates or with their work colleagues. During the COVID-19 pandemic, when it became obvious that the 2020–2021 school year would be 100 percent virtual, educational pods developed by local neighborhood mothers sprouted up in garages and basements and at local YMCAs. Government and formal systems had failed to do anything about physically supervising children's learning so parents could get back to work.

Even Claire told me that by the fall 2020, she had "stood up a miniature private school myself and hired a teacher and recruited families."[37] Like so many other working mothers, she created an educational pod for her kids and other families. And a *New York Times* article from July 22, 2020, titled "Pods, Microschools and Tutors: Can Parents Solve the Education Crisis on Their Own?" demonstrated how all-encompassing the crisis had been for mothers across the country as they dove into mission mode to solve both their children's educational needs and their own needs for childcare.[38] Our bridge had collapsed, but no professional engineers or policymakers were around to save us, so we had to save ourselves.

This knee-jerk instinct puts parents in a lose-lose situation as they struggle to individually solve the problems our nation's childcare crisis brings to their front doors. Just because parents find a detour in a broken system does not mean we should not work on fixing the problem. Their solutions, by definition, are economically inefficient, slowing them down and making them less productive at work and in life. Multiply that by millions of mothers and all of society loses. Our economy becomes less productive, more inefficient.

We are driven by past stereotypes in defining the roles of women. We continually compare women's positions to expectations that society has created for men in the workplace. We have historically overlooked the needs of women. We must envision a society where women have the space and time to flourish under their own leadership and to realize their own visions on their own timeline. It is not about women reaching the goals of a male-driven society, but rather about women creating their own goals and pushing for a society that breaks down barriers that prevent them from succeeding in the ways they see fit. It's about society seeing those goals, acknowledging them, and creating the infrastructure to help make those goals a reality.

Academia often feels like a dying profession these days, but academic economists are good at identifying trends and identifying why one thing causes another. A study using the creation of patents by scientists showed how the career trajectory of baby-boom women scientists looked different than that of men. Men's patent production peaked in their mid-thirties. Women, on the other hand, to the extent they were persistent and stayed in an academic position, maximized their productivity in their forties and fifties.[39]

I was in my forties when this study came out. Others found it sobering, but I was elated: it meant the best was still in front of me. The fact is, women's life trajectories look different from men's, and a lot of that has to do with fertility and childbearing. But that does not mean we should be written off or dismissed, and we should not try to fit ourselves into structures designed for men to thrive, because we won't easily do so. We need to find our own path, the one that makes the best sense for us. And if labor markets cannot adjust, our economy will continue to miss out on untapped potential.

If more infrastructure were available for women to thrive, perhaps we would need the vibe of "Swiftynomics" less. Women would not need to reinvent so frequently because the environment outside their homes would be built for them. Infrastructure that facilitates bringing women back into the fold post birth or once their children go to school would exist, infrastructure like policies that nudge men to be more active caregivers at home and with their children. This type of infrastructure could go a long way to opening more doors and better career matches for men and women in our economy.

THE LAST TIME

Even with female economic power so visible in 2023, a force still pulled on women like riptides churning in the Atlantic Ocean on a stormy day. A large portion of women's economic work inside their homes and for their families was still invisible. This made life challenging for women and made the stress of life difficult. Primary caregivers have never held the majority power in US politics, so policies that bolster high-quality, affordable, and accessible childcare and flexible work schedules have never been successfully prioritized in US politics.

But moms today are aware and active. In recent years, movements and organizations like Moms First, Care Can't Wait, and the Fair Play Institute, which developed from the book *Fair Play* by Eve Rodsky, have continued to expose how gendered assumptions about roles and responsibilities in families leave women at an unfair disadvantage in the home. These movements have driven the unpaid and often ignored work of caregiving and parenting, and of mothering specifically, out from the shadows and into best-selling books and onto streaming services.[40]

In a time of social media, some movers and shakers started blogs to release the stress they felt from parenting—people like Jill Smokler, who created the *Scary Mommy* blog, or the Holderness family enterprise, which created unique business opportunities spoofing the job of parenthood and "adulting."[41] For decades, women entrepreneurs have been tapping into female rage and exhaustion. The pandemic was the latest iteration, and as it dragged on, people like Reshma Saujani, former CEO of Girls Who Code, proposed a Marshall Plan for Moms.

On January 26, 2021, the *New York Times* ran a full-page ad signed by fifty prominent women including Amy Schumer, Tarana Burke, Eva Longoria, and Reshma Saujani demanding a Marshall Plan for Moms.[42] The ad, a letter addressed to President Biden, called on his administration to act in the spirit of the Marshall Plan of 1948 and invest in critical infrastructure that would support mothers' equal participation in the workforce.

The Economic Recovery Act of 1948, signed into law by President Truman, focused on recovery and economic development following World War II and encouraged investments in economic assistance to support infrastructure and economic growth.[43] In a similar spirit, the proposed Marshall Plan for Moms would develop an infrastructure around the caregiving provided by mothers for their families. Exhausted from the additional care responsibilities brought on by the pandemic, mothers wanted change. Their plan argued for payments to stay-at-home mothers in recognition of their care work, investments in reliable, affordable, quality daycare, and policies like paid family and paternity leave. The plan gained national media attention and increased the visibility of the challenges modern mothers experienced in terms of balancing paid work with a disproportionate load of unpaid domestic labor. One of the signatures on the *New York Times* letter was that of Eve Rodsky. She knew the time had come for moms to have nice things.

EXILE

Data shows that during the summer of 2023, women's labor force participation hit its highest level since the federal government began gathering statistics on labor force participation in the early twentieth century, and it has continued to climb.[44] By August 2023, the labor force participation of prime-age women (those ages twenty-five to fifty-four) was 77.6 percent, and it climbed to 78.4 percent by August 2024.[45] Since June 2021, the rate has stayed above 75 percent, including throughout the 2023 summer of the economic woman. This is a new phenomenon, as women's labor force participation usually dips when children are on break and out of school.[46] Mothers with young children (birth to age four) were powering the upward trajectory, with a labor force participation rate 1.4 percentage points above its pre-pandemic peak.[47] Something was shifting with mothers of small children; more of them were staying in or finding their way into the labor market.

For a while, the childcare market coasted on the coattails of the American Rescue Plan Act (ARPA) Childcare Stabilization program, which provided $24 billion in critical aid to more than 200,000 childcare providers supporting as many as 9.5 million children so their parents could work.[48] ARPA also increased the maximum Child and Dependent Care Tax Credit in 2021, allowing families with children under age thirteen earning the median income or less to qualify for up to $8,000 in tax credits toward childcare expenses. ARPA provided child tax credits to parents of minor children. The 2021 credit included anywhere from $2,000 to $3,600 for children under age six and $3,000 for children ages six to eighteen.[49] This lifeline for both parents and childcare providers ended on September 31, 2023, with a care-privileged Congress unwilling to rally enough votes to continue these supports for families.

These pandemic policies supported families without the stigma often attached to other forms of aid; there was no whispering among suspicious neighbors about nonconforming community members being lazy or taking things for granted. We could come together instead of tearing each other apart with distrust and judgement. ARPA credits allowed households without income or with very low income to receive the full credit during tax season. This critical benefit gave families a small cushion to cover expenses associated with caring for small children, but it was swiped away once the economy restabilized after the pandemic.

Eliminating these tax credits had caused a jump in the US poverty level.[50] In 2021 the supplemental poverty rate (which includes earnings, income, and program benefits received) was 7.8 percent, partly because of the child tax credit, which lifted families out of poverty. When the tax credit was eliminated, families sank back into poverty; the supplemental poverty rate for

2022 was a whopping 12.4 percent. More than one in ten Americans were living in poverty, an almost 50 percent increase in one year.

One has to ask why politicians are reluctant to provide aid to families and children. It might have to do with the expectations we have about families being a private endeavor—an expectation that is intrinsically embedded in stereotypically gendered views of the world and in bootstrap mentalities, an expectation driven by a society built for men and those privileged enough to have care provided to them.

The pandemic forced family caregivers to go their own way when it became clear that social structures and supports were not prioritizing their needs. Many women and mothers decided to start their own micro-revolutions, which spawned ideas like the Marshall Plan for Moms and neighborhood educational pods. This is how we know we've got it in us to carve our own path when systems are not working for us. But it was not the pandemic in and of itself that showed us we could do this—we have been doing it all along. When society will not invest in us as mothers, we are left with investing in ourselves, often through paths of reinvention.

SEVEN

Self-Investment

As for me, lately I've been focusing less on what they say I can't
do and more on doing whatever the hell I want.

TAYLOR SWIFT,
2019 *Billboard* Woman of the Decade Award Speech

THE FORTY MINUTES before Taylor Swift appeared on stage for the Eras
Tour were just as methodically planned as the rest of the concert. There was,
of course, a pre-show playlist accompanied by video shorts that bounced off
the stage screen. The playlist was meticulously crafted and featured a mix of
songs with woman-power lyrics and a spattering of tracks by Taylor's musical
friends, including "Diet Mountain Dew" by Lana Del Rey and "Look at Her
Now" by Selena Gomez. The song that made me pause mid-conversation at
the concert was Lesley Gore's "You Don't Own Me." This classic made its
debut in 1963. The composers are listed as Johnny Medora and Dave White
Tricker, two men whose work, along with Lesley's melodic voice, created an
anthem for a generation of women during the civil rights era.

Women show up in this world every day. They wake up, roll out of bed,
and determine how they will present themselves to families, roommates,
neighbors, and colleagues at work. Decisions are made. Will I be assertive,
aggressive, pleasant, demanding, supportive, or helpful? Which of these characteristics do I need to activate to get from point A to point B? If I want the
next promotion, do I need to be handsome, polite, pushy, or daring? Will my
colleagues help or hinder me if I am any of these things? If there is housework
to be done, who in my family do I need to ask, bribe, or strong-arm?

It can be mentally exhausting being a woman in today's economy. We tell
girls and young women they can be or do anything outside of their home, but
we do relatively little to equal the playing field within the home. What if we
could take a step back and imagine a better world for women, a better economy for all? One that does not rely on the gendered expectations of the 1950s?

This chapter is about investing in yourself and taking risks with the belief that you have what it takes to make it, even when others and society might exude doubt.

THE OTHER SIDE OF THE DOOR

Emily Ramshaw and Amanda Zamora harnessed their best start-up personas to create The 19th*, a newsroom that covers women and politics.[1] Its reporting is distributed via traditional news outlets. Emily and Amanda develop content and stories that feature women's voices and cover news that affects women and other groups underrepresented in the media. I was curious as to how the two women started The 19th* and interviewed them.

Amanda was a member of the first group of students to graduate from college after September 11, 2001. She watched the newspaper industry and journalism job opportunities shrink as newspapers were bought up by larger media corporations. The job she thought she would get after college was not available. She ended up falling into digital journalism out of necessity, and eventually into an online producer job. With the help of a motivating mentor, she never looked back. Her reinvention created opportunities for her that she hadn't known existed.

Similarly, Emily Ramshaw knew from a young age that she wanted to follow in her parents' footsteps as a political journalist, and it was around 9/11 that she began her journey as an intern in the Washington bureau of the *Dallas Morning News*. Back home, Emily eventually made her way up working at *The Texas Tribune*, where she ended up recruiting Amanda. It wasn't an easy sell. Amanda had no intention of moving back to Texas.

At *The Texas Tribune*, Emily felt she'd gone as high as she could go professionally as the editor-in-chief, but she still had an itch. The CEO was extraordinary and storied. Emily came to the realization that if she really wanted to lead, it would have to be at an outlet that she created. This itch to lead had started several years earlier, but it wasn't until 2020 that she started to wonder in earnest if there could be—in fact needed to be—a new national nonprofit news platform at the intersection of women, politics, and policy.

Emily started mulling over the idea in earnest. Doubts crept in: She was concerned that she didn't really know how to start something. She felt more comfortable in the number two slot, and she had no experience raising money. She acknowledges that gender may have played a role—that being a woman meant she was best fit to play second fiddle, something women are conditioned to think. But then she went to a conference where she was seated next to a white male journalist with a huge reputation. He asked her what she was going to do next. Emily threw out her idea: "I want to start a nonprofit that's . . . women, politics, and policy." To which he said, "Oh, well, that's such an obvious idea. If you don't do that, somebody else is going to do it first."

That fear, that someone else might do it first, lit a fire in Emily. She called Amanda from the airport on her way home from the conference. With her luggage still in her car, she drove straight from the airport to a coffee shop to meet Amanda and start scheming.

Amanda recalls it as dramatic, weird. Amanda's first thought was "Are you crazy?" Amanda had no idea Emily had been mulling this idea over for years. Even though the idea caught Amanda off guard, she was all in. Emily knew she could not do it without Amanda. Their partnership was strong. They got together over lunch or on weekends and strategized, carrying out thought experiments. This visioning stage created a safe space in which both women could pitch ideas to each other and ponder next steps.

Amanda, who self-identifies as Latina but presents white, had been thinking a lot about race and identity and wanted to figure out how to incorporate the intersection of her own identity with speaking up against systemic racism, oppression, and marginalization. She'd started testing this idea with Emily. For Amanda, the opportunity to engage in a start-up was an opportunity to do political journalism differently—to represent a different, more diverse audience. This new opportunity was a chance for Amanda to fulfill her own personal mission in journalism: to make it more responsive, to make it human centered, and to make it more accessible to the communities it served.

Emily and Amanda wanted to do things differently, disrupt the way journalism was done, not only in terms of reporting, but also in how they structured their organization. They became preoccupied not only with how to report the news but also with what type of stories people would expect The 19th* to produce. They wanted to adjust their operations and culture to align with the way they would report the news.

They both recognized that the structure they began to develop would have been impossible to replicate in traditional newsrooms. Emily knew she lacked the patience for changing a hundred-year-old institution and that, either way, none of it would be easy. But starting anew was, in fact, the fastest route to get the kind of newsroom she and Amanda wanted to see in the world.

Emily and Amanda did not wait in a long line of white male publishers and legacy newsrooms to lead effective change. They did it by building the newsroom they wanted themselves. And in doing that, they created a work and organizational environment that suited them and their lifestyles. The culture revolved around flexibility. Sick days and parental leave were intentionally developed to make it clear that the organization understood that staff members have lives beyond their paid work. They understood and wanted staff to bring their lived experiences to work every day. They wanted the organization to acknowledge all facets of their staffers' lives.

Emily and Amanda's reinvention and the vision they bring to their reporting has brought all of us closer to understanding the lived experiences of women today. Their success should encourage more of us to take risks and redefine the environment around us, actively creating the type of world, society, and economy we want to live in.

THE ALBATROSS

On May 13, 2024, the Gates Foundation made a groundbreaking announcement that would electrify the philanthropic community. Melinda French Gates, who three years earlier had divorced her spouse, was stepping down from her role as co-chair of their foundation, a position she had held for more than twenty-five years.[2] In this "professional divorce" from the Gates Foundation, Melinda took with her $12.5 billion with which to direct her own philanthropic priorities at Pivotal Ventures, a company she created whose mission was to "accelerate social progress by removing barriers that hold people back."[3]

Melinda penned an opinion piece in the *New York Times* describing why she was leaving the Gates Foundation. Some years earlier, someone had advised her, "Set your own agenda, or someone else will set it for you."[4] Melinda was ready to set her own agenda, and she had the resources with which to do it. Her goal was to even the playing field by funding organizations and leaders whose focus was to support the ability of girls and women to advance economically and thrive.

She donated $1 billion of the $12.5 billion in the first year to organizations like New America, the organization founded by Anne-Marie Slaughter, who penned "Why Women Still Can't Have It All" in *The Atlantic*, and Emily and Amanda's nonprofit newsroom The 19th*.* The following year she announced another $1 billion in funding for women's health, dismantling barriers, supporting organization and leadership.[5] Melinda chose to fund organizations that had the potential to make substantial change and improvements to women's economic empowerment and well-being. She focused on leveling the playing field. She was accelerating a goal of equity for all.

. . . READY FOR IT?

Melinda is not alone. MacKenzie Scott is a novelist, mother of four, and ex-wife to the founder of Amazon. In college, she was a research assistant and student of award-winning author Toni Morrison at Princeton University. After being married for twenty-five years, she divorced in 2019 and, as part of the divorce, she received a 4 percent stake in Amazon.[6] Since then, she has given over $16 billion to various charities across the globe that focus on reducing rural poverty, as well as to organizations that increase access to abortion pill delivery services, health and well-being services, and education.[7]

This era of wealthy women walking away from marriages with big money and spending it on reinvesting in women and communities instead of shiny rocket rides into space is not necessarily new, but the attention being paid by the public to how these women are spending their share of the divorce pie is. It received enough attention that Apple TV ran a successful series titled *Loot*, starring Maya Rudolph, about the wealthy divorcée of a tech billionaire.[8]

* Other organizations and individuals funded by Melinda in the first year include the Center for Reproductive Rights; Collaborative for Gender + Reproductive Equity; Collective Future Fund; Community Change; Institute for Women's Policy Research; MomsRising Education Fund; *Ms.* Foundation for Women; National Domestic Workers Alliance; National Partnership for Women & Families; National Women's Law Center; Roosevelt Institute; States United Democracy Center; Time's Up Legal Defense Fund; Washington Center for Equitable Growth; Dr. Alfiee Breland-Noble, founder of The AAKOMA Project; Olympic gold medalist Allyson Felix; filmmaker Ava DuVernay; Crystal Echo Hawk, founder of IllumiNative; Gary Barker, founder of Equimundo: Center for Masculinities and Social Justice; Hauwa Ojeifo, founder of She Writes Woman; former New Zealand Prime Minister Jacinda Ardern; Nobel Peace Prize Laureate Leymah Roberta Gbowee; M. V. Lee Badgett, founding partner of Koppa: The LGBTI+ Economic Power Lab; Richard V. Reeves, founding president of the American Institute for Boys and Men; Sabrina Habib, co-founder and CEO of Kidogo; and Shabana Basij-Rasikh, co-founder of the School of Leadership Afghanistan.

In the series, the divorcée is left to figure out how to run a nonprofit under her name, and we see a comic representation of the disconnect between a super wealthy divorcée and the efforts of a foundation as she struggles to adjust to her new life. While the series is a comedy, it gets at a real-life issue by highlighting that women are coming into their own in terms of extreme wealth, and they are figuring out how best to use their limited time and resources. They often focus on reducing barriers for other women.

This practice of investing one's wealth in programs and projects that accelerate equity for women and other vulnerable groups is just one area where we are seeing women with wealth and resources move the dial. While it might be led by a few wealthy, wise, smart, and caring women, some of whom divorced later in life, it has increased agency for many women and over time has the power to increase equity across the board by concentrating investments in communities that have been historically left behind.

It is not just the wealthy. Every woman, every single one of us, has the agency and internal power to focus on investing in ourselves and building up others around us and in our local communities.

GORGEOUS

On February 21, 2024, I attended a CEO summit in New York City. It was not any ordinary business leader gathering. This summit was organized by the Female Founders Fund and took place at the New York Stock Exchange.[9] I was invited to speak on a panel focused on the economic power of women. Looking out at a room of over two hundred female CEOs, I could not have felt greater pride. These women were an awe-inspiring example of how far women have come in leading their fullest, most adventurous lives in today's economy.

Anu Duggal is a founding partner of the Female Founders Fund, which she started in 2014. A decade later, the fund is managing $125 million in capital across four funds. I talked with Anu about the focus of the fund, and she repeatedly mentioned a common theme that struck me as a mastermind opportunity, similar to when Taylor left an RCA development deal to sign with Big Machine. Taylor had wanted to tap into teenage experiences that until then had been undervalued by the music industry.

Anu's argument was the following: Once launched, a new business tells its success story through the numbers. Is it profitable or not? In Anu's mind, there was an advantage to be found earlier, at the seed or pre-seed stage. Reducing unconscious (and conscious) biases at the beginning of an idea, when the payoff is less clear and investors are mostly going off gut reactions and feelings of connection with the idea producer, could make money, especially if women and women's ideas were being overlooked by the broader (primarily male) venture capital ecosystem. Anu saw an arbitrage moment: "The arbitrage opportunity is that if you can invest early and identify these founders before they take off, then you can deliver great returns. Ultimately, we are sending a message to the venture capital community that [they] are missing out. We want to show that through the investments we are making."

The persistent underinvestment in women's ideas meant that others could make money by fixing or reducing the biases. From Anu's perspective, investors could make money from society's shortsightedness. Anu spotted this opportunity and developed it into an investment thesis, taking advantage of a space that others had long ignored. When I interviewed Anu for this book, she said the idea came from her "own experience as a female founder[,] having raised capital and just recognizing . . . [what] little percentage of venture dollars goes towards companies started by women. That, combined with [a] longer-term macro view . . . owning that initial segment is an investment opportunity."[10] Gary Becker would have been proud. Anu was using discriminatory behavior to make money and increase efficiency while getting others to recognize the inefficiencies of their discriminatory behavior. In the longer term, this could reduce the bias and discrimination that female founders were facing. Anu and her co-founders were proving the current system wrong.

Three months later, I attended another event, The Care Summit, in San Francisco. Sponsored and co-produced by key financial stakeholders like Pivotal Ventures, J. P. Morgan, Ginger Bread Capital, Cake Ventures, famtech.org, The Holding Co., and others, the summit was a first of its kind bringing together both funders and idea founders to discuss critical innovation and new ideas around the technology of care.[11]

The excitement in the room was palpable. The funders and innovators were focused on making technological improvements to the care economy. They recognized the value of these ideas and their future profitability. They had found another arbitrage moment and were harnessing it.

We live in a society where caregivers are increasingly strapped and searching for opportunities to make caregiving easier and less time-intensive where possible, and they are willing to pay for it. This environment exists today because so many women are engaged in the paid labor force and formal economy outside of their homes while simultaneously balancing demanding care needs within their homes. Funders are recognizing this because they themselves are caregivers. Many of the funders producing these events were female or female-led organizations. They could see and value the potential. They were making space for and improving the lives of women and caregivers along the way.

A PLACE IN THIS WORLD

It is not just a handful of female-led venture capitalists that are making a difference for women coming into their financial power. Ellevest is a company created by Sallie Krawcheck that focuses on building female wealth, a company Sallie started after her divorce helped her recognize the need to break down barriers to women's entry into wealth management and resources.[12] Although she became successful at fundraising for Ellevest, Sallie faced initial challenges. Feeling frustrated with some potential investors who doubted women's investment potential and also doubted her, even though she had previously run wealth management services at Merrill Lynch and Smith Barney, Sallie decided to get strategic and focus on intentionally selecting potential investors.

Sallie reinvented her strategy. She went to women with resources who could see her vision and who were excited about supporting it. In one of her first fundraising rounds, she brought together Rethink Impact, former Secretary of Commerce Penny Pritzker, Salesforce, and Venus Williams to support her plans.[13] Her confident attitude helped convince investors to see the opportunity for what it was—an arbitrage moment. Sallie also knew that the return on women's investment would be high because women tend to take fewer risks with investments and play the long game.

Others have tapped into women's financial and investment potential with breakthrough ideas in technology, building financial awareness, and networking. Financial technology company Acorns created an easy-to-use tool to encourage people to save by making small deposits of spare change at regular intervals. Acorns' services focus on those who have historically been excluded from Wall Street investment culture, helping them learn financial confidence.[14] The app builds financial education more generally and makes investing in one's future practical. Acorns is not the only company focused on increasing the comfort level and knowledge of groups that have been excluded from traditional investing.

Claire Wasserman wrote a book called *Ladies Get Paid* that describes tools to help women advocate for themselves and reduce the gender gap in negotiation, pay, and longer-term wealth.[15] Claire started a movement with an interactive space on Slack where women could network and communicate with each other about their own experiences, ask for advice, and share resources. She also offers courses, blogs, and events that help create community for women to advocate for what they deserve and learn from each other.

Along similar lines, Haley Sacks is a self-proclaimed millennial finance expert who calls herself Mrs. Dow Jones. She is CEO of Finance is Fun.[16] I first heard about her when we were tapped to be on a panel together at *Washington Post* Live in February 2024. She ended up in a later session, but I found her social media influencer story fascinating. After trying her hand in the entertainment industry in New York, she ended up following in her father's financial footsteps by building an empire on social media helping Millennial and Gen Z youth, especially women, demystify the world of investment and financial planning.[17] Haley found an opportunity to provide financial education and services to young women (and men) with money to burn, a group traditionally ignored by the establishment.

Every generation has women who carry a flame for the cause of equity between the sexes. They speak, write, and advocate against the structural inequalities holding us back. They use their voices to create awareness and chip away at social structures and norms that keep us from reaching our full economic potential. Today we are experiencing an environment the likes of which we have not seen before. Women have more economic agency, power, and independence than they have ever had at any previous time in history. They have accumulated wealth, which they control—independently and completely. They are focused on investing in priorities that matter to them, like changing labor market structures that have often kept women from these coffers through overt sexism and other barriers, like hefty, unequal amounts of care within families or a lack of innovations in technology that could make caregiving easier or more efficient.

The efforts of previous generations in advancing policies that allow women to vote, get an education, work in male-dominated industries, and independently maintain control of bank accounts and their own finances have made a difference in allowing these women the freedom to create space for the rest of us to excel.

Reproductive health rights are a critical element of policies that help level the economic playing field for women. Following the *Eisenstadt v. Baird* Supreme Court decision in 1972, oral contraception, commonly known as the pill, was made available to all women aged eighteen and over in forty-three states, regardless of marital status.[18] Abortion became legal in 1973 with the Supreme Court decision in *Roe v. Wade*.[19] These laws not only increased women's agency over their own fertility but improved their health and decreased the economic inequalities that women bear from having sex, which, among other things, includes the risk of creating a small human who needs direct care and supervision for years, if not a lifetime.

There have been a handful of landmark economic studies looking at the impact of access to reproductive rights and laws. These studies have generally found that access to contraception and reproductive health services increases the economic power of women by providing them increased choice over when and if to have a child.[20] Almost five decades after *Roe v. Wade* was codified into law, the Supreme Court took up another case, *Dobbs v. Jackson Women's Health Organization*. *Dobbs* removed a national right to abortion services and delegated the legality of abortion to the states. The case received a great deal of input from the public, including from 154 economists who signed their names to an "interest of *Amici Curiae*" (friends of the court) brief.[21]

Led by Caitlin Myers, a professor of economics at Middlebury College, the brief spelled out in detail the research showing the ways in which access to reproductive health rights like abortion has helped mothers, families, and children thrive. It demonstrated that access to abortion significantly reduced teen pregnancies and teen marriage, both of which have negative long-term economic consequences for women and their children. It also highlighted the effect of abortion access on birth rates, educational attainment, work and wages, and children's outcomes.[22]

Other studies have shown that access to oral contraception has had a significant and large positive impact on women's educational attainment and career paths.[23] It is possibly one of the biggest technological advancements of modern history in terms of its impact on women's economic well-being; it has also separated sexuality and sexual desires from fertility and reproduction.

Recently, intrauterine devices (IUDs) have become a more common form of birth control for a couple of reasons. First, they are viable for anywhere from three to ten years and, once inserted, require little to zero maintenance. Second, they reduce and, for some women, even eliminate cramps and monthly bleeding. They also provide birth control that partners may not be aware of, which can give even more agency to women.

The freedom this gives to women in terms of not interrupting their lifestyle with an unexpected or inconvenient monthly bleed and related cramps and headaches is a game changer. The problem with the IUD is that it is painful to insert, and many gynecologists insert the IUD without using pain medication, even though pain medication is readily available. It took an outcry on social media for the Centers for Disease Control (CDC) to craft guidance for medical professionals regarding pain mitigation for IUD insertion.[24] This was another example of the power of women's voices today.

In March 2025, the Miudella, the first copper IUD developed with women's comfort in mind, was approved by the Federal Drug Administration, with six options now available in the United States. Kelly Culwell, head of research and development at Sebela Women's Health, said the reason it took so long to bring a less painful IUD to market was that the research required was expensive and time consuming, and pharma companies would rather spend their resources on developments that yield a higher return on investment.[25] Maybe Anu and Taylor would like to have a word with them.

MY TEARS RICOCHET

The repeal of *Roe v. Wade*, which guaranteed abortion as a fundamental right across the nation, is a temporary setback in the fight for women's freedom and independence. The shift from a national right to a state-determined law has driven state legislators to craft policies and laws that either codifies the right to abortion services or denies it at varying levels. What will happen moving forward in terms of a woman's right to determine her own fertility path remains to be seen. But if Rosie the Riveter has taught us anything, it is that once women get a taste of economic freedoms, they will not permanently go back, even if it means they need to play the long game and reinvent the path not for themselves but for their daughters.

Abortion polices are not the only ones that impact women's economic agency. Divorce laws, access to pensions, and family leave also matter. Unilateral divorce, which requires only one partner to desire a divorce in order for it to proceed, is another policy that has had a positive effect.

Unilateral divorce expanded across the United States in the 1970s. After an increase in divorces in the 1980s and into the 1990s, divorce rates have gone down, partially influenced by fewer overall marriages and increased cohabitation.[26] In 1983, women gained equal access to private pension funds through the Retirement Equity Act.

The Family Medical Leave Act, which guarantees twelve weeks of unpaid leave for the birth or adoption of a child or for family medical emergencies, became law in 1993. Before that, there was no guarantee that if workers left a job temporarily to care for family, it would be available to them upon return. Interestingly, family laws that give women access to resources both within and after marriage increase investments in children's education and necessities.[27] It turns out that women are more likely to reinvest back into the household and their children, so giving them control of the purse strings matters.

THE LUCKY ONE

All the hard-won policies and laws of the twentieth century have made our lives better. They have increased agency, which increases economic independence. I would go a step further to say that women won because their purse strings won.

Today, thanks to organizations like Melinda's Pivotal Ventures and Anu's Female Founders Fund, women have more control over financial institutions, investment opportunities, and power industries than they have had at any other time in history. Women are still a minority in finance, banking, and investment, but this increased control matters because women invest in other women and more clearly understand the barriers holding them back. There is more focus today on funding technology in the care economy and on investing in women inventors and women's ideas than ever before,[28] and more women are in control of companies focused on making improvements in the lives of women, mothers, and caregivers.

In 2024, the March Madness women's college basketball tournament garnered almost ten million more viewers than the men's tournament.[29] Home Depot bought a television commercial spot during the tournament. The commercial showed women doing construction projects independently, with the tagline "When you give a girl a power tool, she becomes an even more powerful woman."[30] Even Home Depot has started to recognize women's economic power and cater to it.

Claudia was right. Women won. Winning has given them more agency and autonomy. This economic autonomy has led to increased financial resources and more control over how, where, and when to invest those resources.[31] These effects are rippling throughout the economy and affect how we show up for work and our families. The impact helps level an uneven playing field. Women today are closer to equity than at any other time in history, even if we still have much more work to do.

STATE OF GRACE

One of the benefits of becoming financially stable is the ability to blend work and family with less concern for the societal constraints and expectations of what showing up for work looks like. Marissa Mayer, former Yahoo CEO, was in the news a decade ago, first for mandating that all employees return to the office, then for building a nursery in her office so she could bring her infant child to work with her.[32] Sheryl Sandberg was criticized for asking for a personal parking spot next to the front door of Facebook headquarters while she was pregnant.[33] For the most part, the criticism came from a recognition that these women in leadership positions had an advantage the rest of us do not. They have access to resources that make their ability to parent and work for pay easier.

Fast forward to today. Women with financial power continue to shape the work environment into a space that gives them better balance. Whether by hiring nannies or having the resources to pay for expensive, high-quality daycare, a certain class of women is staying engaged in paid work. Mothers in the entertainment industry, like Beyoncé and P!nk, bring their children with them on tour—and even on stage.

The truth is, it is hard to be a mom and have a career because for most of us, there is no system in place that that makes it seamless to combine childcare and paid work. In the absence of a robust system of care, mothers (and fathers) are left in an environment like the Wild, Wild West when it comes to care coverage. It is a free-for-all with lengthy waiting lists, inconvenient locations, and stressful challenges. However, instead of raging against famous and wealthy moms with resources, perhaps we should clap for them. They are not the root of our problem. They have done it. They are where we would all love to be—engaged in a job or fulfilling career while using resources to balance parenthood in an efficient manner.

They are not stressed the way we are. They are creating spaces that model a new way of existing—one that works better for women. This is what resources can do. And if we are ever going to have a labor market that maximizes female talent, we need more of this. Instead of fighting and criticizing each other, we should champion each other and encourage more workplaces to look like the blended world these women with resources are building. More childcare, more affordability, more fluidity—a world where employers create spaces for the rest of us to work and parent in a meaningful way. To be honest, the more women and mothers who become financially well off, the more of this we will see in our own communities and in the businesses that they are running, because they get it.

Look at what US Representative Carolyn Maloney was able to spearhead with the support of Ivanka Trump during her father's first administration. Working together, they convinced the administration to adopt a policy giving federal employees twelve weeks of paid parental leave.[34]

US Senator Tammy Duckworth was the first senator to give birth while in office. She championed a policy requiring airports to install breastfeeding pods.[35] In the halls of power, financial and otherwise, women, mothers, and parents have the power to make changes that improve the economic lives of the rest of us and that can influence our own financial power and ability to thrive in the long run. It is time to give ourselves some grace in pursuit of our long-run goals as women. We get further working together.

NOTHING NEW

If Taylor Swift, Beyoncé, and other high-profile women have taught us anything, it is that fine-tuning your talent and becoming a financial powerhouse gives you voice and the ability to craft the type of paid-work world you would like to live in. Finding your talent and harnessing it has the potential to change the dynamic of an entire industry, to shape it toward a model that works better for more of us. Money and marketing prowess has provided these women with opportunities to make society better through leadership and modeling, to make it more flexible for other women (and men too).

Because women have advanced in their education levels and professional careers, more of us control systems and resources that have the power to bend society toward our preferred ways of showing up in the world. Women ages twenty-five to thirty-four now have higher levels of college education than their male counterparts.[36] We should all lean into that, want more of that: a normalization of the way women and caregivers work and the acknowledgment of the need for critical infrastructure like family leave, childcare, and eldercare in our communities.

Women continue to wield their power in the shadows and soft spaces even as an extremely testosterone-driven cohort of men tries to reassert its dominance in American politics. Women are used to working behind the scenes to strategize, maneuver, and mastermind their way to a better environment. As a result, the world will continue to become more accessible for women and caregivers over time, even with temporary setbacks. In the meantime, focus on what you can do to move yourself forward. Think about harnessing a mastermind mentality to get yourself there.

EIGHT

Negotiation and Planning

MASTERMIND

> Thankfully, I left my past in [his] hands and not my future. And hopefully, young artists or kids with musical dreams will read this and learn about how to better protect themselves in a negotiation. You deserve to own the art you make.
>
> TAYLOR SWIFT on Tumblr, June 30, 2019

BEYONCÉ COLLABORATED WITH THE Dixie Chicks to perform "Daddy Lessons" from her album *Lemonade* at the 2016 Country Music Awards (CMAs).[1] While it was widely considered the best performance of the night, to some country music fans, Beyoncé was not country.[2] Television commercials highlighting the performance were pulled at the last minute, leading to concerns they were removed over complaints.

The Beyoncé–Dixie Chicks live performance was so intoxicating that country music radio stations began getting requests to play the song after the CMAs. The stations struggled with whether to play it; most eventually chose not to. The backlash was loud from of a subset of loyal listeners who argued that Beyoncé was not country.[3] Beyoncé was hip-hop or R&B, but not country. The silent, racially driven rationale: Beyoncé was Black, not country.

This idea that country music is all-white is reminiscent of other beliefs built by those in the dominant culture who tell stories of the past from their perspective.[4] Famous Black cowboys and cowgirls go back as far as the 1800s.[5] Stagecoach Mary, considered one of the original cowgirls, was a freed enslaved person born in 1832. She ended up in a school in Ohio after she was orphaned and later followed one of her teachers west to Montana, where she found a job delivering mail in the late 1800s. She protected the mail from thieves while transporting it from the rail station across the countryside.[6]

Another Black cowgirl, Johanna July, born in 1860, was a famous horse trainer who grew up near Eagle Pass, Texas. She was a member of the Black Seminole community, in which women worked in the home and men worked the livestock. Her father broke horses for the US Army, farmed, and raised livestock. Johanna loved horses. Her parents, ignoring gendered norms, let her care for and train the horses. She became a skilled horsewoman and took over her father's work when he passed away.[7]

Early on, African Americans contributed to and influenced the genre that would become country music.[8] Growing up in Texas, Beyoncé was most likely aware of Black cowboy culture and its history and influence on country music. Even if a subset of country music fans complained that she and her music were not, Beyoncé had always been country.

Instead of accepting defeat after being rejected by the CMAs and country music stations, Beyoncé masterminded a plan that would force the country music industry to reckon with its racial stereotypes. It would bring her to the top of the country music charts eight years later.[9] In 2024, Beyoncé released *Cowboy Carter*, the second album of a trilogy. The album soared to the top of *Billboard*'s country music rankings, and country music radio stations were again in a position of having to decide how to handle feedback and whether to play Beyoncé's country music.

Beyoncé publicly challenged the industry at the iHeartRadio Music Awards on April 1, 2024, when she received the Innovator Award, saying the industry needed to be "more open to the joy and liberation that comes from enjoying art with no preconceived notions."[10] Instead of internalizing the noise of those who underestimated and excluded her in 2016, Beyoncé tactfully set in motion a long-term plan to challenge the noisemakers, a plan that would encourage them to check their assumptions while also pushing her talent forward as a force with which to be reckoned. Beyoncé would not bow down. She would be strategic. She would plan. She would mastermind her way to the top.

Beyoncé went on to dominate an NFL game halftime performance carried on Netflix on Christmas Day 2024 with songs from her new album. Over 24 million viewers from around the globe watched the Netflix NFL Christmas Gameday, making it the most-streamed NFL game and halftime show ever.[11]

Change can move as slow as molasses. Even though this time Beyoncé came armed with an entire album, *Cowboy Carter* was shut out of the 2024 CMA awards.[12] Traditional forces would not bend easily. However, *Cowboy Carter* would win Best Country Album and Album of the Year at the 67th annual Grammy Awards in 2025.[13] Persistence, grit, planning, and masterminding paid off. On stage to present her with the Best Country Album award was none other than Taylor Swift. Two women who beat the odds at genre-bending were celebrating Beyoncé's success.

It is not easy being an underestimated individual. You often do not get what you want or deserve. You struggle constantly to be seen, heard, respected. Society sees you differently than you see yourself. Masterminds, though—they are determined, self-motivated. They do the hard work. Underestimate them at your own peril.

When you face doubters, mastermind a long game of how you will prove them wrong. Keep believing in yourself and finding networks that support you, your ideas, and your goals, and you will have a higher chance of achieving them. If others underestimate you, instead of feeling bad, diminished, or defeated, do as Taylor Swift did with *Reputation* or Beyoncé did with *Cowboy Carter* and prove them wrong. If we all do this, we may just be able to move the dial on people's expectations of women and caregivers.

IT WAS NOT ACCIDENTAL

Even with historical advancements in policies that force a reckoning in gender and racial equality, the United States can still feel like the Wild West in terms of equity, especially today. In the US, women earn $0.82 for every dollar earned by men.[14] Broken down by race, this inequality varies. Black women make $0.70 on the dollar, Latina women make $0.65, and Asian women make $0.93. These sticky statistics have remained relatively unchanged for the past three decades. While the Nineteenth Amendment of the US Constitution gave women the right to vote and the US Civil Rights Act of 1964 prohibited discrimination based on race, color, religion, sex, or national origin, women and minorities often remain at a disadvantage in the paid labor market.

However, there are more women in executive leadership positions than at any other point in time and diversity, equity, and inclusion programs reigned strong for a time in human resources departments and on college campuses, although they are currently under attack.[15] Overt sexism in the office setting has decreased.[16] So why do we remain stuck at $0.82? The answer might surprise you. Researchers have shown that over two-thirds of the gender wage gap is due to motherhood or the unequal distribution of unpaid work in the home.[17]

This uneven balance of work in the workplace and work in the home has become so onerous that it has inspired numerous essays and books. It is why Anne-Marie Slaughter wrote "Why Women Still Can't Have It All." It is why research from Claudia has shown that women are more likely to stay engaged with the labor force when work is flexible and employers are not greedy, because it allows workers to better balance the demands of work with the relentless demands of family.[18]

It is why Eve published *Fair Play* in 2019, in which she described her frustration with the assumption that she would be the home manager, chef, maid, and nanny. It is why Kate Washington wrote *Already Toast*, about the unexpected and daunting demands of caring for a gravely ill spouse with two small children at home. Her mastermind spirit forced her raw and unfiltered voice and feelings out into the public domain. It is why Jess Grose, opinion writer for the *New York Times*, wrote *Screaming on the Inside*, highlighting the impossible demands placed on mothers today. Jessica Calarco wrote *Holding It Together* for a similar reason. There are many other examples of caretakers speaking out publicly and acting on the need for more equitable systems. The wage gap and other inequality statistics demand more individuals willing to mastermind—people willing to speak their truth in the public forum to create awareness, destigmatize internalized feelings of failure, and push larger policy efforts that help mitigate and protect.

BY DESIGN

Today's wage gap starts with pregnancy and childbirth. It is mostly nonexistent among younger generations without children; women aged twenty-five to thirty-four with no children at home earn $0.97 on the dollar relative to their male counterparts.[19]

Most women, if they have the resources, take time off after giving birth, both to recover physically and to take care of their newborn infant. This precious time with a new baby is priceless to the parent but costly to their wallet. During this period, other work colleagues continue their grind in the workplace. They may take on extra tasks to help cover for the employee on leave. These colleagues are at the table when opportunities arise to lead new initiatives. They are in front of their supervisor on a regular basis while the new parent is on leave. They can take advantage of opportunities to show their boss they can rise and lead. Even after a new parent comes back to work, say a year later, when a promotion opens up, it is likely that their colleague will be more seriously considered for the position.

Little humans are messy, germy, and require attention. When family caregivers go back to paid work, there is a lot more to balance. It can be challenging to find reliable and consistent daycare, or to find care that fits within the hours one is working for pay. When little kids get sick at daycare, someone must pick them up and care for them at home. This often takes place at an inconvenient time, and it is usually a mother who takes time away from work to deal with these unanticipated events. As she does, the motherhood penalty chips away at her earnings.

Children don't just get sick; they have wellness checks and dentist visits and school registrations and first school days. They have extracurricular activities and school performances. Around the same time, the family care provider's older parents sometimes need help with medical appointments and other activities. Family members with disabilities need help getting around and sometimes with daily activities. All of these activities pull caretakers out of their paid job and away from the workplace and their bosses and colleagues.

Caretakers have the odds stacked against them. Not only are they usually personally invested in providing the best care for their kids, but everyone else expects that from them too. And because of this, they are often not at the table at which decisions about broader resource allocations are made. Caregivers need political representation to get their needs met, yet they have limited time to run for elected office.

In 2018, the Federal Elections Commission ruled that Liuba Grechen Shirley could use campaign funds to cover campaign-related childcare expenses when she ran for a congressional seat in New York. The commission also ruled in favor of congressional candidate MJ Hegar in 2019. Yet despite US Representatives Nikema Williams and Katie Porter's introduction of a bill in 2024 to make this a practice for all federal candidates, it has yet to become law.[20] The 2018 ruling did, however, encourage states to act. Today, thirty-nine states and the District of Columbia allow the use of campaign funds to pay for childcare costs related to official duties.[21] Even when the odds are stacked against us, change is possible.

Women caregivers often carry a disproportionate share of the burden of care because of deep-seated cultural and social norms. When children have two parents in the home, they most likely default to one parent for most of their needs and requests. At least one recent study showed that school systems also default to mom. Even when school principals are told to call fathers, they are likely to call mothers instead.[22] In my own experience during the pandemic, while both my spouse and I were working at home, I was the one my ten- and twelve-year-old children came to when they were bored or hungry or stuck on school work. It was so exhausting that I wrote a piece on *Medium* called "From Warrior to Housemaid—How the Pandemic Changed Me."[23]

If society, schools, family care providers, and even children themselves expect the primary family care provider to be front and center, how can we expect that person to advance at work at a pace similar or equal to those who are not family care providers? Care providers are set up for failure. Mothers and other care providers have a lot going against them in a system made for the care-privileged.

This is especially true in countries that insist that parenting is solely a private endeavor. Even cowgirls get exhausted by the struggle to get society to create social policies that level the playing field. Traditionally led businesses continually underestimate the value mothers and family care providers bring to their organizations—at their own peril. Mothers and related care providers have skill, drive, and leadership skills that bode well in the workforce. I sense another arbitrage moment. Perhaps the workforce needs a reinvention.

THE PAWN

Groups like Moms First and Caring Across Generations[24] and leaders like Ai-jen Poo have spent their careers fighting for the rights of domestic workers and paid care providers. But we still need substantive changes in policies that protect and support family caregivers.

I was curious about the drive of leaders in these organizations, so I asked Ai-jen what drove her passion for the rights of domestic workers. She was quick to point out that she comes from a long line of strong women caregivers. Her grandmother was a nurse and played a pivotal role in Ai-jen's life. She saw firsthand the power of intergenerational care in her own family. Her mom was a chemist, then a doctor. Ai-jen watched both her mother and her grandmother take on challenging roles outside the home and still be expected to take care of everything related to family care within the home. I found that very relatable.

Ai-jen grew up thinking seriously about this. She knew that women and women of color were paid less for doing the same type of work as men and white women. That fact, combined with society's—and often, the family's—disregard for the work they do at home for their families, really affected Ai-jen. As she got older, Ai-jen wondered more and more why women did so much yet had so little power over the big decisions impacting their lives. She felt that if society stopped taking women's work for granted, it would increase women's agency, sense of self-worth, and sense of possibility.

Ai-jen is clear that it is the system that is failing, not the women themselves. And it frustrates her that women internalize the struggle. If we cannot find affordable childcare or the right provider, we often blame ourselves for not being able to solve the crisis, when it is the system that has failed us by not guaranteeing affordable access to high-quality care for both our children and our elder parents. She worries that we focus too much on rallying against each other rather than coming together to work toward winning rights to care and a better life, and society, for all.

Ai-jen thinks there is another critical barrier to achieving a society that values care—cynicism. The belief that it is such a huge obstacle that there is no hope that improvement or change will come. But she remains hopeful, and she thinks what can work is people coming together collectively and finding their agency in connection and relationship to one another. Ai-jen firmly believes that we are motivated by others; that successful women are uplifted by other successful women. Her example of working together collectively is how the organization she founded, the National Domestic Workers Alliance, has been able to push forward and pass critical care-related legislation in eleven states.[25]

Post 2023, there is something else in the air that is new. The pandemic forced unpaid care and domestic work into the light, enough that a handful of organizations developed a similar goal of improving the lives of care providers and making their work visible. These organizations and leaders fight for the rights of unpaid family care providers and domestic workers. Their energy ricochets from one of them to the others, exponentially increasing their political power and clout. Ai-jen is hopeful that these organizations, started by various masterminds in a very grassroots fashion, will have the power to make change.

Kate Washington is one of those leaders who understands the heavy load of unpaid family care. Kate was a mother of two young children when her spouse became ill with cancer. In her book *Already Toast*, she writes about the challenges associated with the invisibility of family care and the sacrifices she and her family made to provide intensive care to her spouse during his illness and recovery in a system that assumes invisible care is available.* Kate became a strong advocate for viewing the family firm as a public, not private, good, one that is best protected and supported through public policy interventions

---

* Invisible care is defined as the work, usually of another family member, done within the home and for loved ones that requires time, energy, and effort and is not compensated and is often undervalued and ignored.

like monthly payments to caregivers, affordable quality childcare, supported public schooling, and comprehensive health care.

What all of these women have in common is their observations of the toll caregiving takes on family members when society takes them for granted. Their personal and family experiences turned them into advocates for a larger cause. They advocate for a more just system that recognizes both the work provided in family homes across the country, predominantly by women, and the value that work contributes to society as a public good. Their goal is to create systems that reciprocate and better support those around us who do care work. They strive for a system that folds care workers into the larger economic ecosystem by valuing unpaid and paid care work as economic in nature. It is only through this recognition that policymakers can begin to consider the ways in which these policies hinder or provide suboptimal support to a large swath of society.

CRIMINALLY SCHEMING

For years an arguably perverse gender vibe has lingered in academia. Want to study for a PhD while female? The advice you will often be given is "Do not have children." If you do decide to have children, dedication to your craft will be challenged, even threatened, because those in academia may not think you are serious enough about your science.

The mastermind in me birthed two amazing children during my PhD program and then went on to take a non-academic position in government, where equity among the genders and caregiver PhD economists was more balanced.[26] I could not worry about the future of my career with children. But women should not have to make these choices or feel unsupported by the system if they want to have children. Men do not have this dilemma.

For years women in academia and other corners of the male-dominated labor force have hidden their fertility or chosen not to have children because of how it might affect their career advancement. There is an entire cohort of older women in academia and science from the baby-boom generation who gave up having a family for academia. Of baby-boom women in science, only 27 percent of mothers received tenure, compared to 48 percent of fathers and 46 percent of other women.[27] Younger women today are often counseled to wait until they get tenure, the equivalent to job security in academia, before having children—putting many of them into their mid-thirties or later before having children, when fertility is biologically on the decline.

Academic men do not face this level of scrutiny surrounding their fertility decisions. They can have children during their studies, pre-tenure, post-tenure, without any negative impact or hit to their image—even if their performance declines temporarily during their child's younger years. They can more easily hide their children when convenient. Colleagues assume their spouse will take on the work of caring for children, and men with kids are more likely to advance than their female counterparts. The stark contrast in the treatment of men and women in academia slows progress for all because we leave talent, skills, and discovery on the table when we assume the birth of a child means the death of a woman's career.

So strong are these signals to women that they are easily visible in academic studies. Recall the study by Petra Moser, economic historian at the New York University School of Business, and colleagues that examined the peak productivity of academic scientists as defined by the creation of patents. Patents formally link a new idea, technology, or concept with the creator. Petra and coauthors showed that academic men's patenting patterns peaked in their thirties, while academic women's patent development peaked in their forties.[28] Women's peak came after their fertile years, assuming they were able to successfully fight gender bias and stay in academia. Those who were able to stay became just as successful as their male counterparts, but their timing was delayed.

Another study looked at the impact of tenure extensions for parents.[29] In academia, assistant professors start a new job with what is sometimes called a tenure clock, or a limited amount of time before they go up for promotion to tenure. Starting in the 1980s, some universities implemented policies allowing for an extension to the tenure clock for professors, men or women, who had children pre-tenure. The goal was to give them extra time to better balance producing babies with producing research, thereby acknowledging that those with small children who do not make tenure before the clock expires might be talented, productive researchers, but that their timing might be different than it is for those without children. The underlying goals of the policy seemed legit—even, dare I say, forward thinking.

The policies were randomized, and a few years later academics did what academics do and studied the impact of the policy. The preconceived thinking was that the policy would help retain more women in academia. But what actually happened baffled many in the field. While the mothers who were given the extension were more likely to stay in academia, the gap between men and women had widened. Why? Mothers used their extension to focus on caring for their new infant and the family. Fathers used the extra time to produce more scientific papers. This study is a key piece of evidence showing that creating gender-neutral policies to help women advance can have unexpected results and can even backfire. In this case, the policy made academic men even more productive than they previously were and accelerated their success because the demands on them within the household were not the same as they were for women.

In an even more recent study by female academic economists who were tired of getting called first by their children's schools even after they asked the schools to call their spouses, gendered expectations in parenting was disproportionately impacting women's work productivity in a negative way. In their paper titled "Who You Gonna Call?," Kristy Buzard, Laura Gee, and Olga Stoddard found that mothers were 1.4 times more likely to get called by schools than fathers, even if they had asked the school to call fathers first.[30]

Taking time for wellness visits, dentist visits, sickness, and other activities required to grow happy and healthy children reduces the time dedicated to one's job or career. Less time at work translates into being less likely to take the next leadership role or advancement opportunity, which leads to a decreased likelihood of getting promoted.

These studies are key examples of why policies are needed to promote equity, not equality. While equality implies equal exposure and experience for all (like the changed gender-neutral tenure clock policy), equity acknowledges that we all start with different endowments or resources, and that this variation in original resource allocation, as well as in expectations on how we spend our time, should be seriously considered when crafting policies to help women advance.

Given gendered assumptions about care work within households, most women need additional support in the workplace. Their needs should be addressed through laws and social policies that keep them engaged in using their talent to advance economic growth while also allowing them to give care to family members without stretching them thin and running them into exhaustion. Policy cushions should be developed that make care transitions easier, more affordable, and accessible, allowing them to maximize their talent and energy in a way that benefits all of us.

GROUNDWORK

Most in search of a gender-supportive economy realize that it is equally important to argue for gender equity in the household and family life.

Because of this, today's movement may look different than those of prior generations. Younger men are more aware of and more likely to engage in unpaid household chores than they were in the past.[31] Employers are more aware of gender inequalities in the workplace, and many groups in society have been pushing for policies that infuse more equity at work and at home.

The modern movement toward gender equity is inward facing—it focuses on reducing inequalities in informal care work in the home, allowing women more time to focus on career and paid care. This movement focuses on increasing cushions that allow women and parents to care for their families and then bounce back without much drag on their paid work path.

There are two clear paths to achieving this. Either men step up more at home or governments provide more formalized support that reduces the burden of care responsibilities that is disproportionately placed on women.[32] Neither of these options is novel. Both are possible. They just require the social and political will to prioritize gender equity, to allow women's talent to shine outside the home without them being driven to exhaustion, and to allow men's caregiving nature to shine at home. It is about time we gave back to female caregivers and repaid them for all they have given us to date.

We may be much closer to gender equity in the workplace than at any other point in the past, but the environment outside of the workplace is still filled with inequities. When my children were young, I worked as an economic researcher for a statistical agency. I would daydream at my desk about the lives of my non-caregiver colleagues when they went home at the end of day. I imagined them kicking off their shoes, cracking open a beer, and watching a basketball game. When I got home from work, after commuting forty-five minutes on a metro train with two cranky, hungry kids under age five, I would rush to make dinner. We would feed the kids, clean up, give them baths and get them ready for bed, then read them books until they went to sleep. I was so exhausted that the minute they went to bed, so did I. Sometimes I fell asleep while reading to them, only to wake up the next day and do it all over again.

Between work and family, I had essentially zero personal time. As an economist, I also knew that if either my spouse or I took time off from work to focus on caring for our kids during the workday, our lifetime earnings trajectory would change. And it was unlikely we would be able to afford a small townhome or even a small apartment for our growing family in Washington, DC, on one salary. Like the families discussed in Heather Boushey's book *Finding Time*, we needed both incomes to thrive—not to mention the fact that I had just invested thirteen years of time and money in post-secondary schooling to study something I loved. We put our daycare payments for an infant and toddler on our credit card to be paid at some future date.

This grind happens to parents, especially mothers, at all income levels; some women even work more than one job to make ends meet, like my mother did. These issues are common today in the United States and other parts of the globe. Having an able-bodied adult who stays home and cares for the family is a luxury many of us can no longer afford. We urgently need larger structural solutions to the challenges most of us face—like how to successfully raise the next generation of children.

BEING A MASTERMIND

For many women, the experience of feeling muzzled, cornered in a room full of others' minimal expectations, or pushed to the back is not uncommon. Instead of feeling bad, diminished, or defeated, try using the experience to reinvent yourself, to propel yourself into your next era. Figure out the long game of how to prove the doubters wrong or how to maneuver around, over, or through them.

The best advice Taylor Swift may have imparted to us through her actions to date is this: In a world where you can be anything, be a mastermind. Set your long-term goals for you and only you, goals that speak to you, that burn deep in your soul, and then figure out how to go and get them.

The path will not be linear. It will require reinvention. The majority of those who responded to the Swiftynomics survey said they reinvented their paths.[33] It won't be easy. You will probably fail. The goalposts will move because you have limited control over the environment around you. Every day, every hour, every minute, you will learn new information that forces (sometimes uncomfortable) updates. But all that any of us can do is keep forging forward with determination. Moving forward with a mastermind mentality increases the odds that you will get where you belonged all along.

PLAY THE LONG GAME

Remember when US gymnast Simone Biles got the twisties and left the 2020 Tokyo Olympics team competition?[34] Everyone seemed to have an opinion about her departure. I remember being pleasantly surprised to hear the words of support and encouragement that bubbled up in the national and international media. But there were some who wrote Simone off, declared her career over. Simone, though, became a skilled mastermind. She was playing the long game.

Overwhelmed by media pressure and a lack of in-person support in Tokyo, Simone knew she needed to work through her challenges. And while some declared her career over, she was consciously and unconsciously observing other strong, determined reinventionists around her. She owed nothing to anybody except herself, but what she owed to herself ran deep.[35]

We all face setbacks. We all get jumbled up in our heads as stress increases and life becomes more complicated. It is how we choose to handle those challenges, to overcome the failures, that makes us masterminds. Simone knew that. She'd been taking notes, acquiring strength, determination, and grit from others who had fallen in the eyes of the public. The most important person in Simone's comeback story was herself.

Simone drew on the same kind of grit and determination to rewrite her own story that drove Taylor Swift to write and release her *Reputation* album and Beyoncé to write and release *Lemonade* and *Cowboy Carter*. We all benefitted from the strategic masterminding these women did to prove to themselves that their hurdles were surmountable, to define for themselves how their talent would be seen by a society that had rejected them, criticized them, or written them off.

This mastermind-style long game best describes women in today's economy. They thrive and persist simply because they are not willing to be boxed in by old rules often steeped in stereotypes that hold them back from being the best versions of themselves. They resist where they can and plan when they can't.

Everyone loves a comeback story, and on August 1, 2024, at the Paris Olympics, Simone helped her team win gold in gymnastics and then went on to win three additional individual medals in all-around, beam, and floor routines.[36] In the four years between Tokyo and Paris, Simone had put in the work. She defined a path that was uniquely hers, and she did it for herself. That was obvious if you spent any time watching her performances in Paris; she was nervous but having so much fun. She had set goals and she superseded them. In the spirit of taking notes and of endgames, Simone chose to start her floor routine with "Are You Ready for It" by Taylor Swift.

In support, Beyoncé recorded an advertisement for NBC television for Simone, her team, and other athletes, her voice filled with pride.[37] Taylor

Swift narrated a separate stream of promotional pieces in support of the women athletes at the games, who won 65 percent of all US gold medals and made up 50 percent of all Olympic athletes.[38] Simone was following in Beyoncé's and Taylor's footsteps, knowing that revenge is best served cold and is most fulfilling when you are in it for yourself and only yourself. Simone had one goal: to prove to herself that she was still the greatest of all time (G.O.A.T.), and she did just that. She won four medals: three gold and one silver.[39]

EFFORTLESS

Protecting ourselves in a world not originally built for our needs can feel overwhelming and exhausting. If our protective layers are thin, we are easily prodded and maneuvered into submission. In a world that was not built for us, we sometimes need to bubble-wrap our souls, hearts, and minds to protect them.[40] Build yourself your own world, one that you run, and protect it at all costs. That often means being proactive instead of reactive. Instead of reacting to misogynistic or racist behavior with anger or spite, acknowledge it, call it out when it is safe to do so, and then push it aside, out of your way. In these times of social media influence and digital attention grabbing, be mindful not to collect and internalize other people's baggage. It will do you no service.

Imagine the world you want to live in and speak your truth. As a caregiver and woman, my truth is that I do not live in a professional world built to make me successful. I live in a world where others have perceptions that do not live up to the reality that I want to live. In my real-world experience, being bold and female means that others will easily complain about me to supervisors, or even directly to me, when I do not do what they expect or want me to do. In their world, I am here to support them and not the other way around. I spent years getting angry and frustrated when colleagues complained about an ask that I made or a thing that I did. Rarely was I able to convince them to see how their behavior was gendered.

But I played the long game and, in the meantime, wrapped myself in bubble wrap. I focused on the goals just beyond my reach, spoke out to those who mattered when they would listen, and just chose to let go of the noise my colleagues were making. At the end of the day, it was the quality of my work, my innovative visions, and my willingness to work hard that pushed me into better spaces. Having a bubble-wrap mentality helped me not get sucked into believing the rhetoric and challenges others were imposing on me. It helped me thrive and push past them.

Where we are not unified, we need to unify. There is power in numbers in our workplaces, social spaces, and even in our families. We need to advocate for each other, especially those of us who wield more power in society due to social constructs around age, race, ethnicity, and family makeup. We need to promote those who best understand our needs and are interested in prioritizing equity. We need to manifest the world we want to see. Backlash is to be expected; it means we are making progress. It means change is in the air.

END GAME

I attended a workshop at the Brookings Institution in the spring of 2024 at which Claudia Goldin was the keynote speaker.[41] She outlined the history of formal childcare in the United States in three acts. Act One focused on the years following the Great Depression, when federally funded nurseries provided early childhood education and jobs for unemployed teachers. Act Two came during World War II, when federally funded daycare sites were developed so mothers could work in factories to support the war effort, and it ended in the 1970s, when President Nixon vetoed universal childcare. Act Three is the post-pandemic era, in which telework, remote work, and flexible schedules have become more common and more mothers than ever are able to work *while* mothering. Notice that in all three acts, mothers worked for pay, even as the childcare available to them differed. In many respects, Nixon's veto of universal childcare in the 1970s solidified a dominant value at the time that taking care of children was an independent endeavor, the responsibility for which rested on parents and families.

Despite this restrictive policy stance, which clearly muted women's economic opportunities outside the home, many women thrived. Those who have, have done so through the support of their families, friends, and mentors. And, while many of us have struggled to lean in, like Anne-Marie Slaughter highlighted, still we persist. Through her own reinvention, Anne-Marie remains an active, authentic voice in the policy space and has a successful career as a policy leader and author on women's leadership.[42] She has crisply articulated her frustrations in writing, and in doing so, made a mastermind move by shifting shame and blame off her own shoulders and onto the rightful owner—society. She bravely declared that she had lost an unfair and unjust fight.

Ai-jen Poo closed out the Brookings Institution Care Economy Workshop in a way that reminded me of what Anne-Marie had accomplished. Ai-jen's positivity was infectious. Even in a world where care is often ignored and those who provide either paid or unpaid care work are often undervalued, Ai-jen was hopeful. Hopeful because the past few years had brought more change, improvements, and willingness than she had ever previously seen. To her, it felt like we were moving in a positive direction, even if there was still much work to be done.

What I have learned from these women is that if we want a lifestyle and a society that treat us better and prioritize our needs, we can achieve them. We get there by acknowledging our already existing power, getting out and voting for our priorities, and uniting instead of dividing ourselves. Working together, we win, hands down. Even when there are disparities among groups of women in terms of advancement, working together, we are more likely to succeed.

Girls and women are no longer bending to dominant attitudes when they contradict their health and well-being. They are surrounding themselves with those who support and believe in them. They are figuring out how to success-fully stick up for themselves within their careers and professions, and it shows.[43] The fact that we can see it demonstrates the increasing power and influence they have in society.

What if I told you that the ability to effect larger societal change has existed in you, and in us, all along? Girls can run the world—in fact, even given all the struggles mentioned, what if they already do? There is a power within us that in combination with the political influence given to us with the right to vote in 1920, the taste of economic independence gained by our grandmothers and great-grandmothers during World War II thanks to the Lanham Act, and the landslide of equitable policies and laws passed between 1963 and 1973 has given us more education, freedom, and economic inde-pendence than women have enjoyed at any other point in time.

Look at what we have done. We are closer than ever to electing the first female president of the United States, an accomplishment already achieved in about one-third of United Nations member states.[44] Traditional methods used to divide and conquer us are not working. Famous women stick together rather than letting themselves be pitted against each other. Beyoncé showed up for Taylor Swift's Eras Tour concert film and Taylor went to Beyoncé's concert tour movie opening in London.[45] After surviving the pandemic, mothers who stay home to take care of their children may no longer be willing to believe their struggle is different than mothers who work for pay, and vice versa.[46] Our power is untapped and unused choice, the freedom to choose the path that works best for each of us.

Women make up half of humanity but our needs, our priorities, in fact, the entirety of our work has been largely ignored and undervalued. Girls do run the world, and it is time we told the rest of the world to start acting like it.

TIED TOGETHER WITH A SMILE

The women who came before us figured out that we all need support, especially in the shared cause of creating a society that more accurately reflects the lived experiences and aspirations of the women around us. We return the favor by supporting others and calling out bad behavior when we see it. As seen through the #MeToo movement started by Tarana Burke,[47] women are getting more comfortable publicly calling out harmful behavior and moving shame onto its rightful owner—the perpetrators and a society that tolerates them. For the benefit of the women who come after us, it is our duty to continue the fight by highlighting inappropriate behavior when it happens and believing survivor stories.

When you live in an economy and society built for others, maneuvering around landmines can be challenging and overwhelming. Sometimes people do not take you seriously. Sometimes you are unaware of the insider's club or how to advance. Maybe managers and leaders do not see you in that way. Perhaps needing time off to handle family care is interpreted as you not being as dedicated to your work as others are. This is especially true when those in charge have lots of care privilege and live in a family where others take care of them and their needs, including childcare.

When we create buffers around our needs, we craft new realities within a domain we control. The easiest way to create a buffer is to speak our truth and describe our reality to those around us. It is critical to invite men and others with care privilege to meet us in this space. We shine when we are no longer willing to put up with a status of lesser or to struggle silently to fit into a system not designed for us. Let's invite everyone else to meet us in these new buffer zones we create, in spaces where we are not held back and neither are they—spaces with equal opportunity for equity, safety, and advancement at work and in the home.

When I interviewed Claire Cain Miller about women in today's economy, she highlighted a prominent barrier to reducing mothers' stress and mental load: child-rearing is viewed as a very individualized task.[48] During the mid-twentieth century, people were fighting for women's education, careers, and equal incomes. The fight for childcare and paid leave, however, failed, reducing the potential for creating buffers that support women and mothers who work. According to Claire, the lack of buffers is exemplified by a school day that ends at 3:00 p.m. and a three-month break from school over the summer, during which many adults must continue to work.

Claire had recently attended a dinner with other mothers at her children's school. One mother had been carpooling another mother's child to dance class while she worked. These women were friends. Their daughters were friends, and minimal effort was involved in bringing the child along with them, but the mother who could not drive because of work appeared overly grateful for the help, hyper-aware of what she perceived as a real burden on the other mother and a potential failure on her part to handle the dilemma privately. It struck Claire like a ton of bricks—we, as a society, have such an aversion to relying on community for help and support.

Claire gets enraged when she thinks back to the pandemic and school closures because there was little or no help for parents even as their family care duties increased. There were no airline bailouts for parents, although temporary child tax credits were put in place to help with financial and economic challenges associated with the pandemic.[49] There was no bending of quarantine closure rules for schools like there was for liquor stores, which received exemptions to remain open for public health reasons. The argument for liquor stores was that this helped mitigate burdening hospitals with alcoholics going through withdrawal. Apparently having a multitude of school-age children climbing the walls in their homes while their parents' mental health deteriorated as they tried to work from home and help their kids adjust to remote school was less of an issue.

There were even childcare bailouts to help formal childcare businesses reopen during the summer of 2020. But any support to cover the intense time commitment required to cover the family care needs provided by parents was minimal to nonexistent. Parents and the care needs of children were, for the most part, highlighted in the media but essentially ignored by policymakers. The increased care burden parents experienced while also trying to maintain paid work was viewed as a pandemic side effect that parents needed to manage privately. Meanwhile schools, backed by strong teachers' unions, remained closed much longer than most other businesses and organizations.

Claire highlighted that "raising the next generation of children [is] a good for society. This is the next generation of workers. It is the next generation of taxpayers. It is the next generation of people paying into social security. There are a lot of ways that you can justify why it [child-rearing] is important."[50] Claire lamented that whenever she publishes a story on children, paid leave, screen time, or anything that touches on child-rearing, remarks pop up in the comments section from individuals saying things like "It is your fault for having children. You didn't need to have them." Even during the pandemic, comments such as "Why did you have children if you did not want to spend all day with them?" were common. Some readers compared having children to hobbies like owning a horse or tending a vegetable garden.

To Claire, this misses the point. Should the government subsidize hobbies? It is not the same thing because raising the next generation of healthy, educated adults who carry on the legacy of citizenship and voting is a benefit to society, and there are clear consequences if we cannot execute it successfully. Claire mentioned that parenting has become harder and more complex as society advances. We need to get better at asking for and offering help and support at a broader communal level.

This, perhaps, is our moment. A moment for schools, policymakers, and public institutions to revisit how our communities support the role and infrastructure of raising our next generation of adults and workers. Maybe it is time we got serious about masterminding public policies and programs that prioritize the needs of caregivers. And we should probably do it before the generations of today decide that raising the next generation on a pedestal of privacy may just be too much to bear.

SAME ROOM SAME TIME

Once children become adults, their ability to survive often depends on the infrastructure in place around them, including friends and family, and their ability to work for pay. Working for pay is the most direct route to economic freedom. Yet the organizations for which women work often reflect the lived experiences of men, especially in sports. Until recently, that is.

The Kansas City Current, a professional women's soccer team in the US National Women's Soccer League, opened a stadium in 2024 in Kansas City,

Missouri. It is the first stadium built solely and entirely for a women's professional team in any sport. No more sharing a stadium with a professional men's team or collegiate and, in some instances, community or high school teams. No more waiting for leftover scraps of time on the pitch calendar. Perhaps influenced by Megan Rapinoe and the other women's national team players who, a decade earlier, pushed for pay equity in the sport, those who spearheaded the effort to build the stadium were focused on building a home for fans of women in soccer.[51]

The original co-owners of the team and the stadium, Angie and Chris Long and Brittany Mahomes, focused on creating an environment specifically designed for women, rather than one that replicated the men's soccer stadium experience. The stadium was developed to accommodate caregivers and welcome female athletes. As a first-season ticket holder, I noticed various important subtleties upon entering the stadium. There were breastfeeding and sensory family rooms available to attendees with infants and children with sensory issues. There was a wall of photos of the first women's national soccer team and a video documentary available for all attendees to see. Next to the locker rooms, the text of Title IX was displayed on a wall in big, bold letters, and players go past it every time they walk out onto the pitch.

During the 2024 season, the KC Current social crew did a "show us your baby" segment to the song "Circle of Life" from *The Lion King* at the beginning of games. Parents held their babies up in the air just like Mufasa did with baby Simba. Fertility and the lived experiences of women as care providers was celebrated, embedded into the culture of the team and stadium. At almost every game, starting goalie Adrianna (AD) Franch was accompanied by her small daughter as she stepped off the team bus and walked into the stadium.

The KC Current leaned into motherhood as a natural extension of the athletes' professional lives. The team chose to do what more governments, societies, and businesses would do if they were led by women: adapt the organization to the lives of women and caregivers in a way that allows them to continue to shine professionally without asking them to choose between work and family or pressuring them to hide their family life and caregiver responsibilities while at work. By leaning into how women present their true selves, the KC Current organization is showing us what our lives could look like if women were fully accepted in professional spaces.

In January 2023, Brittany's spouse, Patrick, became a co-owner of the club.[52] A little more than a year later, he gave a speech at the TIME100 Gala where he said, "I'd like to raise a glass to a new era in sports. An era when the women's game is finally getting the attention it deserves."[53] While there will always be work needed to increase gender equity, he was correct that we are in a new era, one in which women will continue to shine, break records, and reach for the stars.

In our lives, we are always in either a reinvention or an era. Which one are you in right now? Always be willing to reinvent yourself without shame or doubt. Always be willing to play the long game. Know that along the way, those with the most power in society will try to divide and conquer. Do not fall for it. We are always stronger together.

Cannot get your needs met in a men's stadium? Work toward building your own. Tired of roles and jobs in your industry that limit your ability and ignore the depth of your talent? Work with a group of like-minded individuals to mastermind your own space. Tired of being told you cannot be X, Y, or Z? Do what Beyoncé did and forge ahead anyway, without the doubters. They will eventually catch up, or not, but you have the power to ignore them and mastermind your own path.

Conclusion

IS IT OVER NOW?

I'm trying to tell you that losing things doesn't just mean losing.
A lot of the time, when we lose things, we gain things too.

TAYLOR SWIFT,
2022 New York University Commencement Speech

LIVING IN A WORLD not originally designed for you can be challenging.
Your talent may go unnoticed; your skills may be invisible. It can be hard to
be seen as a leader or as experienced enough to advance. You may not be
taken seriously. Many of us cling to Taylor's lyrics because she is in the mainstream, articulating our lived experiences through all our eras. She bolsters
us, helps us feel less isolated in an economic world originally envisioned by
and for the ease of men and the care-privileged.

Taylor is but one figure in a line of inspiring women. The women of today
are the mark left on society by every generation before them. We are the
products of the labor of the women before us. As Claudia highlighted, the
previous generations gave us ten years (1964–1973) of critical policies and laws
that have propelled women into new domains.[1] They made the world and our
economic infrastructure friendlier to women.

We should feel proud of these prior generations. Thanks to them, we have
become women less likely to be intimidated by misogynistic behaviors and
attitudes. We call them out when we encounter them. We no longer let a
male-dominated society define us, but rather strive to redefine and reshape
society, stereotypes, and attitudes so they work for us. No longer lost in the
shame-and-blame games of yesteryear that controlled women's behaviors, we
stand up for ourselves and each other. This matters because our girls and boys
are watching, and they represent the next generation of change.

Although we may not initially believe it, the women of today have similar wants, desires, and goals as the women of prior generations. But they also have more opportunities in the workplace, making for different struggles at home. No matter the decade, women have always found ways to pave their path, influence society and family, and survive. How they do it might be a relic of their time, but women create community, reinvent themselves to fit the situation, and mastermind their path forward when they can. They make decisions on how to spend household money and control certain resources. They invest time and resources in their communities and raise the next generation.

Today's younger generation will continue to push and resist, to be their true authentic selves, to call out bad behavior when they see it, and to follow their passions. Will they see the micro economies of their homes become more equitable? Will they see the labor market become more accommodating of their way of life? These questions are at the heart of *Swiftynomics*.

SUBURBAN LEGENDS

On July 21, 2024, Vice President Kamala Harris was named to the Democratic ticket for president.[2] In the first twenty-four hours after President Biden's decision to drop out of the race, Kamala's campaign raised $250 million.[3] Supporters organized Zoom calls within hours. One of the first calls was hosted by an online group called "Win with Black Women," which had been organizing for about four years and held regular Sunday night meetings. Around 44,000 people logged in on Zoom to strategize in support of the new nominee.[4] A different online meeting later in the week broke records, with over 130,000 women joining a call titled "White Women: Answer the Call! Show Up for Kamala Harris."[5] Within a few days, "Swifties for Kamala" gained more than 128,000 followers on social media platforms like X (formerly Twitter) and Instagram.[6]

After Kamala's first presidential debate in early September, Taylor Swift announced she was voting for Kamala and encouraged others to register to vote and to do their research in order to make an informed vote for the person whose values best aligned with theirs.[7] In the twenty-four hours following her announcement, more than 400,000 people visited the Vote.org site.[8] While the 2024 presidential election did not go to a woman, Kamala still holds the honor of being the first female vice president of the

United States. She moved mountains for the rest of us. I, for one, could not be prouder.

Even with the 2024 election setback and the persistent drag of a society not willing to support a more-than-qualified first female president (twice), women have made strides. Wherever pushback toward competent women leaders still exists, there are supporters waiting to help clear her path forward, to find alternative routes to keep us advancing.

We know this because women represent us in increasing numbers in the halls where decisions are made. In 2025, women made up one-fourth (26 percent) of the members of the US Senate and almost one-third (29 percent) of members of the US House of Representatives.[9] In 2023, just under 33 percent of state legislators and twelve state governors were women.[10] Strides to bring women's voices into the political fold continue.

Even with the current administration launching political attacks on diversity, equity, and inclusion (DEI) programs, it is only a matter of time before the United States sees its first female president. The writing is on the wall. Just as Rosie the Riveter never gave up the long game of working for pay and economic agency for her daughters and granddaughters after World War II, even as paid work opportunities were stripped from her, we will not give up on this goal.

HOW YOU GET THE GIRL

To understand the modern woman in today's economy, we must understand that her goal is equity, both inside and outside the home. She yearns to live in the gloriously non-misogynistic, multicolored, sparkly glow that Taylor Swift and others have worked to create for us.

Swiftynomics is all about seeing beyond the construct that currently holds us back. It is about creating the economy and society we want to live in by using our talent, intellect, and grit to design structures and pathways that meet our needs. It is about using the power given to us by those who came before us to reinvent and reposition ourselves in ways that maximize our hidden and overt potential.

The main goals of this book have been to provide the reader with a better understanding of women as economic agents, uncover and highlight our strengths, bring forth an enlightened economic view of women from the past, and present ideas for promoting women's well-being and economic success (broadly defined) as we move into the future. Gender inequity is not a problem for women to solve. It is a societal challenge we must all take on.

The role of care provider is inherently a selfless one; a care provider's job is to put others first. Because of this, the needs of care providers are rarely acknowledged, let alone met, and burnout is inevitable. Direct family care providers need more support in, and opportunities to step outside of, their role. If they are not given this, birth rates will continue to plummet as younger women shift their priorities. They see the silent sacrifices of care that drag us down, and they are not signing up for that.[11] But it does not have to stay this way.

Figuring out how to recognize and formally value the contributions of women's informal work and economic activity is critical to our success. The longer it takes for society to figure this out, the more damage is done to the economy, because we cannot maximize economic growth when half the members of society find it challenging to contribute their fullest while balancing care responsibilities. Where women and family care providers can, they should stand up for themselves with the persistence of a Frances Perkins, Dolores Huerta, Dolly Parton, Madonna, Beyoncé, Taylor Swift, or any of the other women who have decided to bet on themselves, make their own rules, and determine what they will and will not put up with.

Policies that support work environments that help family care providers thrive benefit everyone. They benefit the workplace because family care providers are talented individuals with something unique to contribute. When talents more precisely align with jobs, labor markets become more efficient. Economies grow because waste decreases, productivity increases, and individual flourish.

The women and care providers of today are exhausted and need policies that break traditional norms. They need policies that reflect reality, acknowledge their exhaustion, and improve their quality of life. These policies should support the economic independence of women and direct family care providers while allowing them to fill a direct care role at home should they so choose.

Women and their allies should break free from the current traditional norms that hold us back. It does us no good to accept a fate of being perpetually overworked and stressed out. Be a mastermind and challenge society to see the totality of your work and economic contributions in combination with your care roles. Champion policies that give family care providers the support they need to care for their families while not damaging their job or career, including policies that encourage men to engage more at home so women can flourish at paid work.

Creating a nation where public policies broadly support human development within communities is necessary. Childcare is a public good: investing in quality development opportunities for children creates independent, well-rounded, healthy individuals regardless of their family's initial endowments. This redistribution of resources allows children to flourish and sets them on a path to become productive adults, thereby fostering economic growth and contributing positively to society.

If systems that support the public good—childcare, schooling, health care—are made available equally across the country, as was originally done with public schools, public libraries, railroad systems, and national parks in the early and mid-twentieth century, societal benefits accrue. Workers are less likely to miss work due to family illness, crime decreases, and self-sufficiency increases because basic needs are met that allow individuals to thrive at home and at work.

An economy that recognizes the critical and essential value of care also understands that without support, equality, and infrastructure around care responsibilities, care providers are at a disadvantage because society undervalues them and takes their unpaid work for granted. We desperately need a system in which the care work is more equally distributed.

The United States spent $700 billion to bail out our banks and financial system in 2008, $30 billion to bail out the auto industry in 2009, and $54 billion to save airlines during the pandemic in 2021, so why can't we implement the steps recommended below?[12] The industry of informal family care providers and formal paid care workers, predominantly women, is too important for us to fail it. Care providers are critical to the establishment of our next generation of adults, our future. Excluding care work from economic statistics is a failure that allows Economic Man to continue devaluing care provider rights to resources. Arguing that the family firm is a private endeavor and not worthy of government support is shortsighted.

To change things, we need to:

- Pay women and parents for their invisible labor
  - Compensate mothers with stipends in the form of robust child credits, the kind of credit—a base salary, if you will—that is paid monthly regardless of whether they work for pay outside the home. Those working outside the home could use this base salary to cover other costs, like childcare.

- Provide universal paid parental leave after a birth or adoption.
- Develop policies that encourage men to engage in more care and invisible household labor
  - Install paid paternity leave that is universally available and provides the father or second caregiver specific extensions of leave that if not taken, are forfeited.
  - Provide incentives that encourage men to do more household work, like normalizing paid time off for children's doctor appointments or paying family members for managing calendars and chores.
- Offer universal childcare
  - Invest in before- and after-school care and early childhood education programs.
  - Provide access to universal, high-quality, affordable childcare for children ages birth to five. Just as public school access is an educational and human right across the country, so should early childhood education and care be.
- Create public policies, laws, or guidelines for businesses that establish rules for flexible work that do not hamper career advancement
  - Measure employee effort by productivity versus being physically in an office seat or on site.
  - Implement telework policies and procedures that include weekly in-office days and flex days.
  - Develop laws for work reentry after a major family event and rules around employee evaluations post reentry.
- Formalize the production of data and statistics that shine a light on women and care providers as full economic agents—a dashboard of statistics on the care economy
  - Invest in the development of official national statistics similar to what my team and I have developed at the University of Kansas, called The Care Board (https://thecareboard.org)
    - Improve data collection measures to enhance statistics that provide a comprehensive view of the care economy, care providers, and the true cost of care.

Economic Man will warn us that these ideas are costly and inefficient, but Economic Woman knows they are not. Economic Man will think that they will encourage people to have babies, which in today's environment he may see as positive, but he will worry that direct family care providers will leave the paid labor market in droves to live off government coffers. He will also be concerned about the possibility of abuse of and fraud in the system.

Economic Woman knows these tactics of division and distrust; she has seen them before. Economic Man, with all his inherent privilege, may spit and sputter, but Economic Woman will remind him of her invisible heart.[13] She will remind him that raising the next generation of workers is a noble task and one of the most challenging, inspiring, and also soul-crushing endeavors she (and he) will endure in their lifetime.

She will clarify for him that those government coffers only exist because of her and her foremothers' hard (invisible) work in raising him. If she does not deserve this investment of the funds she helped develop, then it is unclear who does. Economic Woman knows her day has come. She has listened intently to the lyrics of Taylor Swift, and she knows she deserves all that is coming her way.

I KNOW [POLICY] PLACES

The family firm (i.e., our households) and investments in the health and well-being of the next generation are public goods. As such, they are resources that are best protected through broad public investments and public policy interventions on behalf of families.

While I have outlined a few specific options above, the policy options are vast. If we can wrangle political power away from Economic Man, we can provide child credits to parents. Parents could choose to stay at home to care for the next generation of workers, or they could choose to work for pay and use the funding to pay for high-quality childcare. Research shows that we should direct this credit into the mother's coffer, who, on average, is more likely to reinvest the money directly into her children and household.[14]

Universal paid parental leave is critical. Evidence has shown that the best policies encourage fathers' engagement by providing an extended period of leave for fathers that, if not taken, is forfeited.[15] Encouraging fathers to engage more directly with the care of their children early on has shown to benefit fathers, mothers, and children and to have a lasting impact throughout childhood.

Why take away leave if fathers do not use it, rather than giving it to mothers? Research has shown that because of traditional gender norms in most societies, men need a pull—a carrot, if you will—to leave their workplace to care for an infant. Structuring a policy in a way that takes the choice away from men and puts the blame on the policy itself allows men to take family leave without the associated shame and stigma they may feel from their friends, family, and employer. If, on the other hand, parents are given a total amount of leave time to distribute as they see fit, because of gender norms and differences in pay, the mother usually ends up taking all of it, to the detriment of her career.

Families critically need affordable, high-quality healthcare, education, and childcare in order for society to advance. If families underinvest in the next generation, either because they cannot afford the services or because services are not available and markets, like the childcare market, are not working, we all lose. Innovations that reduce the cost of healthcare and promote quality education and accessible childcare should be actively and urgently pursued by government and private entities.

Societies and governments often waver in their level of commitment to workers. Governments swing between allowing employers and big business too much power and then installing rights for workers when big employers abuse their privileges. This is what Frances Perkins fought for in the early twentieth century, and it is what we must fight for now, except that now, it is time to rebalance power between those who receive care and those who give it.

One step toward increasing care provider power within the larger society is through the democratization and modernization of data collection, production, and distribution.[16] We need to gather, reconcile, and make public regularly available data on the amount of invisible work care providers do and the roles their work plays in advancing the well-being of others and the economy. Only through access to data on caregiving can we focus on creating new policies and improve existing ones to support care providers.

In 2023, I began a project at the University of Kansas called The Care Board.[17] The mission was to quantify the economic contributions of care work, which encompasses various activities such as daycare, preschool care, in-home care, nursing home care, janitorial work, nanny care, and housework. By gathering existing statistics from administrative sources like public assistance programs or tax records, we can provide a centralized repository of accessible data. In order to craft informed, data-driven policies, we need more initiatives like this that record documented acts of service and care activities that benefit society as a whole.

COLD AS YOU

On June 24, 2022, Nina Totenberg and Sarah McCammon did something they probably never expected they would have to do. Their job as public radio journalists meant that they had to report on the overturning of *Roe v. Wade*, which legalized abortion rights throughout the United States and had been considered a constitutional right since the 1970s.[18] In *Dobbs v. Jackson Women's Health Organization*, the US Supreme Court deferred the matter of abortion rights back to the states. It was no longer considered a right under the US Constitution. State governments were now delegated with determining the fate of abortion rights within their borders.

This ruling was not only about the right to life or the rights of the fetus, but also, critically, about the rights of women to determine their own economic agency and future. Children require resources. Biologically, it is easier for men than women to avoid expending the resources required for children they either intentionally or unintentionally create. We live in a society that normalizes it when men shirk the cost of unwanted children, which then moves the entire cost of these children onto women. No or restricted access to reproductive health services like birth control and abortion services creates a gender inequity that has life-long effects for women. Not acknowledging this fact while also imposing greater restrictions on women's freedom of choice is disingenuous to half of the population. Access to the right to abortion services is, in and of itself, a gender equity policy.

I WISH YOU WOULD

When we live for ourselves, we see women's economic resiliency grow. We live in an era until it stops working for us, until we stop growing, and then we reinvent. Reinvention does not imply that everything changes. Rather, it means that we minimize or change the things in our lives that are holding us back. It means being authentic about who we are and who we want to be.

There are large inequalities in the world today. Women often start out with an inequality in endowments related to care and expectations on how we show up as economic agents. These unequal initial endowments imply that efficient models driven by mathematical equations have important limitations when it comes to moving toward a society that engages with and harnesses diversity for the benefit of all. Policies and legislation that redistribute resources through taxation and other policies can correct for unequal endowments. Another option is for individuals to persist by reinventing their economic goals, contributions, and paths.

In addition to studying policy options, we should start expanding the frontier of research and modeling in order to reshape the traditional economy into a more inclusive one, one that accounts for and records all types of economic activities, including those within the home. We need models that more accurately reflect women's economic activities to help move the field of economics into a more inclusive, comprehensive, and accurate science, one that studies decision-making with limited resources, as well as growth and macroeconomic trends that make care visible. Like the macroeconomic models of yesteryear that were named after the men who created them, our care model could be called the Barbie-Ken-Alan-Midge model, if you will, and incorporate invisible labor into the mix.

Today you have the right to vote (or you will gain it when you turn eighteen), and you should vote for those who want the same rights you do and who have beliefs similar to your own. Your greatest superpower is your ability to vote, a power given to us by the women who came before us. The longer-term impact would happen decades later, through expanded rights for women that enhanced women's economic power in the middle of the twentieth century. The women who helped expand the right to vote may or may not have understood the crucial importance their achievement would take on decades or even a century later, but we are here as proof.

BLANK SPACE

Some may believe Taylor Swift has beaten men at their game, but I think she is simply playing her own game. Continually underestimated by the likes of Kanye West, Colorado DJ David Miller, and Scooter Braun, Taylor has a determination that all women possess but few of us activate. She pushes back, leans on support systems, and reinvents her life by masterminding future spaces for herself.

Taylor does not get bogged down by the sexist and misogynistic behaviors of others. Women in today's economy thrive, advance, and create meaning best when they focus on playing their own games. When there are blocks in the road, they reinvent themselves. They become their own masterminds, determined to achieve their goals no matter in which era they find themselves.

Some might argue that for Taylor, the struggles are over. Challenged by a society, culture, and an industry not made to benefit her, she used her best mastermind strategies to create a path forward. She perfected the art of escaping confines. She leaned into the power of women's experience and voices. In doing so, she developed a movement, a "Swiftynomics" movement, if you will. She focused on providing art and experiences that other women (and men) who are thriving as economic beings want. She swerved around barriers by rerecording her music and, eventually, acquiring enough funds through the success of the Eras Tour to buy back her original catalogue. With patience, time, talent, and resources, she found her way back to owning all her own art. She did all of this by leaning into her authentic self.

Taylor thought outside the box when necessary. She called people out when needed. Taylor Swift has won. So, is it over now for Taylor? Probably not. She will continue to experience challenges in how society views her as she ages and maintains her billionaire status or in what others see as appropriate in how she dresses or who she dates or marries. People will assume she will settle down and leave her career for a spouse and children. She may start building a family, but she won't give up her career for it. She will continue being who she is and doing what she loves even as she incorporates herself fully into some future version of a family life that she creates, because that is what women do today. (It is also why we are so exhausted.)

A portion of society will continue to dismiss or be confused by her successes. How could a woman who likes cats and glitter be considered so transformative, so awe inspiring? They do not and probably will not get it. The joy in this is that they do not need to. Taylor will continue to reinvent herself in a new era, continue to thrive and live her best life.

Perhaps even more important is *your* next reinvention. I have no doubt that you are up to the challenge. This is what we can all learn from Taylor and the women whose stories are told in the pages of this book. When life gives us lemons, we do not always have to accept them. And when there is no other option but to accept them, we can plan, strategize, and maneuver (or mastermind) ourselves into a future space where instead of lemons, we have lemonade.

Even when it is tough, do what you want to. Be open to feedback and other points of view, but do not let others pressure or shame you into changing your chosen direction. Do not bring others' baggage into your mental space and physical home. There are barriers that will seem impossible to ignore or remove, maybe because your safety would be at risk or because others control resources you need to succeed or advance. When a barrier seems impossible to ignore or remove in the short run, let it be while you mastermind your way into a future position that more closely aligns with where you want to go.

At the end of the day, "Swiftynomics" is about surrounding yourself with those who support your longer-term vision of yourself. Find yourself mom-ager-level support among family, friends, and coworkers. Find the people who believe in you. Fight to get all the complex aspects of your life and your goals as an economic being recognized in both your personal space and in public policy. Believe in your goals and trust your path, just like Taylor did. If you do, great things can happen. We will be here cheering you on the whole way. Just know that it is not over. You've only just begun. Use the black space. Fill it with you.

Afterword

WHO ARE THE WOMEN in your life who came before you? How have they influenced who you have become? How have their stories been memorialized? Knowing your herstory is healing and powerful. I encourage you to search for the abandoned and not-so-abandoned stories of the women who made you. We all have a herstory, and this is mine . . .

My paternal grandmother, Doris, was born in Fargo, North Dakota, to a homemaker and a decently successful businessman. As I learned during our kitchen table chats, Doris was destined to be an opera singer. She was musically trained, and a passion for singing burned deep inside her, but the norms of the time drove her to give up her singing career when she married my grandfather. Doris would never work for pay, but her passion and love for music lived on deep within her. And even though she never worked outside her home, her labor produced vibrant gardens, perfect family meals, scores of elaborate holiday treats, painstaking attention to the likes and desires of her four darling children, and squeaky-clean corners in even the most abandoned rooms of her home.

My mother, Melody, led a feisty middle-of-the-country youth with her parents and siblings in Fargo, North Dakota. Third in a line of four and the only girl, she learned boldness, defensiveness, and bravery early on. Her father, having lived his own rough and tumble life as an orphan, gently pushed her out of the nest, like a robin nudging its chicks, when she was fifteen, dropping her in front of the Northwestern Bell Telephone Company for an ad-hoc interview for a job advertised in the local newspaper. This became her first job, and with it she saved enough money by age eighteen to buy herself a brand-new 1968 Mercury Cougar.

The envy of her entire high school class, her newfound economic status allowed her to experience freedoms of which most girls and boys her age only dreamed. The economic freedom of work gave her options. She boldly and bravely divorced my father in 1978, when the stigma of divorce dripped out of the veins of a country in the middle of a culture war that predominantly blamed women for marriage failures and stigmatized single parenthood and out-of-wedlock births.

Her mother and my maternal grandmother, Elsie Nypan, was born to salt-of-the-earth farmers and lived her early years on her parents' farm near Litchfield, North Dakota. The eldest of four, she was determined to explore the world. She left the farm at an early age, rented a room in the city, completed high school, and trained to be a teacher. She taught Laura Ingalls Wilder–style, in a one-room schoolhouse, until she met and married my grandfather. Predominantly a spouse and mother, she made room for paid jobs once her children were of school age.

Elsie would persist, intermittently, in paid labor. Her obituary is a rolling resume of jobs held throughout adulthood. Reading how she dove in and out of the workforce is dizzying. In addition to rural schoolhouse teacher, her jobs included sales associate at a J. C. Penney department store and secretary at the North Dakota State University Housing Office, where she worked her way up to office manager before retiring. An obituary-resume: perhaps the telltale sign of a woman determined to be seen and remembered for her contributions not only within her home, but also to the community outside of it.

Elsie's mother, Gunhilde, was the daughter of Norwegian immigrant farmers and herself a farmer's wife. She lived long past her husband's death, but with the Atlantic-crossing adventurous spirit that ran through her veins, she had survival skills. Legendary for her delicious *lefse*, a Norwegian flatbread made with potatoes, flour, cream, and butter, Gunhilde was best known for her economic independence in her older years. Every Friday, she would walk her plump, aged-by-the-sun-scorched-plains self the mile and a half from her retirement apartment "in town" to the local grocery, carrying a woven basket of freshly baked *lefse* to sell. According to family legend, as the smell of warm, steamy *lefse* wisped through the streets and into open windows, she accrued a following of paying customers who, their mouths drooling, rushed to the grocery store to purchase her *lefse* before it ran out, *Strega Nona*– and Pied Piper–style.

My grandmother Elsie sprouted from strong, wildly wicked female stock on both sides of her family. In 1670, her (and my) many-times-great-grandmother, Lisbet Nypan, was the second-to-last documented Norwegian women burned at the stake for witchcraft. Lisbet lived in the rural countryside of

Norway with her husband. They had four children. She knew how to make a living with her skills and talent in a man's world, collecting herbs to concoct medicinal remedies and selling her herbal medicine to sick neighbors and ill village folk. She also read salt as a method of healing; she would pray over the salt and feed it to the sick and injured. Her strategies were a mix of Christian prayer, black arts, and folk medicine. As legend has it, one day the neighbor's cows became ill and died. Lisbet, then in her sixties, her children fully grown, was blamed for causing the cows' death. At the time, a conviction carried a sentence of death by fire. A trial ensued, and Lisbet and her husband were found guilty. She was burned at the stake. He was beheaded.

My mother-in-law Teresa's story has always intrigued me. She grew up in the rural deep south of Chile. Her parents and her parents' parents stem from the legendary Mapuche tribes of the most southern parts of South America. Mapuche women are famous for the important roles they play as medicinal healers, spiritual counselors, and community leaders. The Mapuche are unrivaled in their warrior stance and fierce determination. They have thrived persistently in the face of serious adversity; they never give up.

Teresa grew up in the countryside with her parents and siblings. When she was ten years old, she and two sisters went to study in the closest city, Temuco, where she attended boarding school and finished high school. After high school, she found work with a foreign-owned company until that company left Chile when the Allende government came into power. After losing her job, she traveled with two friends to the capital city of Santiago in search of work.

Teresa eventually married a Santiaguino and had three children, one of whom became my spouse. Once she married and had children, Teresa stopped working for pay outside the home. She became an expert in many economic activities, including cooking, daycare, concocting natural medicine recipes for common illnesses, and perfecting the art of cleanliness. (Marie Kondo has nothing on Teresa.)

What I have always found amazingly interesting about Teresa is how she gave up everything she knew to pursue better opportunities for herself and, eventually, her children. Her sacrifices were monumental and entirely economic in nature even though she never worked for pay past the age of twenty-five, when she married. Her entire married life, she worked from the time she woke up until the time she went to bed. She crafted weekly meal plans that she shopped for on Saturdays at the local farmers' market. Her home functioned like a well-oiled business. Her drive for efficiency and to eliminate waste would have been noteworthy for even the best of the best CEOs.

She raised two boys and a girl. With each one, she was determined to support their achievements through education, which she saw as the best path toward a better life for each of them, including her daughter. She did not raise her daughter to be second to anyone. Just as she never encouraged her boys to adopt her culinary talents, she never expected that of her daughter either. Her children all graduated from college and became professionals—two are lawyers and one is an engineer with an MBA. She is so proud of who and what they have become. I, in turn, am in awe of her.

The boldly brave economically active women in my herstory were defined by and helped to define my generation of women. Even though their lives and opportunities looked different than those of the men they grew up with, these women were *always* economically active, every single day of their lives. Whether that economic activity presented itself in the form of working in the labor market for pay; working on their family farms or in their homes cooking meals, washing clothes, and making beds; or volunteering at community events, *every single day* they worked—and worked *hard*. They worked to develop a world that created opportunity, advancement, and adventure for their next of kin, yet their economic activity was rarely accurately captured in national statistics on work and the economy. We should change that. We should change it not only for them, but for ourselves and our children who come after us.

I was determined to go to college far away from home and ended up in Minneapolis, Minnesota. College was easy for me, adventurous. I saw girls and boys studying side by side. I lived off campus, with male and female roommates. I went on to study for a master's degree as I tried to figure out what to do with my life post-college. When I finally married, at the age of twenty-six, I still believed equality was quite possible.

But marriage and kids can change you, not only physically and emotionally, but because family members' expectations change. Partner up and people want to know when you are getting married. Get married and they want to know when you are having kids. Whether we like it or not, gaining a lifetime partner pulls at the most traditional expectations in the core of our souls. We often convert to more traditional gendered roles not out of awareness or intention, but out of necessity and unconscious biases from childhood woven into the seams of our being.

Moving from Minneapolis to Washington, DC, after finishing my PhD was exhausting, mostly because I was pregnant and had an eighteen-month-old, but we made it work. For me, stepping out of the labor force was never an option. I had spent too much time investing in my education and career aspirations. As an economist, I knew too much about the devastating effect of parenthood and the motherhood penalty on lifetime earnings. So I found a job that was at least manageable with a small family and continued working as a research economist for the federal government, even as balancing the impossibility of fitting everything into a twenty-four-hour day fried my nerves and left me exhausted to my core. My brain was full of good ideas and determination, and I wanted to use all of it to make an influence outside the home, but it came at a cost.

Somehow, I survived. My kids are now fifteen and seventeen. They still need support and attention but of a different kind. It is for them that I fight this fight. My hope is that when they enter adulthood and start building their own families, we will have moved the dial slightly more toward schedules that benefit the lives of women, mothers, and parents. My hope for them is that they will not be as exhausted, will have lives that balance better, and that they will continue to fight toward an equitable economy for all.

ACKNOWLEDGMENTS

This book stands on the shoulders of giants. During the pandemic, as I worked on providing data that told an accurate story of mothers' labor supply, I realized how much I enjoy writing for the general public about women and the economy. In my pursuit of book writing, I received critical advice and guidance early on from Claudia Goldin, who kindly introduced me to my dedicated agent, Lucy Cleland. After writing and rewriting (read: failing and re-failing) book proposals to find the right fit and angle, I finally found a theme that stuck—perhaps the one that was always meant to be.

At that point, Nancy Folbre, like a fairy godmother, generously mentioned the name of a brilliant editor, Michelle Lipinski. The rest, if you will, is herstory. Were it not for these four women (plus the extremely generous time invested by two anonymous reviewers), and their belief in my ability to tell stories that bring women's economic power to life, this book would not exist.

I am also extremely grateful to Ben Casselman for an early discussion of a book title, where we laughed at the possibility of overlaying my obsession with Taylor Swift, as a superb example of Economic Woman in her prime, with economic theories of women and work, until it became obvious that no other path would do. Tamara Tinkham deserves credit for believing in me without a sliver of doubt and actively encouraging me to pursue writing this book.

It takes a village, and I am so lucky mine is robust. Numerous individuals, from the generations before and after mine, scoured the manuscript looking for holes, errors, and missing links. Without their critical eyes and internal wisdom, this book would not be nearly as bold and beautiful. I will never be able to fully thank them all here, but I will try. I will always be eternally grateful to Pilar McDonald, who stepped in last minute with gusto to review and corral all the loose ends; Lucie Prewitt, who poured blood, sweat, and tears into developing the *Swiftynomics* survey and who has been my ride-or-die throughout this entire process; and Lilly Springer, a Swiftie at heart (and an economist) who joined me in the front seat from the beginning of this adventure, reading and re-reading early versions of the manuscript, and on whom I could always count for solid Swiftie leads that fit perfectly into various sections of the book. The figures and tables in this book would not look nearly as nice as they do without the amazing technical assistance and careful eye of Yurong Zhang and Anna Ratcliffe. Others who have contributed in various ways include Boyeon Park, Italia Maria Galindo, Joseph Bommarito, and Yana van der Meulen Rodgers, all of whom saw my vision and provided critical support, editing, and guidance, for which I am forever grateful.

The influencers of this book are too many to be named, but they are women I adore, admire, and aspire to emulate. To these women, I will always be eternally grateful; I am so thankful for their friendships and encouragement. In addition, I thank Alexia Saavedra Vera for letting me hear about all her youthful adventures, which brought me energy and an increased desire to write this book for the next generation. To Franco Maldonado, my dearest godson, I will always be thankful that you were visiting me as I was on the last leg of book writing. You provided endless critical, useful distraction and joy in our shared passion for sporting events, which helped mitigate the stress of finishing the manuscript.

To my amazing, compassionate spouse, Mauricio, and my uniquely courageous children, Magdalena (Maddie) and Santiago, I will be forever grateful for your patience, support, and encouragement—even during the embarrassing times when you had to explain why your economist professor spouse and mother was writing a book about a pop singer. I thank my parents, who raised me in the best way possible given the turbulence of their lives. This book is what it is because of you.

Without interviews, this book would be less engaging, less informed, and, perhaps, generally uninteresting. Being interviewed takes courage and time. I am grateful to all the women who took time out of their day to let me talk with them about their lives, their eras, and their reinventions. Finally, my huge appreciation to all those who were willing to take the *Swiftynomics* survey and help us learn more about the real-life reinventions, eras, and pathways of women today.

NOTES

INTRODUCTION

1. Maddie Ellis, "Taylor Swift Debuts 'Tortured Poets' at Concert," Yahoo Entertainment, May 10, 2024, www.yahoo.com/entertainment/taylor-swift-debuts -tortured-poets-030533806.html; Ryan Hudgins, "Taylor Swift Files Trademark for 'Female Rage: The Musical,'" *Us Weekly*, May 13, 2024, www.usmagazine.com/celebrity -news/news/taylor-swift-files-trademark-for-female-rage-the-musical/.

2. Brad Simmons, "Why Teenage Girls Are the Key to Cultural Relevance," *Forbes*, May 30, 2024, www.forbes.com/sites/bradsimms/2024/05/30/teenage-girls -are-the-key-to-cultural-relevance/.

3. Misty L. Heggeness, "Taylor Swift Isn't the Economic Force. It's Her Fans," *Time*, April 18, 2024, https://time.com/6968040/taylor-swift-swifties-economic-force/.

4. James P. Smith and Finis R. Welch, "Chapter 7: Black/White Male Earnings and Employment: 1960–70," in *The Distribution of Economic Well-Being*, ed. F. Thomas Juster (Cambridge, MA: National Bureau of Economic Research, 1977), 233–302, www.nber.org/chapters/c4374; Cordelia W. Reimers, "Labor Market Discrimination Against Hispanic and Black Men," *Review of Economics and Statistics* 65, no. 4 (1983): 570–79, https://doi.org/10.2307/1935925; John Bound and Harry J. Holzer, "Industrial Shifts, Skills Levels, and the Labor Market for White and Black Males," Working Paper No. 3715, National Bureau of Economic Research, May 1991, https://doi .org/10.3386/w3715; Chinhui Juhn, "Labor Market Dropouts and Trends in the Wages of Black and White Men," *ILR Review* 56, no. 4 (July 1, 2003), 643–62, https://doi .org/10.1177/001979390305600406; Robert W. Fairlie and Bruce D. Meyer, "Trends in Self-Employment Among White and Black Men During the Twentieth Century," *Journal of Human Resources* 35, no. 4 (2000): 643–69, https://doi.org/10.2307/146366.

5. Claudia Goldin, *Career and Family: Women's Century-Long Journey Toward Equity* (Princeton, NJ: Princeton University Press, 2021).

6. Karli Bendlin and Megan Gibson, "Taylor Swift's Eras Tour: A Timeline of the Ticketmaster Fiasco," *People*, https://people.com/music/taylor-swift-eras-tour -ticketmaster-timeline/.

7. Rachel Treisman, "The Senate's Ticketmaster Hearing Featured Plenty of Taylor Swift Puns and Protesters," NPR, January 24, 2023, www.npr.org/2023/01/24/1150942804/taylor-swift-ticketmaster-senate-hearing-live-nation; Ben Sisario and Matt Stevens, "Ticketmaster Cast as a Powerful 'Monopoly' at Senate Hearing," *New York Times*, January 24, 2023, www.nytimes.com/2023/01/24/arts/music/ticketmaster-taylor-swift-senate-hearing.html.

8. Bendlin and Gibson, "Taylor Swift's Eras Tour."

9. Roger Dooley, "Taylor Swift's Record-Breaking Tour Has One Flaw: Merch Issues," *Forbes*, www.forbes.com/sites/rogerdooley/2024/07/17/taylor-swifts-record-breaking-tour-has-one-flaw-merch-issues/.

10. Gabe Hauari and Bryan West, "How Many Shows Were in Taylor Swift's Eras Tour? Here's When It Started and How Long It Lasted," *USA Today*, www.usatoday.com/story/entertainment/music/2024/12/09/when-did-taylor-swift-eras-tour-start/76858107007/.

11. Conor Murray, "These Cities Reported the Biggest Economic Boosts from Taylor Swift's Eras Tour—As Tour Wraps Up In Vancouver," *Forbes*, December 6, 2024, www.forbes.com/sites/conormurray/2024/12/06/these-cities-reported-the-biggest-economic-boosts-from-taylor-swifts-eras-tour-as-tour-wraps-up-in-vancouver/.

12. Kate Perez, "Swifties' Friendship Bracelet Craze Creates Spikes in Jewelry Sales During Eras Tour," *USA Today*, August 8, 2023, www.usatoday.com/story/money/retail/2023/08/08/taylor-swift-friendship-bracelets-driving-michaels-sales/70549834007/.

13. Saraiva, "Welcome to 'Swiftonomics.'"

14. Taffy Brodesser-Akner, "My Delirious Trip to the Heart of Swiftiedom," *New York Times*, October 12, 2023, www.nytimes.com/2023/10/12/magazine/taylor-swift-eras-tour.html.

15. Emily Yahr and Maham Javaid, "They Couldn't Get Taylor Swift Tickets. So They Got Jobs at the Venues," *Washington Post*, July 27, 2023, www.washingtonpost.com/arts-entertainment/2023/07/27/taylor-swift-eras-tour-fans-venue-jobs/; Meghan Powers, "Taylor Swift Fans Are Working at Concerts to See 'Eras' Tour," *New York Post*, July 28, 2023, https://nypost.com/2023/07/28/taylor-swift-fans-are-working-at-concerts-to-see-eras-tour/.

16. BGS Press, "Quake It Off: Taylor Swift Concerts Shake Edinburgh," *British Geological Survey* (blog), June 13, 2024, www.bgs.ac.uk/news/quake-it-off-taylor-swift-concerts-shake-edinburgh/; Jillian Sykes and Alli Rosenbloom, "Taylor Swift Fans 'Shake It Off,' Causing Record-Breaking Seismic Activity During Seattle Shows," CNN, www.cnn.com/2023/07/27/entertainment/taylor-swift-seismic-activity/index.html.

17. Bryan West, "Watching the Eras Tours for Free, Thousands of Swifties 'Taylor-gate' in Munich, Germany," *USA Today*, July 27, 2024, www.usatoday.com/story/entertainment/music/2024/07/27/taylor-swift-eras-tour-free-munich-taylor-gate/74449359007/; Charlotte Phillipp, "Taylor Swift Is Amazed by Massive Crowds Tailgating at Munich Eras Tour Show: 'I Feel So Incredibly Welcomed,'"

People, July 29, 2024, https://people.com/taylor-swift-amazed-by-crowds-tailgating
-munich-eras-tour-night-1-8684876.

18. Andrea Dresdale and Mason Leib, "'Taylor Swift: The Eras Tour' Concert Film Coming to AMC Theaters: How to Get Tickets," Good Morning America, August 31, 2023, www.goodmorningamerica.com/culture/story/taylor-swift-eras
-tour-movie-theaters-102826293.

19. Kelly Tyko, "Taylor Swift's Movie Twist: Dancing and Singing Encouraged," Axios, October 12, 2023, www.axios.com/2023/10/12/taylor-swift-movie-tickets
-eras-tour-amc.

20. Ty Roush, "Taylor Swift's 'The Eras Tour' Movie Earns $26 Million in Presale Tickets—AMC's Single-Day Record," *Forbes*, September 1, 2023, www.forbes
.com/sites/tylerroush/2023/09/01/taylor-swifts-the-eras-tour-earns-26-million-in
-presale-tickets-amcs-single-day-record/.

21. Pamela McClintock, "Taylor Swift: Eras Tour Movie Could Top $100M Opening Weekend," *Hollywood Reporter*, September 5, 2023, www.hollywoodreporter.com
/movies/movie-news/taylor-swift-eras-tour-movie-1235581725/.

22. Kyle Denis, "'Exorcist' Release Date Shifts Due to Taylor Swift 'Eras Tour' Movie," *Billboard*, August 31, 2023, www.billboard.com/culture/tv-film
/taylor-swift-eras-tour-movie-exorcist-believer-release-date-moves-1235404723/;
Brenna Cooper, "Meg Ryan's Rom-Com Changes Release Date Due to Taylor Swift Movie," Digital Spy, September 4, 2023, www.digitalspy.com/movies
/a44986420/meg-ryan-what-happens-later-release-date/; Nina Braca, "Taylor Swift Forcing Movies to Change Their Release Dates," UPROXX, September 8, 2023, https://uproxx.com/movies/taylor-swift-eras-tour-movie-releases-changes-the
-exorcist/.

23. David Sims, "Taylor Swift Did What Hollywood Studios Could Not," *The Atlantic*, October 16, 2023, www.theatlantic.com/culture/archive/2023/10
/taylor-swift-eras-tour-movie-theaters/675653/.

24. Chris Eggertsen, "Taylor Swift Eras Tour Concert Film Ditched Studios for Deal with AMC," *Billboard*, September 1, 2023, www.billboard.com/pro/taylor-swift
-eras-tour-concert-film-deal-amc/.

25. Sarah Krouse and Anne Steele, "Women Own This Summer. The Economy Proves It," *Wall Street Journal*, August 10, 2023, www.wsj.com/economy/consumers
/the-summer-women-flexed-their-spending-power-dc2ce92c.

26. See https://pinksummercarnival.com/.

27. Mary Whitfill Roeloffs, "Coco Gauff's US Open Victory Trounced Men's Final in Viewership—In Rare Win for Women's Sports," *Forbes*, September 13, 2023, www.forbes.com/sites/maryroeloffs/2023/09/13/coco-gauffs-us-open-victory
-trounced-mens-final-in-viewership-in-rare-win-for-womens-sports/.

28. Andrew Das, "US Soccer and Women's Players Agree to Settle Equal Pay Lawsuit," *New York Times*, February 22, 2022, www.nytimes.com/2022/02/22
/sports/soccer/us-womens-soccer-equal-pay.html.

29. Tamara Palmer, "5 Takeaways from Beyoncé's New Album 'Renaissance,'" Grammy.com, July 29, 2022, www.grammy.com/news/beyonce-new-album

-renaissance-2022-takeaways-review-uncle-jonny-club-culture-lgbtqia-collaborators
-jay-z-break-my-soul.

30. Lucy-Jo Finnighan, "Barbie Box Office: How Much Has It Made?" Dexerto, September 18, 2023, www.dexerto.com/tv-movies/barbie-box-office-how-much -has-it-made-2220313/.

31. Katie Hafner and Amy Scharf, "Female Scientists Who Worked on A-Bomb Mostly Absent from 'Oppenheimer,'" editorial, *Washington Post*, August 10, 2023, www.washingtonpost.com/science/2023/08/10/oppenheimer-manhattan-project -women-scientists-bomb/.

32. Rebecca Rubin, "Summer Box Office Hits $4 Billion After All, Thanks to 'Barbie' and 'Oppenheimer,'" *Variety*, September 3, 2023, https://variety.com/2023 /film/box-office/summer-box-office-hits-4-billion-barbie-oppenheimer-1235712314/.

33. NCAA, "Women's College Volleyball All-Time Attendance Records," December 17, 2023, www.ncaa.com/news/volleyball-women/article/2023-12-17 /womens-college-volleyball-all-time-attendance-records.

34. Isabel Gonzalez, "Caitlin Clark, Iowa Break Women's College Basketball Attendance Records with Exhibition Game at Kinnick Stadium," October 15, 2023, www.cbssports.com/womens-college-basketball/news/caitlin-clark-iowa-break-womens -college-basketball-attendance-record-with-exhibition-game-at-kinnick-stadium/.

35. Melissa Kravitz Hoeffner, "The Rise and Rise of Women's Sports Bars," *Vogue*, March 12, 2024, www.vogue.com/article/rise-of-womens-sports-bars.

36. Abdul Azim Naushad, "Golden Globes 2024 Jo Koy's Jokes: What Did He Say About Barbie & Taylor Swift?," Yahoo Entertainment, January 8, 2024, www .yahoo.com/entertainment/golden-globes-2024-jo-koy-151229539.html; Pamela Paul, "'Barbie' Is Bad. There, I Said It," *New York Times*, January 24, 2024, www .nytimes.com/2024/01/24/opinion/barbie-movie-oscars.html; Katrina vanden Heuvel, "Why Does the Barbie Movie Have Republicans in Such a Tizzy?" *The Guardian*, July 20, 2023, www.theguardian.com/film/barbie/2023/jul/20/all; Brittany Wong, "The 'Barbie' Movie Is Ending Relationships Left and Right," Huffington Post, July 31, 2023, www.huffpost.com/entry/barbie-movie-breakup_l _64c3052ce4b044bf98f44379.

37. Misty L. Heggeness, "It's Not Just Barbie Snubbed at the Oscars. This Is How Female Talent Got Ignored During Awards Season," *Fast Company*, March 10, 2024, www.fastcompany.com/91050390/barbie-snubbed-oscars-female-talent-got -ignored-during-awards-season.

38. Heggeness, "It's Not Just Barbie."

39. "Home," Geena Davis Institute, https://geenadavisinstitute.org/.

40. In Vibrant Company (invibrantcompany), "Often portrayed as helpless in films, women in real life are nature's ultimate crisis managers, multitaskers, and action-takers. Comment below if you agree 👏 This old video of Reese Witherspoon at the Glamour magazine Women of the Year awards is currently trending again for good reason. Head to invibrantcompany.com to read features on countless other women who are getting things done. 💪 #invibrantcompany #vibrantwoman #reesewitherspoon #glamourmagazine #womanoftheyear #whatcantwomendo #womenareamazing

#womenarepowerful #multitasking #doer #crisismanagement #problemsolver." Instagram, December 5, 2024, www.instagram.com/reel/DDMkoNvu-5Z/.

41. Brent Lang and Rebecca Rubin, "Reese Witherspoon's Hello Sunshine Sold for $900 Million to Media Company Backed by Blackstone," *Variety*, August 2, 2021, https://variety.com/2021/film/news/reese-witherspoon-hello-sunshine -sold-1235032618/; Elsa Keslassy, "Reese Witherspoon Unveils Hello Sunshine Sister Label, Sunnie, for Gen Z at Cannes Lions," *Variety*, June 18, 2025, https://variety .com/2025/tv/global/reese-witherspoon-hello-sunshine-sunnie-genz-cannes -lions-1236435091/.

42. "Our Team," The 19th*, https://19thnews.org/team/.

43. Madeline Berg, "How Reese Witherspoon Has Become the World's Richest Actress," *Forbes*, August 2, 2021, www.forbes.com/sites/dawnchmielewski/2021 /08/02/how-reese-witherspoon-has-become-the-worlds-richest-actress/; Terry Gross, "'This Changes Everything': Geena Davis on Empowering Women in Hollywood," NPR, August 7, 2019, www.npr.org/2019/08/07/749067994/this-changes-everything -geena-davis-on-empowering-women-in-hollywood; Melissa Houston, "What Taylor Swift Teaches Women About Business," *Forbes*, December 1, 2023, www.forbes.com /sites/melissahouston/2023/12/01/what-taylor-swift-teaches-women-about-business/.

44. Mariel Padilla, "Defend and Deny: What We Know About Trump and Accusations of Sexual Misconduct," The 19th*, October 26, 2023, https://19thnews .org/2023/10/donald-trump-associates-sexual-misconduct-allegations/.

45. Amanda Goh, "Jo Koy Was the Wrong Host for the Golden Globes, and His 'Jokes' About Taylor Swift and 'Barbie' Prove It," Business Insider, January 8, 2023, www.businessinsider.com/jo-koy-taylor-swift-barbie-awkward-jokes-host-golden -globes-2024-1.

46. "Real-Time Sahm Rule Recession Indicator," October 4, 2024, https://fred .stlouisfed.org/series/SAHMREALTIME; Federal Reserve Bank of St. Louis, "Release: Economic Data," *FRED Economic Data*, https://fred.stlouisfed.org /release?rid=456; Talia Murray, "Recession: What Is the Sahm Rule and Why Is Everyone Talking About It?," CNBC, August 5, 2024, www.cnbc.com/2024/08/05 /recession-what-is-the-sahm-rule-and-why-is-everyone-talking-about-it.html.

47. Steven D. Levitt and Stephen J. Dubner, *Freakonomics: A Rogue Economist Explores the Hidden Side of Everything* (New York: HarperCollins, 2005).

1. REINVENTION

1. "Taylor Swift—Look What You Made Me Do," YouTube, 2017, www.youtube .com/watch?v=3tmd-ClpJxA.

2. "Watch *60 Minutes Overtime*: Taylor Swift on Being an Outsider—Full Show," CBS, 2020, www.cbs.com/shows/video/pIyHii9bkqajGqjJhq76d_DhoSbT6xbP/.

3. Paul Grein, "Taylor Swift Is Hot as Ever, 17 Years After Her Debut Album: See Where Other Chart Titans Stood at the Same Point," *Billboard*, October 24, 2023, www.billboard.com/lists/taylor-swift-17-years-after-debut-artist-comparison/.

4. "An Oral History of Taylor Swift's '1989' Secret Sessions," *Nylon*, October 26, 2023, www.nylon.com/entertainment/oral-history-of-taylor-swifts-1989-secret -sessions.

5. "Walk the Blurred Lines: Country Music's Cross-Over Popularity," Nielsen, October 2014, www.nielsen.com/insights/2014/walk-the-blurred-lines-country -musics-cross-over-popularity/.

6. Kelsie Gibson, "Kanye West Infamously Stormed Taylor Swift's VMAs Speech 15 Years Ago: A Recap of the Viral Moment in Music History," *People*, September 11, 2024, https://people.com/revisiting-taylor-swift-and-kanye-west -2009-mtv-vmas-moment-8710574.

7. The Editors, "Buckle Up for the Full History of Kim Kardashian and Taylor Swift's Drama," *Cosmopolitan*, April 24, 2024, www.cosmopolitan.com/entertainment /celebs/a60566989/kim-kardashian-taylor-swift-feud-timeline/.

8. Mehera Bonner, Gretty Garcia, and Samantha Olson, "Taylor Swift and Scooter Braun's Drama, Explained," *Cosmopolitan*, June 17, 2024, www.cosmopolitan .com/entertainment/celebs/a29807801/taylor-swift-scooter-braun-scott-borchetta -tyrannical-control-amas-netflix-doc/.

9. Mehera Bonner, "The Story Behind Taylor Swift Sending Kelly Clarkson Flowers After Every Re-Recording Is So Special," *Cosmopolitan*, November 10, 2023, www.cosmopolitan.com/entertainment/celebs/a45802072/taylor-swift-sends-kelly -clarkson-flowers/.

10. Bonner, "The Story Behind Taylor Swift Sending Kelly Clarkson Flowers."

11. Noah Yoo, "Taylor Swift Accuses Scooter Braun and Scott Borchetta of Blocking Her from Performing Her Old Music," Pitchfork, November 14, 2019, https://pitchfork.com/news/taylor-swift-accuses-scooter-braun-and-scott-borchetta -of-blocking-her-from-performing-her-old-music/.

12. Marc Schneider, "Taylor Swift Buys Back Her Masters from Shamrock, Reclaiming Her First Six Albums," *Billboard*, May 30, 2025, www.billboard.com /pro/taylor-swift-regains-control-master-recordings-shamrock/; Hugh McIntyre, "Taylor Swift's 'Reputation' Soars to No. 1 Following Her Groundbreaking News," *Forbes*, May 31, 2025, www.forbes.com/sites/hughmcintyre/2025/05/31/taylor -swifts-reputation-soars-to-no-1-following-her-groundbreaking-news/; Em Casalena, "Taylor Swift's 'Reputation' Has Officially Re-Entered the Top 5 of the Billboard 200—Eight Years After Its Release," *American Songwriter*, June 9, 2025, https://americansongwriter.com/taylor-swifts-reputation-has-officially-re-entered -the-top-5-of-the-billboard-200-eight-years-after-its-release/.

13. Kase Wickman, "Scooter Braun Says He's Retiring," *Vanity Fair*, www .vanityfair.com/style/story/scooter-braun-retires-music-manager-ariana-grande-justin -bieber.

14. Michael Gracey, P!nk, Remi Bakkar, Khasan Brailsford, and Eva Gardner, dirs., *P!nk: All I Know So Far*, 2021, Amazon Prime.

15. Beyoncé, dir., *Renaissance: A Film by Beyoncé*, 2023, AMC Theatres.

16. Joanna Reposi Garibaldi and Camila Grandi, dir., *Mon Laferte, Te Amo*, Netflix/Blackstar Content, August 1, 2024.

17. Lewis A. Coser, "Greedy Organizations," *European Journal of Sociology* 8, no. 2 (1967): 196–215, www.jstor.org/stable/23998539; Rose Laub Coser and Gerald Rokoff, "Women in the Occupational World: Social Disruption and Conflict," *Social Problems* 18, no. 4 (1971): 535–54, https://doi.org/10.2307/799727; Guenther Roth, review of *Greedy Institutions: Patterns of Undivided Commitment*, by Lewis A. Coser, *American Political Science Review* 71, no. 2 (1977): 632–34, https://doi.org/10.2307/1978360; Claudia Goldin, *Career and Family: Women's Century-Long Journey Toward Equity* (Princeton, NJ: Princeton University Press, 2021).

18. Interview with Eve Rodsky, September 20, 2023.

19. Interview with Eve Rodsky.

20. Fair Play Policy Institute, www.fairplaypolicy.org/.

21. "First Partner Jennifer Siebel Newsom," www.gov.ca.gov/about/first-partner/.

22. Jennifer Siebel Newsom, dir., *Fair Play*, 2022, www.fairplaylife.com/documentary.

23. Misty Heggeness et al., "Reinvention: The Path to Career and Life Fulfillment Is Non-Linear," unpublished manuscript, June 2025.

24. Caroline Criado Perez, *Invisible Women: Data Bias in a World Designed for Men* (New York: Harry N. Abrams, 2021).

25. Misty L. Heggeness et al., "An Introduction to Care Privilege and Policymaking in the United States," *Applied Economic Perspectives and Policy*, forthcoming September 2025.

26. Claudia Goldin, "Nobel Lecture: An Evolving Economic Force," *American Economic Review* 114, no. 6 (2024): 1515–39, https://doi.org/10.1257/aer.114.6.1515.

27. Misty L. Heggeness, "Taylor Swift Isn't the Economic Force. It's Her Fans," *Time*, April 18, 2024. https://time.com/6968040/taylor-swift-swifties-economic-force/.

28. Heggeness, "Taylor Swift Isn't the Economic Force."

29. CNN, "Taylor Swift Could Break $2 Billion for 'Eras' Tour," August 18, 2023, www.cnn.com/videos/world/2023/08/18/exp-taylor-swift-eras-tour-reader-081802pseg2-cnni-world.cnn; Kookiekoo (u/kookiekoo), "The trailer for NBC's 'The Swift Effect' documentary series has been released. Premiering on Peacock on November 25!" Reddit post, R/TaylorSwift, November 23, 2024, www.reddit.com/r/TaylorSwift/comments/1gyo1mi/the_trailer_for_nbcs_the_swift_effect_documentary/.

30. Hugh McIntyre, "Taylor Swift Is Making an Insane Amount of Money Every Night on the Eras Tour," *Forbes*, October 14, 2023, www.forbes.com/sites/hughmcintyre/2023/10/14/taylor-swift-is-making-an-insane-amount-of-money-every-night-on-the-eras-tour/?sh=62220b1c300b.

31. Abha Bhattarai, Rachel Lerman, and Emily Sabens, "The Economy (Taylor's Version)," *Washington Post*, October 13, 2023, www.washingtonpost.com/business/2023/10/13/taylor-swift-eras-tour-money-jobs/.

32. Bhattarai et al., "The Economy (Taylor's Version)."

33. Matthew Fox, "Taylor Swift's Effect on the Economy Has Caught the Eye of the Fed," Business Insider, July 14, 2023, https://markets.businessinsider.com/news

/stocks/taylor-swifts-economic-impact-catches-attention-federal-reserve-hotel
-revenue-2023-7; Board of Governors of the Federal Reserve System, "Beige Book,"
July 12, 2023, www.federalreserve.gov/monetarypolicy/beigebook202307.htm.

34. Office of the Mayor of London, "Taylor Swift's Record-Breaking The Eras
Tour to Generate £300m for the Capital's Economy—As London Confirms Status
as the World-Leader for Music," June 20, 2024, www.london.gov.uk/taylor
-swifts-record-breaking-eras-tour-generate-ps300m-capitals-economy-london
-confirms-status.

2. SURVIVAL

1. Katrine Marçal, *Who Cooked Adam Smith's Dinner? A Story of Women and
Economics*, trans. Saskia Vogel (New York: Pegasus Books, 2016).

2. Discussion with Shelly Lundberg, July 17, 2024.

3. The closest is perhaps a 2007 article by economists Betsey Stevenson and
Justin Wolfers that highlights a shift from a 1950s household economy to today's
households, in which couples partner up based on consumption complementarities
instead of production complementarities. See Betsey Stevenson and Justin Wolfers,
"Marriage and Divorce: Changes and Their Driving Forces," *Journal of Economic
Perspectives* 21, no. 2 (2007): 27–52, www.aeaweb.org/articles?id=10.1257/jep.21.2.27
.www.aeaweb.org/articles?id=10.1257/jep.21.2.27.

4. Michele Bee and Maxime Desmarais-Tremblay, "The Birth of *Homo economicus*: The Methodological Debate on the Economic Agent from J.S. Mill to V.
Pareto," *Journal of the History of Economic Thought* 45, no. 1 (2022): 1–26.

5. Adam Smith, *The Wealth of Nations*, 5th ed. (W. Strahan and T. Cadell, London, 1789); Andreu Mas-Colell et al., *Microeconomic Theory* (Oxford: Oxford University Press, 1995); Richard H. Thaler, "From *Homo economicus* to *Homo sapiens*,"
Journal of Economic Perspectives 14, no. 1 (2000): 133–41, https://doi.org/10.1257
/jep.14.1.133.

6. Sarah Archer, "Tidying Up with Marie Kondo Isn't Really a Makeover Show,"
The Atlantic, January 4, 2019, www.theatlantic.com/entertainment/archive/2019/01
/tidying-up-with-marie-kondo-netflix-show-kon-mari-review/579400/.

7. Alexis Jones, "Marie Kondo Admits She Has 'Kind of Given Up' on Extreme
Tidiness, Says Her House 'Is Messy,'" *People*, January 27, 2023, https://people.com
/home/marie-kondo-admits-she-has-kind-of-given-up-on-tidying-up/.

8. Paul Romer, "Mathiness in the Theory of Economic Growth," *American
Economic Review* 105, no. 5 (2015): 89–93, http://doi.org/10.1257/aer.p20151066; Tim
Harford, "Down with Mathiness!," https://timharford.com/2015/06/down-with
-mathiness/; Paul Pfleiderer, "Chameleons: The Misuse of Theoretical Models in
Finance and Economics," *Economica* 87, no. 345 (2020): 81–107, https://doi
.org/10.1111/ecca.12295; Alan Jay Levinovitz, "The New Astrology: By Fetishis-
ing Mathematical Models, Economists Turned Economics into a Highly Paid
Pseudoscience," Aeon, https://aeon.co/essays/how-economists-rode-maths-to

-become-our-era-s-astrologers; George A. Akerlof, "Sins of Omission and the Practice of Economics," *Journal of Economic Literature* 58, no. 2 (2020): 405–18, https://doi.org/10.1257/jel.20191573/.

9. Dan Pilat and Sekoul Krastev, "Homo Economicus," The Decision Lab, https://thedecisionlab.com/reference-guide/economics/homo-economicus; Richard H. Thaler, *Misbehaving: The Making of Behavioral Economics* (New York: W. W. Norton, 2015), 158.

10. Gary S. Becker, *The Economics of Discrimination* (Chicago: University of Chicago Press, 1957).

11. Misty L. Heggeness, "Swifties vs. NFL Fans: An Economist Explains What Happens When Two Rabid Fan Bases Collide," *Fast Company*, October 8, 2023, www.fastcompany.com/90962560/swifties-vs-nfl-fans-an-economist-explains-what-happens-when-two-rabid-fanbases-collide.

12. Sam Lansky, "2023 Person of the Year: Taylor Swift," *Time*, December 6, 2023, https://time.com/6342806/person-of-the-year-2023-taylor-swift/.

13. Abbey White, "NFL Commissioner Says Taylor Swift and Travis Kelce's Romance Is 'Great for the League,'" *Hollywood Reporter*, November 22, 2023, www.hollywoodreporter.com/tv/tv-news/nfl-commissioner-taylor-swift-travis-kelce-romance-1235675409/; Natasha Dye and Juliet Pennington, "Chiefs Coach Andy Reid Is 'Happy for Both' Travis Kelce and Taylor Swift: 'She's Got a Great Guy' (Exclusive)," *People*, December 18, 2023, https://people.com/chiefs-coach-andy-reid-happy-for-both-travis-kelce-and-taylor-swift-exclusive-8417408.

14. Joe Drape and Ken Belson, "The E-Sports Generation: Pro Sports Leagues Are Chasing Gen Z Where It Plays," *New York Times*, January 12, 2022, www.nytimes.com/2022/01/12/sports/video-games-nfl-gamers-gen-z.html.

15. Ben Blatt and Francisca Paris, "Is Taylor Swift Actually Increasing NFL Ratings?," *New York Times*, February 10, 2024, www.nytimes.com/2024/02/10/upshot/taylor-swift-nfl-ratings.html.

16. Courtney Kane, "Want to Reach Female Viewers? The NFL Asks Marketers If They're Ready for Some Football," *New York Times*, December 22, 1999, www.nytimes.com/1999/12/22/business/media-business-advertising-want-reach-female-viewers-nfl-asks-marketers-if-they.html; Katherine Rosman and Ken Belson, "Promised a New Culture, Women Say the NFL Instead Pushed Them Aside," *New York Times*, February 8, 2022, www.nytimes.com/2022/02/08/sports/football/nfl-women-culture.html; Natalie Kitroeff, "NFL Hones Message for Its Female Fans," *New York Times*, January 5, 2023, www.nytimes.com/2013/01/06/sports/football/nfl-hones-message-for-its-female-fans.html.

17. Paul A. Samuelson, "Social Indifference Curves," *Quarterly Journal of Economics* 70 (February 1956): 1–22, https://doi.org/10.2307/1884510.

18. Becker, Gary S. *A Treatise on the Family*. Cambridge, MA: Harvard University Press, 1993.

19. Shelly J. Lundberg (@ShellyJLundberg), "A very good book, but Becker's story of specialization was based on women's 'heavy biological commitment to the bearing and feeding of children' plus complementarities between this and other household

work (e.g. taking care of older children at home)," Twitter (now X), March 25, 2023, https://x.com/ShellyJLundberg/status/1639802701331730432; Shelly J. Lundberg (@ ShellyJLundberg), "This is the 'actual argument' explaining why women are more efficient at home. They learned to be more skilled at home while breastfeeding the baby. I don't think it ever occurred to Becker that one could work and breastfeed," Twitter, March 25, 2023, https://x.com/ShellyJLundberg/status/1639814239690031104.

20. Stevenson and Wolfers, "Marriage and Divorce."

21. Motoko Rich, "It's the Economy, Honey," *New York Times*, February 11, 2012, https://users.nber.org/~jwolfers/aboutme/Economics%20of%20Family%20Life.pdf; Marilyn Waring, *If Women Counted: A New Feminist Economics* (San Francisco: Harper, 1990).

22. Edorado Ciscato and Simon Weber, "The Role of Evolving Marital Preferences in Growing Income Inequality," *Journal of Population Economics* 33, no. 1 (2020): 307–47, https://doi.org/10.1007/s00148-019-00739-4.

23. Romer, "Mathiness in the Theory of Economic Growth," 89–93; Harford, "Down with Mathiness!"; Pfleiderer, "Chameleons," 81–107; Akerlof, "Sins of Omission," 405–18.

24. Elizabeth L. Campbell and Oliver Hahl, "Stop Undervaluing Exceptional Women," *Harvard Business Review*, July 22, 2022, https://hbr.org/2022/07/stop-undervaluing-exceptional-women.

25. Becker, *Economics of Discrimination*; Gary S. Becker, "Altruism in the Family and Selfishness in the Market Place," *Economica* 48, no. 189 (1981): 1–15.

26. Raj Chetty et al., "Income Segregation and Intergenerational Mobility Across Colleges in the United States," *Quarterly Journal of Economics* 135, no. 3 (2020): 1567–633, https://doi.org/10.1093/qje/qjaa005; William A. Darity Jr. et al., "A Tour de Force in Understanding Intergroup Inequality: An Introduction to Stratification Economics," *Review of Black Political Economy* 42 (2015): 1–6, https://doi.org/10.1007/s12114-014-9201-2; Raj Chetty et al., "Using Differences in Knowledge Across Neighborhoods to Uncover the Impacts of the EITC on Earnings," *American Economic Review* 103, no. 7 (2013): 2683–721, https://doi.org/10.1257/aer.103.7.2683.

27. This tale mimics the true story of Virginia O'Hanlon, who, in 1897, wrote to the New York newspaper *The Sun* asking if Santa Claus was real, to which the newspaper editor replied in a famous letter, "Yes, Virginia, there is a Santa Claus." For more information see https://guides.loc.gov/chronicling-america-yes-virginia.

28. Kristy Buzard et al., "Who You Gonna Call? Gender Inequality in External Demands for Parental Involvement," *The Quarterly Journal of Economics*, 2025, qjaf027, https://doi.org/10.1093/qje/qjaf027.

29. Julie A. Nelson, *Feminism, Objectivity, and Economics* (New York: Routledge 1995); Julie A. Nelson, *Economics for Humans* (Chicago: University of Chicago Press, 2006).

30. Interview with Julie Nelson, September 4, 2024.

31. Peter Baker, "The Women Who Are Reshaping Economics," *New York Times*, January 10, 2018, www.nytimes.com/2018/01/10/us/politics/women-economics.html.

32. Interview with Kate Bahn, February 29, 2024.

33. Lisa Rein, "As Federal Government Evolves, Its Clerical Workers Edge Toward Extinction," *Washington Post*, January 14, 2014, www.washingtonpost.com/politics/as-federal-government-evolves-its-clerical-workers-edge-toward-extinction/2014/01/14/ded78036-5eae-11e3-be07-006c776266ed_story.html.

34. Charlotte Alter, "Nobel Laureate Claudia Goldin Told the 'Big and Bold' Story Other Economists Ignored," *Time*, February 21, 2024, https://time.com/collection/women-of-the-year/6691521/claudia-goldin/.

35. "All Prizes in Economic Sciences," NobelPrize.org, www.nobelprize.org/prizes/lists/all-prizes-in-economic-sciences/.

36. Emmanuelle Auriol et al., "Underrepresentation of Women in the Economics Profession More Pronounced in the United States Compared to Heterogeneous Europe," *PNAS* 119, no. 16 (2022): e2118853119, www.pnas.org/doi/pdf/10.1073/pnas.2118853119.

37. Carolyn Shaw Bell, "Report of the Committee on the Status of Women in the Economic Profession," *American Economic Association* 63, no. 2 (1973): 508–11.

38. Anusha Chari, "Report on the Committee on the Status of Women in the Economics Profession," *AEA Papers and Proceedings* 113 (2023): 815–39.

39. David Keyton, Paul Wiseman, and Michael Carey, "Nobel Economics Prize Goes to Harvard's Claudia Goldin for Research on the Workplace Gender Gap," Associated Press, October 9, 2023, https://apnews.com/article/nobel-prize-economy-224c204c0cc20843636e5525d6a61673.

40. "Claudia Goldin—Banquet Speech," NobelPrize.org, December 10, 2023, www.nobelprize.org/prizes/economic-sciences/2023/goldin/speech/.

41. "Claudia Goldin—Banquet Speech."

42. Emily Peck, "Policymakers Used to Ignore Child Care. Then Came the Pandemic," *New York Times*, May 9, 2021, www.nytimes.com/2021/05/09/business/child-care-infrastructure-biden.html.

43. Claudia Goldin, "Why Women Won," Working Paper No. 31762, National Bureau of Economic Research, October 2023, https://doi.org/10.3386/w31762.

44. Interview with Julie Nelson, September 4, 2024.

3. MISOGYNY

1. Char Adams and Abigail Edge, "Witnesses Say They Saw Former DJ Grab Taylor Swift's Butt," *People*, https://people.com/music/taylor-swift-groping-trial-witnesses-back-up-claims/.

2. Roisin O'Connor, "Taylor Swift: 5 of the Most Powerful Quotes from Her Sexual Assault Trial Testimony," *The Independent*, August 15, 2017, www.independent.co.uk/arts-entertainment/music/news/taylor-swift-sexual-assault-trial-win-one-dollar-best-quotes-groped-dj-david-mueller-latest-a7893631.html.

3. Ken Baker and McKenna Aiello, "Taylor Swift Wins Groping Trial After Jury Decides DJ David Mueller Assaulted and Battered Pop Star," E! Online, August 14,

2017, www.eonline.com/news/873385/taylor-swift-groping-trial-jury-decides
-dj-david-mueller-assaulted-and-battered-pop-star.

4. Guinness World Records, "Youngest Solo Winner of the BRITs' Global Icon Award," www.guinnessworldrecords.com/world-records/660297-youngest-brits
-global-icon-award-winner; Alyssa Bailey, "Taylor Swift Shouted Out Selena Gomez and Joe Alwyn in Candid BRIT Awards Speech," *Elle*, May 11, 2021, www.elle.com
/culture/celebrities/a36399766/taylor-swift-selena-gomez-joe-alwyn-brit-award-speech
-shoutouts/.

5. Scott Bomboy, "The Vote That Led to the 19th Amendment," National Constitution Center, August 18, 2023, https://constitutioncenter.org/blog/the
-man-and-his-mom-who-gave-women-the-vote.

6. Eliana Dockterman, "The True Story Behind *Bombshell* and the Fox News Sexual Harassment Scandal," *Time*, December 16, 2019, https://time.com/5748267
/bombshell-true-story-fox-news/; Mariel Padilla, "Defend and Deny: What We Know About Trump and Accusations of Sexual Misconduct," The 19th*, October 26, 2023, https://19thnews.org/2023/10/donald-trump-associates-sexual-misconduct
-allegations/.

7. Ben Casselman and Jim Tankersley, "Harvard Suspends Roland Fryer, Star Economist, After Sexual Harassment Claims," *New York Times*, July 10, 2019, www
.nytimes.com/2019/07/10/business/economy/roland-fryer-harvard.html; Ben Casselman and Jim Tankersley, "Women in Economics Report Rampant Sexual Assault and Bias," *New York Times*, March 18, 2019, www.nytimes.com/2019/03
/18/business/economy/women-economics-discrimination.html; Jennifer Gerson, "On #EconTwitter, #MeToo Anger Is Boiling Over," The 19th*, October 28, 2022, https://19thnews.org/2022/10/me-too-movement-economics-twitter
-misconduct/.

8. Gerson, "On #EconTwitter, #MeToo Anger Is Boiling Over"; Catarina Saraiva, "'Cesspool' Website Under Fire as Economists Confront Harassment," Bloomberg, January 8, 2023, www.bloomberg.com/news/articles/2023-01-08/
-cesspool-website-under-fire-as-economists-confront-harassment; Christopher Beam and Catarina Saraiva, "An Influential Economics Forum Has a Troubling Surplus of Trolls," Bloomberg, March 15, 2024, www.bloomberg.com/news/features
/2024-03-15/ejmr-economics-forum-posts-unmask-field-s-racism-and-sexism.

9. Eric R. Pedersen, Elizabeth J. D'Amico, Joseph W. LaBrie, David J. Klein, Coreen Farris, and Beth Ann Griffin, "Alcohol and Sexual Risk Among American College Students Studying Abroad," *Prevention Science: The Official Journal of the Society for Prevention Research* 21, no. 7 (2020): 926–36. https://doi.org/10.1007
/s11121-020-01149-9; Matthew Kimble, William F. Flack Jr., and Emily Burbridge, "Study Abroad Increases Risk of Sexual Assault for Female Undergraduates," Office of Justice Programs, US Department of Justice, October 2012, www.ojp.gov/ncjrs
/virtual-library/abstracts/study-abroad-increases-risk-sexual-assault-female
-undergraduates.

10. Saraiva, "'Cesspool' Website Under Fire."

11. Laurel Wamsley, "Anger in Spain After Soccer Chief Kisses a Player at Women's World Cup Ceremony," NPR, August 23, 2023, www.npr.org/2023/08/22/1195252925/spain-world-cup-kiss-luis-rubiales-jennifer-hermoso.

12. "The FIFA Disciplinary Committee Opens Disciplinary Proceedings Against Luis Rubiales, President of the Spanish FA," Inside FIFA, August 24, 2023, https://inside.fifa.com/legal/media-releases/the-fifa-disciplinary-committee-opens-disciplinary-proceedings-against-luis-rubiales.

13. Rodrigo Orihuela, "Disgraced Head of Spanish Soccer Luis Rubiales Finally Resigns," *Time*, September 11, 2023, https://time.com/6312552/luis-rubiales-spain-football-chief-resigns-kiss-scandal/; "Luis Rubiales' Mother Discharged from Hospital After Going on Hunger Strike," BBC Sport, August 30, 2023, www.bbc.com/sport/football/66664374.

14. "Rubiales' Mother Discharged from Hospital amid Hunger Strike," ESPN, August 30, 2023, www.espn.com/soccer/story/_/id/38291712/rubiales-mother-hospitalised-hunger-strike-fa-row; "Luis Rubiales' Mother Discharged from Hospital after Going on Hunger Strike."

15. Camilla Alcini, "Spain's Women's Soccer Coach Fired amid Kiss Controversy," ABC News, September 5, 2023, https://abcnews.go.com/Sports/spains-womens-soccer-coach-fired-amid-kiss-controversy/story?id=102933709.

16. Graham Keeley, "Spain's Soccer Chief Luis Rubiales Quits in Kiss Scandal," Reuters, September 10, 2023, www.reuters.com/sports/spains-soccer-chief-luis-rubiales-announces-resignation-2023-09-10/.

17. Matt Bonesteel and Beatriz Rios, "Former Spanish Soccer President Found Guilty of Sexual Assault," *Washington Post*, February 20, 2025, www.washingtonpost.com/sports/2025/02/20/luis-rubiales-guilty-sexual-assault/.

18. Tiffanie Turnbull, "Bob Ballard: Olympics Commentator Axed over Sexist Remark," BBC News, www.bbc.com/news/articles/cprq88oyzoxo; Ariana Brockington, "Olympics Commentator Bob Ballard Fired over Sexist Remark. Here's What He Said," Today, July 29, 2024, www.today.com/news/paris-olympics/bob-ballard-olympics-commentator-fired-sexist-remark-rcna164200.

19. Mesfin Fekadu, "#MeToo's Tarana Burke on Diddy Allegations: 'The Zeitgeist Has Changed and People Are Ready to Believe the Survivors,'" *Hollywood Reporter* (blog), April 5, 2024, www.hollywoodreporter.com/news/music-news/diddy-allegations-metoo-founder-tarana-burke-1235867216/.

20. Alex Brotherton, "Coventry Elected First Female IOC President as Coe Beaten," BBC, March 20, 2025, www.bbc.com/sport/olympics/articles/cy4v91e3e1wo.

21. Angela Yang, "Political Ad Ignites Conservative Anger over Women Possibly Hiding Their Votes from Their Husbands," NBC News, November 3, 2024, www.nbcnews.com/politics/politics-news/political-ad-ignites-conservative-anger-women-possibly-hiding-vote-hus-rcna178584.

22. Emily Davies, "In a Bathroom Stall, a Simple Message: Vote Harris. No One Will Know," *Washington Post*, November 3, 2024, www.washingtonpost.com/politics/2024/11/03/harris-wife-trump-husband-ad/.

23. US Census Bureau, "Census Bureau Releases New Educational Attainment Data," press release, February 24, 2022, www.census.gov/newsroom/press-releases/2022/educational-attainment.html.

24. Katherine Schaeffer, "The Data on Women Leaders," Pew Research Center Fact Sheet, September 27, 2023, www.pewresearch.org/social-trends/fact-sheet/the-data-on-women-leaders/; Richard Fry, "Women Now Outnumber Men in the US College-Educated Labor Force," *Pew Research Center* (blog), September 26, 2022, www.pewresearch.org/short-reads/2022/09/26/women-now-outnumber-men-in-the-u-s-college-educated-labor-force/.

25. Emma Hinchliffe, "Women CEOs Run 10.4% of Fortune 500 Companies. A Quarter of the 52 Leaders Became CEO in the Last Year," *Fortune*, June 5, 2023, https://fortune.com/2023/06/05/fortune-500-companies-2023-women-10-percent/.

26. Esther Duflo, "Women Empowerment and Economic Development," *Journal of Economic Literature* 50, no. 4 (2012): 1051–79, https://doi.org/10.1257/jel.50.4.1051; Shelly Lundberg et al., "Do Husbands and Wives Pool Resources?" *Journal of Human Resources* 32, no. 3 (1996): 464–80, https://doi.org/10.2307/146179; Misty L. Heggeness, "Improving Child Welfare in Middle Income Countries: The Unintended Consequence of a Pro-Homemaker Divorce Law and Wait Time to Divorce," *Journal of Development Economics* 143 (March 1, 2020): 102405, https://doi.org/10.1016/j.jdeveco.2019.102405; Ho-Po Crystal Wong, "Credible Commitments and Marriage: When the Homemaker Gets Her Share at Divorce," *Journal of Demographic Economics* 82, no. 3 (2016): 241–79, https://doi.org/10.1017/dem.2016.9; Claudia Martínez, "Intrahousehold Allocation and Bargaining Power: Evidence from Chile," *Economic Development and Cultural Change* 61, no. 3 (2013): 577–605, https://doi.org/10.1086/669260; Marcos A. Rangel, "Alimony Rights and Intrahousehold Allocation of Resources: Evidence from Brazil," *The Economic Journal* 116, no. 513 (2006): 627–58, https://doi.org/10.1111/j.1468-0297.2006.01104.x.

27. Abdul-Aziz Seidu et al., "Women's Autonomy in Household Decision-Making and Safer Sex Negotiation in Sub-Saharan Africa: An Analysis of Data from 27 Demographic and Health Surveys," *SSM-Population Health* 14 (2021): 100773, https://doi.org/10.1016/j.ssmph.2021.100773; Michael Bittman et al., "When Does Gender Trump Money? Bargaining and Time in Household Work," *American Journal of Sociology* 109, no. 1 (2003): 186–214, https://doi.org/10.1086/378340; Matthias Doepke et al., "The Economics and Politics of Women's Rights," *Annual Review of Economics* 4 (2012): 339–72, https://doi.org/10.1146/annurev-economics-080511-110928; Anna Aizer, "The Gender Wage Gap and Domestic Violence," *American Economic Review* 100, no. 4 (2010): 1847–59, https://doi.org/10.1257/aer.100.4.1847; Vijetha Koppa, "Can Information Save Lives? Effect of a Victim-Focused Police Intervention on Intimate Partner Homicides," *Journal of Economic Behavior and Organization* 217 (January 2024): 756–82, https://doi.org/10.1016/j.jebo.2023.11.001; Duflo, "Women Empowerment and Economic Development."

28. Tami Luhby, "Taylor Swift Is a Hero to Food Banks from Coast to Coast," CNN Business, August 13, 2023, https://edition.cnn.com/2023/08/13/business/taylor-swift-food-bank-donations/.

29. Hannah Dailey, "Taylor Swift's Donations Cover a Year of Meals for UK Food Bank," *Billboard*, June 27, 2024, www.billboard.com/music/music-news /taylor-swift-uk-food-bank-donations-cover-year-of-meals-1235719076/.

30. Randi Richardson, "Beyoncé to Donate $2 Million to Students and Small Business Owners During Renaissance Tour," Today, April 20, 2023, www.today .com/popculture/music/beyonce-2-million-renaissance-tour-donation-students -entrepreneurs-rcna80706.

4. CARE WORK

1. Rebecca Rubin, "Inside 'Barbie's' Pink Publicity Machine: How Warner Bros. Pulled Off the Marketing Campaign of the Year," *Variety*, July 23, 2023, https:// variety.com/2023/film/box-office/barbie-marketing-campaign-explained-warner -bros-1235677922/.

2. Taylor Swift statistics (@TSstatistics), "This #Barbie is the music industry! #TaylorSwift," Twitter (now X), April 4, 2023, https://x.com/TSstatistics /status/1643361378235740160; "This Barbie Is the Music Industry," Pinterest, www .pinterest.com/pin/948289265267878213/.

3. "Everything You Need to Know About Taylor Swift's Family," *Harper's Bazaar*, www.harpersbazaar.com/celebrity/latest/a46539860/taylor-swift-family -guide-everything-to-know/.

4. "Who Are Taylor Swift's Parents? Meet Scott and Andrea Swift Swept Up in Daughter's Travis Kelce Romance," Sporting News, www.sportingnews.com/us /nfl/news/taylor-swift-parents-scott-andrea-swift/a53190a18da8173433d5919c.

5. Misty L. Heggeness, "Taylor Swift Isn't the Economic Force. It's Her Fans," *Time*, April 18, 2024, https://time.com/6968040/taylor-swift-swifties-economic -force/.

6. Benjamin Bridgman et al., "Accounting for Household Production in the National Accounts: An Update 1965–2020," *BEA Survey of Current Business* 102, no. 2 (2022), https://apps.bea.gov/scb/issues/2022/02-february/pdf/0222-household -production.pdf.

7. Sarah Jane Glynn, "An Unequal Division of Labor," Center for American Progress report, May 18, 2018, www.americanprogress.org/article/unequal-division -labor/; Misty L. Heggeness, "The Girly Economics of Care Work: Implications for Economic Statistics," *AEA Papers and Proceedings* 113: 632–36, 2023, https://doi .org/10.1257/pandp.20231108.

8. Heggeness, "The Girly Economics of Care Work."

9. "Home," US Bureau of Labor Statistics, www.bls.gov/.

10. Kyle Buchanan, "Greta Gerwig on the Blockbuster 'Barbie' Opening (and How She Got Away with It)," *New York Times*, July 25, 2023, www.nytimes .com/2023/07/25/movies/greta-gerwig-barbie-movie.html?smid=url-share.

11. Saumya, "Barbie Beats Up Captain Marvel in Box Office," M9 News, August 14, 2023, www.m9.news/hollywood/barbie-beats-up-captain-marvel-in-box-office/;

Eddie Makuch, "Barbie Beats Batman to Become Warner Bros. Biggest Movie Ever in the US," GameSpot, August 16, 2023, www.gamespot.com/articles/barbie-beats -batman-to-become-warner-bros-biggest-movie-ever-in-the-us/1100-6516921/; Emily Olson, "'Barbie' Beats 'Oppenheimer' at the Box Office with a Record $155 Million Debut," NPR, July 24, 2023, www.npr.org/2023/07/24/1189760422/barbie -oppenheimer-box-office-ticket-sales.

12. Chip Cutter, "'Barbie' Surpasses $1 Billion at the Box Office," *Wall Street Journal*, August 6, 2023, www.wsj.com/articles/barbie-surpasses-1-billion-at-the -box-office-3ce00733.

13. Heggeness, "The Girly Economics of Care Work."

14. Sarah Krouse and Anne Steele, "Women Own This Summer. The Economy Proves It," *Wall Street Journal*, August 10, 2023, www.wsj.com/economy/consumers /the-summer-women-flexed-their-spending-power-dc2ce92c; Leslie Albrecht, "Beyoncé, 'Barbie,' and Taylor Swift Have Put a Spotlight on the Rising Power of the 'Female Dollar,'" MarketWatch, August 5, 2023, www.marketwatch.com/story /barbie-beyonce-and-taylor-swift-and-the-rising-power-of-the-female-dollar -9acba515; Bilal Qureshi, "How Three Female Artists Lead This Summer's Billion-Dollar Pop Culture Revival," NPR, August 14, 2023, www.npr.org/2023/08/11 /1193283472/barbie-taylor-swift-beyonce.

15. Tommy McArdle, "Read the Powerful 'Barbie' Monologue About Being a Woman that America Ferrera Performed '30 to 50' Times," *People*, July 28, 2023, https://people.com/read-the-powerful-barbie-monologue-about-being-a-woman -that-america-ferrera-performed-30-to-50-times-7565806.

16. Maja Egnell, "Gender Bias: Balancing on the Tightrope," RHR International, July 13, 2023, https://rhrinternational.com/blog/gender-bias-balancing-on -the-tightrope-2/.

17. Lois Shearing, "Women Are Using the 'Barbie Test' on Their Boyfriends," *Cosmopolitan*, July 27, 2023, www.cosmopolitan.com/uk/love-sex/relationships /a44661142/boyfriend-barbie-test/; Amber Raiken, "Woman Reveals She Broke Up with Her Boyfriend Over His 'Uncomfortable' Reaction to Barbie," *The Independent*, August 4, 2023, www.independent.co.uk/life-style/boyfriend-reaction -barbie-movie-reddit-b2387744.html.

18. Lana Wilson, dir., *Miss Americana*, Netflix, 2020.

19. "Grandparents in Sweden Can Now Get Paid to Take Care of Their Grand-kids," AP News, https://apnews.com/article/sweden-parental-leave-grandparents -stepparents-a2dc2a77530cf8f52a39bc8c830482ec.

20. Audrey Redford and Angela K. Dills, "The Political Economy of Drug and Alcohol Regulation During the COVID-19 Pandemic," *Southern Economic Journal* 87, no. 4 (2021): 1175–209, https://doi.org/10.1002/soej.12496.

21. Melinda Wenner Moyer, "School Pods: A Solution for Parents During Coronavirus," *New York Times*, July 22, 2020, www.nytimes.com/2020/07/22/parenting /school-pods-coronavirus.html; Anna Silman, "Parents Tell the Truth About Their COVID-19 Learning Pods," The Cut, December 8, 2020, www.thecut.com/2020/12 /parents-tell-the-truth-about-their-covid-19-learning-pods.html; Eilene Zimmer-

man, "Learning Pods: A Solution for Parents During the Pandemic," *New York Times*, October 14, 2020, www.nytimes.com/2020/10/14/education/learning/pods-microschools-pandemic.html.

22. Melinda Wenner Moyer, "Pods, Microschools and Tutors: Can Parents Solve the Education Crisis on Their Own?," *New York Times*, July 22, 2020. www.nytimes.com/2020/07/22/parenting/school-pods-coronavirus.html.

23. Personal communication, Tamara Tinkham, November 4, 2020.

24. Personal communication, Dani Sandler, fall 2020.

25. Thomas Gold and Melissa Steel King, "Pods in Action: The Boston Community Learning Collaborative," Center on Reinventing Public Education, April 15, 2022, https://crpe.org/pods-in-action-the-boston-community-learning-collaborative/.

26. Jessica Calarco, *Holding It Together: How Women Became America's Safety Net* (New York: Portfolio, 2024).

27. Günseli Berik et al., "Feminist Economics of Inequality, Development, and Growth," *Feminist Economics* 15, no. 3 (July 1, 2009): 1–33, https://doi.org/10.1080/13545700903093524.

28. Esther Duflo, "Women Empowerment and Economic Development," *Journal of Economic Literature* 50, no. 4 (2012): 1051–79, https://doi.org/10.1257/jel.50.4.1051; Shelly Lundberg et al., "Do Husbands and Wives Pool Resources?," *Journal of Human Resources* 32, no. 3 (1996): 464–80, https://doi.org/10.2307/146179; Misty L. Heggeness, "Improving Child Welfare in Middle Income Countries: The Unintended Consequence of a Pro-Homemaker Divorce Law and Wait Time to Divorce," *Journal of Development Economics* 143 (March 1, 2020): 102405, https://doi.org/10.1016/j.jdeveco.2019.102405; Ho-Po Crystal Wong, "Credible Commitments and Marriage: When the Homemaker Gets Her Share at Divorce," *Journal of Demographic Economics* 82, no. 3 (2016): 241–79, https://doi.org/10.1017/dem.2016.9; Claudia Martínez, "Intrahousehold Allocation and Bargaining Power: Evidence from Chile," *Economic Development and Cultural Change* 61, no. 3 (2013): 577–605, https://doi.org/10.1086/669260; Marcos A. Rangel, "Alimony Rights and Intrahousehold Allocation of Resources: Evidence from Brazil," *The Economic Journal* 116, no. 513 (2006): 627–58, https://doi.org/10.1111/j.1468-0297.2006.01104.x; Dev R. Acharya et al., "Women's Autonomy in Household Decision-Making: A Demographic Study in Nepal," *Reproductive Health* 7 (2010): 15, https://doi.org/10.1186/1742-4755-7-15; Siwan Anderson and Mukesh Eswaran, "What Determines Female Autonomy? Evidence from Bangladesh," *Journal of Development Economics* 90, no. 2 (2009): 179–91, www.sciencedirect.com/science/article/abs/pii/S0304387808001089; Michael Bittman et al., "When Does Gender Trump Money? Bargaining and Time in Household Work," *American Journal of Sociology* 109, no. 1 (2003): 186–214, https://doi.org/10.1086/378340; Xinwei Dong, "Intrahousehold Property Ownership, Women's Bargaining Power, and Family Structure," *Labour Economics* 78 (2022): Article C, https://doi.org/10.1016/j.labeco.2022.102235; Kaveh Majlesi, "Labor Market Opportunities and Women's Decision Making Power Within Households," *Journal of Development Economics* 119 (March 1, 2016): 34–47,

https://doi.org/10.1016/j.jdeveco.2015.10.002; Abdul-Aziz Seidu et al., "Women's Autonomy in Household Decision-Making and Safer Sex Negotiation in Sub-Saharan Africa: An Analysis of Data from 27 Demographic and Health Surveys," *SSM-Population Health* 14 (2021): 100773, https://doi.org/10.1016/j.ssmph .2021.100773; Hannah Uckat, "Leaning In at Home: Women's Promotions and Intra-Household Bargaining in Bangladesh," Policy Research Working Paper No. 10370, World Bank, 2023, http://hdl.handle.net/10986/39586.

29. Shelly Lundberg and Robert A. Pollak, "Separate Spheres Bargaining and the Marriage Market," *Journal of Political Economy* 101, no. 6 (1993): 988–1010, https://doi .org/10.1086/261912; Shelly Lundberg and Robert A. Pollak, "Noncooperative Bargaining Models of Marriage," *American Economic Review* 84, no. 2 (1994): 132–37, www .jstor.org/stable/2117816; Shelly Lundberg and Robert A. Pollak, "Bargaining and Distribution in Marriage," *Journal of Economic Perspectives* 10, no. 4 (1996): 139–58, https://doi.org/10.1257/jep.10.4.139; Lundberg et al., "Do Husbands and Wives Pool Resources?"; Heggeness, "Improving Child Welfare in Middle Income Countries."

30. Bharati Basu and Pushkar Maitra, "Intra-Household Bargaining Power and Household Expenditure Allocation: Evidence from Iran," *Review of Development Economics* (2020), https://doi.org/10.1111/rode.12636; Rangel, "Alimony Rights," 627–58; Uckat, "Leaning In at Home"; Namizata Binaté Fofana et al., "How Micro-finance Empowers Women in Côte d'Ivoire," *Review of the Economics of the Household* 13 (2015): 1023–41, https://doi.org/10.1007/s11150-015-9278-6.

31. Shing-Yi Wang, "Property Rights and Intra-Household Bargaining," *Journal of Development Economics* 107 (March 1, 2014): 192–201, https://doi.org/10.1016 /j.jdeveco.2013.12.003.

32. Lundberg et al., "Do Husbands and Wives Pool Resources?"; Heggeness, "Improving Child Welfare in Middle Income Countries."

33. Matthias Doepke et al., "The Economics and Politics of Women's Rights," *Annual Review of Economics* 4 (2012): 339–72, https://doi.org/10.1146/annurev -economics-080511-110928; Marie Hyland et al., "Gendered Laws and Women in the Workforce," *American Economic Review: Insights* 2, no. 4 (2020): 475–90, https:// doi.org/10.1257/aeri.20190631.

34. Duha T. Altindag et al., "Child-Custody Reform and the Division of Labor in the Household," *Review of Economics of the Household* 15, no. 3 (2017): 833–56, https://doi.org/10.1007/s11150-017-9374-7; Daniel Fernández-Kranz and Jennifer Roff, "The Effect of Alimony Reform on Married Women's Labor Supply: Evidence from the American Time Use Survey," IZA Discussion Paper No. 14949, Institute of Labor Economics (IZA), 2021.

35. Anne E. Winkler, "The Impact of Gender Inequality in Education and Labor Force Participation on Economic Growth: New Evidence for a Panel of Countries," IZA Discussion Paper No. 4050, Institute of Labor Economics (IZA), 2009, https:// wol.iza.org/uploads/articles/289/pdfs/womens-labor-force-participation.pdf; Rachel Heath and S. Jayachandran, "Financing Innovation: Evidence from R&D Grants," NBER Working Paper No. 22766, National Bureau of Economic Research, 2016, www.nber.org/system/files/working_papers/w22766/w22766.pdf.

36. Alan Rappeport and Niraj Chokshi, "Crippled Airline Industry to Get $25 Billion Bailout, Part of It as Loans," *New York Times*, April 14, 2020, www.nytimes.com/2020/04/14/business/coronavirus-airlines-bailout-treasury-department.html; "Rescuing the American Auto Industry," Obama White House Archives, https://obamawhitehouse.archives.gov/node/73621.

37. Jacki Lyden, "Missed Summer Learning Spells Out Long-Term Struggles," NPR, audio transcript, August 4, 2013, www.npr.org/transcripts/208946952; Motoko Rich, "To Increase Learning Time, Some Schools Add Days to Academic Year," *New York Times*, August 5, 2012, www.nytimes.com/2012/08/06/education/some-schools-adopting-longer-years-to-improve-learning.html.

38. "Agrarian Roots? Think Again. Debunking the Myth of Summer Vacation's Origins," PBS News, September 7, 2014, www.pbs.org/newshour/education/debunking-myth-summer-vacation.

39. Flynn Lebus et al., "Can Snow Clearing Be Sexist?," *FSG: Reimagining Social Change* (blog), March 6, 2020, www.fsg.org/blog/can-snow-clearing-be-sexist/.

40. Misty L. Heggeness, Joseph Bommarito, and Pilar McDonald, "The Challenge to Recognize 'Care Privilege' in the Field of Economics," *Oxford Review of Economic Policy*, forthcoming; Caroline Criado Perez, *Invisible Women: Data Bias in a World Designed for Men*. New York: Harry Abrams, 2021.

41. Chabeli Carrazana, "The 'Open Secret' in Most Workplaces: Discrimination Against Moms Is Still Rampant," The 19th*, April 27, 2023, https://19thnews.org/2023/04/workplace-discrimination-mothers-open-secret/.

42. Rachel Minkin and Juliana Menasce Horowitz, "Gender and Parenting," part 1 of "Parenting in America Today," Pew Research Center, January 24, 2023, www.pewresearch.org/social-trends/2023/01/24/gender-and-parenting/; Josie Cox, "Why Women Are More Burned Out Than Men," BBC, October 3, 2021, www.bbc.com/worklife/article/20210928-why-women-are-more-burned-out-than-men.

43. Kim Parker and Wendy Wang, "How Mothers and Fathers Spend Their Time," chap. 4 of "Modern Parenthood: Roles of Moms and Dads Converge as They Balance Work and Family," Pew Research Center, March 14, 2013, www.pewresearch.org/wp-content/uploads/sites/20/2013/03/FINAL_modern_parenthood_03-2013.pdf; David Richter et al., "Long-Term Effects of Pregnancy and Childbirth on Sleep Satisfaction and Duration of First-Time and Experienced Mothers and Fathers," *Sleep* 42, no. 4 (2019): 1–10, https://doi.org/10.1093/sleep/zsz015; Kelly Sullivan, "Sleep Duration and Feeling Rested Are Differentially Associated with Having Children Among Men and Women (P3.060)," *Neurology* 88, no. 16 (2017), https://doi.org/10.1212/WNL.88.16_supplement.P3.060.

44. Calarco, *Holding It Together*.

45. Patricia Resnick wrote the script for the movie *9 to 5* (1980); Tara Murtha, "Why '9 to 5' Is Still Radical Today," *Rolling Stone*, December 18, 2015, www.rollingstone.com/feature/9-to-5-turns-35-and-its-still-radical-today-50499/.

46. TED: The Economics Daily, "How Parents Used Their Time in 2021," July 22, 2022, Washington, DC: US Bureau of Labor Statistics, www.bls.gov/opub/ted/2022/how-parents-used-their-time-in-2021.htm.

47. Elaine Schwartz, "The Fines That Create Unintended Consequences," *Econlife* (blog), September 18, 2018, https://econlife.com/2018/09/unintended-consequences-from-fines/.

48. Heather Boushey, *Finding Time: The Economics of Work-Life Conflict* (Cambridge, MA: Harvard University Press, 2016). Ever since the 1980s, it has been almost impossible for middle-class families to survive off one income, and today more women work outside of the household due to family budget needs rather than for personal spending money.

49. Claire Cain Miller, "The 'Silver Lining to the Pandemic' for Working Mothers," *New York Times*, October 28, 2023, www.nytimes.com/2023/10/28/upshot/mothers-remote-work-pandemic.html; Rachel Wolfe and Justin Lahart, "More Women Are Working Than Ever. But They're Doing Two Jobs," *Wall Street Journal*, July 13, 2024, www.wsj.com/economy/jobs/more-women-are-working-than-ever-but-theyre-doing-two-jobs-bf93b9bf; Abha Bhattarai and Luis Melgar, "Women Are Rejoining the Workforce Faster Than Men Are," *Washington Post*, February 13, 2023, www.washingtonpost.com/business/2023/02/12/women-workforce-jobs-flexibility-remote/; Scott Horsley, "Women Are Returning to the Job Market in Droves, Just When the US Needs Them Most," NPR, July 5, 2023, www.npr.org/2023/07/05/1185723117/working-women-jobs-workforce-pandemic-economy-employers-labor.

50. Michael Horrigan and Diane Herz, "Planning, Designing, and Executing the BLS American Time Use Survey," *Monthly Labor Review*, October 2004, www.bls.gov/opub/mlr/2004/10/art1full.pdf.

51. Author's calculations using the 1970 decennial census and the 2022 American Community Survey, US Census Bureau, ipums.org.

52. Madeline Holcombe, "Why Fewer People Are Choosing to Have Kids," CNN, July 26, 2024, www.cnn.com/2024/07/26/health/childless-adults-pew-research-wellness/index.html; Peggy O'Donnell Heffington, *Without Children: The Long History of Not Being a Mother* (New York: Seal Press, 2023).

53. Katherine Schaeffer and Carolina Aragão, "Key Facts About Moms in the US," *Pew Research Center* (blog), May 9, 2023. www.pewresearch.org/short-reads/2023/05/09/facts-about-u-s-mothers/.

54. Dean Spears, "The World's Population May Peak in Your Lifetime. What Happens Next?" *New York Times*, September 18, 2023, https://www.nytimes.com/interactive/2023/09/18/opinion/human-population-global-growth.html.

55. Damien Cave, Emma Bubola, and Choe Sang-Hun, "Long Slide Looms for World Population, with Sweeping Ramifications," *New York Times*, May 22, 2021, www.nytimes.com/2021/05/22/world/global-population-shrinking.html.

56. Theresa Andrasfay and Noreen Goldman, "Reductions in 2020 US Life Expectancy Due to COVID-19 and the Disproportionate Impact on the Black and Latino Populations," *Proceedings of the National Academy of Sciences* 118, no. 5 (February 2, 2021): e2014746118, https://doi.org/10.1073/pnas.2014746118.

57. Martha J. Bailey et al., "The Missing Baby Bust: The Consequences of the COVID-19 Pandemic for Contraceptive Use, Pregnancy, and Childbirth Among

Low-Income Women," *Population Research and Policy Review* 41, no. 4 (August 2022): 1549–69, https://doi.org/10.1007/s11113-022-09703-9; Melissa Schettini Kearney and Phillip Levine, "The US COVID-19 Baby Bust and Rebound," Working Paper No. 30000, National Bureau of Economic Research, April 2022, https://doi.org/10.3386/w30000; Martha J. Bailey et al., "The COVID-19 Baby Bump in the United States," *Proceedings of the National Academy of Sciences* 120, no. 34 (August 22, 2023): e2222075120, https://doi.org/10.1073/pnas.2222075120; Misty Heggeness et al., "New Parent Labor Supply in Adaptive Markets," January 18, 2025, https://papers.ssrn.com/sol3/papers.cfm?abstract_id=5102602.

58. "2024 Gender Pay Gap Report (GPGR)," Payscale, February 20, 2024, https://www.payscale.com/research-and-insights/gender-pay-gap-2024.

59. "19th Amendment to the US Constitution: Women's Right to Vote (1920)," Milestone Documents, National Archives, www.archives.gov/milestone-documents/19th-amendment.

60. Raija Haughn, "The History of Women and Loans," Bankrate, September 19, 2023, www.bankrate.com/loans/personal-loans/history-of-women-and-loans/.

61. Pub. L. No. 93-495 (1974) states, "Equal Credit Opportunity Act—States that it is the purposes of this Act to require that financial institutions and other firms engaged in the extension of credit make that credit equally available to all creditworthy customers without regard to sex or marital status. Makes it unlawful for any creditor to discriminate against any applicant on the basis of sex or marital status." See www.congress.gov/bill/93rd-congress/house-bill/11221.

62. Michelle Fox, "Women Aren't Investing at the Same Rate as Men. Here's Why It Matters—and How the Gap Can Be Closed," CNBC, March 9, 2023, www.cnbc.com/2023/03/09/how-to-close-the-gender-investing-gap.html.

63. Julia Boorstin, "Survey: It's Still Tough to Be a Woman on Wall Street—but Men Don't Always Notice," CNBC, June 26, 2018, www.cnbc.com/2018/06/25/surveyon-wall-street-workplace-biases-persist---but-men-dont-see-t.html; Gregg Greenberg, "Adding and Retaining Women on Wall Street Are Goals for 2024," InvestmentNews, January 3, 2024, www.investmentnews.com/practice-management/adding-and-retaining-women-on-wall-street-are-goals-for-2024/247533; Fox, "Women Aren't Investing at the Same Rate as Men."

64. Fox, "Women Aren't Investing at the Same Rate as Men"; Meagan Drew and Sienna Wrenn, "Survey: Women Are Confident Money Managers Who Crave Shame-Free Support," Investopedia, May 14, 2024, www.investopedia.com/her-money-mindset-survey-8647284; "Women Taking On More Financial Responsibility," Allianz Life, February 6, 2024, www.allianzlife.com/about/newsroom/2024-Press-Releases/Women-Taking-On-More-Financial-Responsibility?cmpid=shared-facebook; "Bank of America Study Finds 94% of Women Believe They'll Be Personally Responsible for Their Finances at Some Point in Their Lives," Bank of America, June 22, 2022, https://newsroom.bankofamerica.com/content/newsroom/press-releases/2022/06/bank-of-america-study-finds-94--of-women-believe-they-ll-be-pers.html.

65. Therese Jefferson, "Women and Retirement Pensions: A Research Review," *Feminist Economics* 15, no. 4 (2009): 115–45, https://doi.org/10.1080

/13545700903153963; Martie Gillen and Hyungsoo Kim, "Older Women and Poverty Transition," *Journal of Applied Gerontology* 28, no. 3 (2009): 320–41, https://doi.org/10.1177/0733464808326953.

66. Claudia Goldin, *Career and Family: Women's Century-Long Journey Toward Equity* (Princeton, NJ: Princeton University Press, 2021).

67. Tracy McVeigh, "The Biggest Financial Risk for Women Today? Embarking on a Relationship," *The Guardian*, March 18, 2017, www.theguardian.com/lifeandstyle/2017/mar/19/divorce-women-risk-poverty-children-relationship; Lyz Lenz, "In My Marriage Money Was a Trap. After My Divorce It Was My Freedom," *Time*, February 13, 2024, https://time.com/6588974/money-marriage-trap-lyz-lenz-essay/.

68. Gillian Paull, "Children and Women's Hours of Work," *The Economic Journal* 118, no. 526 (2008): F8–F27, https://doi.org/10.1111/j.1468-0297.2007.02114.x; Patricia Cortés and Jessica Pan, "Children and the Remaining Gender Gaps in the Labor Market," *Journal of Economic Literature* 61, no. 4 (2023): 1359–1409, https://doi.org/10.1257/jel.20221549.

69. Jeremy Burke and Amalia R. Miller, "The Effects of Job Relocation on Spousal Careers: Evidence from Military Change of Station Moves," *Economic Inquiry* 56, no. 2 (2018): 1261–77, https://doi.org/10.1111/ecin.12529.

70. Angelina Grigoryeva, "Own Gender, Sibling's Gender, Parent's Gender: The Division of Elderly Parent Care Among Adult Children," *American Sociological Review* 82, no. 1 (2017): 116–46, https://doi.org/10.1177/0003122416686521.

71. Danielle DeSimone, "Over 200 Years of Service: The History of Women in the US Military," USO, February 28, 2023, www.uso.org/stories/3005-over-200-years-of-service-the-history-of-women-in-the-us-military.

72. Sarah Smarsh, "Growing Up In America's Heartland," *Saturday Evening Post*, January 28, 2020, www.saturdayeveningpost.com/2020/01/growing-up-in-americas-heartland/.

73. Emilie Stoltzfus, "Child Care: The Federal Role During World War II," Congressional Research Service Report for Congress, RS20615, 2000.

74. Chris M. Herbst, "Universal Child Care, Maternal Employment, and Children's Long-Run Outcomes: Evidence from the US Lanham Act of 1940," *Journal of Labor Economics* 35, no. 2 (2017): 519–64, www.jstor.org/stable/26553263.

75. Jack Rosenthal, "President Vetoes Child Care Plan as Irresponsible," *New York Times*, December 10, 1971, www.nytimes.com/1971/12/10/archives/president-vetoes-child-care-plan-as-irresponsible-he-terms-bill.html.

76. Rosenthal, "President Vetoes Child Care Plan."

77. Ari Shapiro, "How Politics Killed Universal Child Care in the 1970s," NPR, podcast transcript, October 13, 2016, www.npr.org/transcripts/497850292.

78. Rosenthal, "President Vetoes Child Care Plan."

79. Deborah Dinner, "The Universal Childcare Debate: Rights Mobilization, Social Policy, and the Dynamics of Feminist Activism, 1966–1974," *Law and History Review* 28, no. 3 (2010): 577–628, https://doi.org/10.1017/S0738248010000581.

80. Shapiro, "How Politics Killed Universal Child Care."

81. Boushey, *Finding Time*.

82. Bureau of Labor Statistics, "Employment Characteristics of Families—2024," news release, April 23, 2025, USDL-25-0564, US Department of Labor, www.bls.gov/news.release/pdf/famee.pdf.

83. Joseph P. Ferrie et al., "Mobilizing the Manpower of Mothers: Childcare Under the Lanham Act During WWII," Working Paper No. 32755, National Bureau of Economic Research, July 2024, www.nber.org/papers/w32755.

84. Nik Popli and Abby Vesoulis, "The House Just Passed Biden's Build Back Better Bill. Here's What's in It," *Time*, November 19, 2021, https://time.com/6121415/build-back-better-spending-bill-summary/.

85. Daniella Diaz, "Manchin Says He Won't Vote for Build Back Better Act," CNN, December 19, 2021, www.cnn.com/2021/12/19/politics/joe-manchin-build-back-better/index.html.

86. Heggeness et al., "Reinvention: The Path to Career and Life Fulfillment Is Non-Linear," unpublished manuscript, June 2025.

5. GENERATIONS

1. Kathryn Knight, "Taylor Swift's 'Timeless' Lyrics Are Inspired by Her Grandmother Marjorie," Capital FM, July 7, 2023, www.capitalfm.com/news/music/taylor-swift-timeless-lyrics-grandmother-marjorie/.

2. Mauricio Ginestra, "Meet Taylor Swift's Grandmother Marjorie Findlay: A Fellow Singer with Plenty of Latino Connections," Latin Times, January 4, 2025, www.latintimes.com/meet-taylor-swifts-grandmother-marjorie-findlay-fellow-singer-plenty-latino-connections-570878.

3. Hannah Dailey, "Taylor Swift Recalls Surprising Her Mom with Secret 'Fearless' Track During Mother's Day Concert," *Billboard*, May 15, 2023, www.billboard.com/music/music-news/taylor-swift-surprising-mom-best-day-mothers-day-show-1235329527/; Melody Chiu, "Taylor Swift's Most Heartbreaking Song on Lover Is About Her Mom Andrea's Battle with Cancer," *People*, August 23, 2019, https://people.com/music/taylor-swift-lover-mom-andrea-cancer-song/.

4. Frances Osborne, *The Bolter: The Story of Idina Sackville, Who Ran Away to Become the Chief Seductress of Kenya's Scandalous "Happy Valley Set"* (New York: Vintage, 2008).

5. Rune Blix Hagen, "The Era of Early Modern Witch-Hunts in Europe. A Short Overview—Time, Place, Numbers, and Gender," August 14, 2024, https://munin.uit.no/bitstream/handle/10037/35314/article.pdf?sequence=4; *The Nordic Storyteller: Essays in Honour of Niels Ingwersen*, ed. Susan Brantly and Thomas A. DuBois (Newcastle, UK: Cambridge Scholars, 2009).

6. Taylor Swift, "Happy belated Independence Day from your local neighborhood independent girlies 😎 See you tonight Kansas Cityyy," Instagram, July 7, 2023, www.instagram.com/taylorswift/p/CuZeFNrOdT-/.

7. Brenna Ehrlich, "Who Is Rebekah Harkness, Star of Taylor Swift's 'The Last Great American Dynasty'?" *Rolling Stone* (blog), July 24, 2020, www.rollingstone.com/music/music-news/rebekah-harkness-taylor-swift-1033497/.

8. Katie Schultz, "Taylor Swift's Rhode Island Mansion: Here's Everything You Need to Know," *Architectural Digest*, August 26, 2024, www.architecturaldigest.com/story/taylor-swifts-rhode-island-mansion-heres-everything-you-need-to-know; Craig Unger, *Blue Blood: The Story of Rebekah Harkness and How One of the Richest Families in the World Descended into Drugs, Madness, Suicide, and Violence* (New York: William Morrow & Company, 1988).

9. Ellise Shafer, "Taylor Swift Reveals Meaning of 'Fortnight,' 'Clara Bow,' 'Florida!!!' and More 'Tortured Poets Department' Tracks in Amazon Music Commentary," *Variety*, April 22, 2024, https://variety.com/2024/music/news/taylor-swift-tortured-poets-department-meaning-fortnight-clara-bow-florida-1235977904/.

10. David Stenn, *Clara Bow: Runnin' Wild* (New York: Cooper Square Press, 1988).

11. Stenn, *Clara Bow*.

12. Misty L. Heggeness, "The Girly Economics of Care Work: Implications for Economic Statistics," *AEA Papers and Proceedings* 113: 632–36, 2023, https://doi.org/10.1257/pandp.20231108.

13. Negley Harte, "Professor Phyllis Deane: Leading and Influential Figure in the Field of Economic History," *The Independent*, September 30, 2012, www.the-independent.com/news/obituaries/professor-phyllis-deane-leading-and-influential-figure-in-the-field-of-economic-history-8191322.html.

14. Luke Messac, "Women's Unpaid Work Must Be Included in GDP Calculations: Lessons from History," The Conversation, June 20, 2018, http://theconversation.com/womens-unpaid-work-must-be-included-in-gdp-calculations-lessons-from-history-98110.

15. Phil Davison, "Obituary: Professor Phyllis Deane, Economic Historian," *The Scotsman*, October 8, 2012, www.scotsman.com/news/obituaries/obituary-professor-phyllis-deane-economic-historian-1604586.

16. Negley Harte, "Professor Phyllis Deane: Leading and influential Figure in the Field of Economic History," *The Independent*, September 30, 2012, www.independent.co.uk/news/obituaries/professor-phyllis-deane-leading-and-influential-figure-in-the-field-of-economic-history-8191322.html.

17. For more information, see www.bea.gov/data/special-topics/household-production.

18. Joanna Rostek, *Women's Economic Thought in the Romantic Age: Towards a Transdisciplinary Herstory of Economic Thought* (New York: Routledge, 2021).

19. Sarah Chapone (1699–1764) was a married feminist activist with five children who wrote *The Hardships of the English Laws in Relation to Wives* (1735). Mary Wollstonecraft (1759–1797) was a writer and women's rights advocate best known for *A Vindication of the Rights of Woman* (1792). She argued that men were not superior to women, but rather that women lacked education, and she advocated for

the education of daughters. Mary Hays (1759–1843) was a feminist who wrote about women's education and independence and gender equity in the six-volume *Female Biography; or, Memoirs of Illustrious and Celebrated Women of All Ages and Countries*. Mary Robinson (1758–1800) was a poet, actress, and advocate of women's rights. Her achievements included publishing fourteen volumes of poetry. She had a brief romance with the young Prince of Wales (later George IV). She died in debt and despair. Priscilla Wakefield (1751–1832) was a Quaker woman known for pursuing social reform. Priscilla was more focused on women's obligations and duties than their civic rights. To Adam Smith she would argue that "all useful labour was productive labour, and that the labour of women, whether within the household or in the market sphere, was useful and productive. . . . To devalue women's labor was, in effect, to devalue women themselves" (https://www.priscillawakefield.uk /economist.html). Mary Ann Radcliffe (1746–1818) was a writer who, in 1799 at the age of fifty-three, published *The Female Advocate; or An Attempt to Recover the Rights of Women from Male Usurpation*. She had seven children and an alcoholic husband who wasted all her inheritance and disappeared. Mary linked women's oppression to their economic dependency on men and suggested that, given the options available for women's work at the time, prostitution was the most profitable profession. Jane Austen (1775–1817) wrote six novels about middle-class life in England during the nineteenth century, including *Pride and Prejudice*. She wrote of love and marriage, resource allocation, and the fate of women in a society that did not value their talents.

20. Cultures of Knowledge and the Bodleian Libraries, University of Oxford, "The Correspondence of Sarah Chapone," on *Early Modern Letters Online (EMLO)*, ed. Howard Hotson and Miranda Lewis, http://emlo-portal.bodleian.ox.ac.uk /collections/?catalogue=sarah-chapone; Sylvana Tomaselli, "Mary Wollstonecraft," *Stanford Encyclopedia of Philosophy*, ed. Edward N. Zalta and Uri Nodelman, https:// plato.stanford.edu/entries/wollstonecraft/; "Mary Hays," The New Historia, https:// thenewhistoria.org/schema/mary-hays/; "Mary Robinson," Poetry Foundation, www.poetryfoundation.org/poets/mary-robinson; Priscilla Wakefield, "Responding to Adam Smith," www.priscillawakefield.uk/economist.html; "Radcliffe, Mary Ann," The Women's Print History Project, https://womensprinthistoryproject.com /person/620; "Mary Radcliffe," Brooklyn Museum, www.brooklynmuseum.org /eascfa/dinner_party/heritage_floor/mary_radcliffe.

21. Joanna Rostek, "Women's Economic Thought in the Romantic Age," virtual seminar, International Association for Feminist Economics, June 24, 2024.

22. Kirstin Downey, *The Woman Behind the New Deal: The Life and Legacy of Frances Perkins—Social Security, Unemployment Insurance, and the Minimum Wage* (New York: Anchor, 2010).

23. Downey, *The Woman Behind the New Deal*.

24. Downey, *The Woman Behind the New Deal*.

25. Downey, *The Woman Behind the New Deal*.

26. Downey, *The Woman Behind the New Deal*.

27. Social Security Administration, "Frances Perkins," https://ssa.gov/history/fpbiossa.html; Downey, *The Woman Behind the New Deal*.

28. Downey, *The Woman Behind the New Deal*.

29. Downey, *The Woman Behind the New Deal*.

30. Stacey K. Sowards, *¡Sí, Ella Puede! The Rhetorical Legacy of Dolores Huerta and the United Farm Workers* (Austin: University of Texas Press, 2019), 35, 36.

31. "Dolores Huerta," *Encyclopedia Britannica*, www.britannica.com/biography/Dolores-Huerta; Sowards, *¡Sí, Ella Puede!*, 9, 13.

32. Jad Abumrad, *Radiolab Presents: Dolly Parton's America*, podcast, October 15, 2019, https://radiolab.org/podcast/radiolab-presents-dolly-partons-america.

33. "Uncle Bill Owens Archives," Dolly Parton Official Website, https://dollyparton.com/tag/uncle-bill-owens.

34. Arden Lambert, "Inside Dolly Parton and Porter Wagoner's Legendary Feud," Country Thang Daily, August 3, 2021, www.countrythangdaily.com/dolly-parton-porter-wagoner-feud/.

35. Madonna, "Woman of the Year Full Speech: Billboard Women in Music 2016," https://www.youtube.com/watch?v=c6Xgbh2E0NM.

36. Mary Gabriel, *Madonna: A Rebel Life* (New York: Little, Brown, 2023).

37. Gabriel, *Madonna*.

38. Gabriel, *Madonna*.

39. "Taylor Swift & the NFL: A Love Story? Introduction," YouTube, 2024, https://www.youtube.com/watch?v=OwSofZnbFPc; "Roger Goodell Calls the 'Taylor Swift Effect' a Positive," YouTube Shorts, 2024, https://www.youtube.com/watch?v=cgEH2GXRQKA.

40. Sam Lansky, "2023 Person of the Year: Taylor Swift," *Time*, December 6, 2023, https://time.com/6342806/person-of-the-year-2023-taylor-swift/.

41. Gabriel, *Madonna*.

42. Keith Caulfield, "Taylor Swift Surpasses Elvis Presley for Most Weeks at No. 1 on Billboard 200 Among Soloists," *Billboard*, December 31, 2023, www.billboard.com/music/chart-beat/taylor-swift-elvis-presley-billboard-200-chart-number-one-weeks-1235574100/.

43. Gabriel, *Madonna*.

44. Claudia Goldin, "Why Women Won," Working Paper No. 31762, National Bureau of Economic Research, October 2023, https://doi.org/10.3386/w31762.

45. Goldin, "Why Women Won."

46. Goldin, "Why Women Won."

47. Joseph P. Ferrie et al., "Mobilizing the Manpower of Mothers: Childcare Under the Lanham Act During WWII," Working Paper No. 32755, National Bureau of Economic Research, July 2024, www.nber.org/papers/w32755; Chris M. Herbst, "Universal Child Care, Maternal Employment, and Children's Long-Run Outcomes: Evidence from the US Lanham Act of 1940," *Journal of Labor Economics* 35, no. 2 (2017): 519–64, www.jstor.org/stable/26553263.

48. Access was granted on March 23, 1972, with the US Supreme Court decision in *Eisenstadt v. Baird*; "A Timeline of Contraception," PBS American Experience, www.pbs.org/wgbh/americanexperience/features/pill-timeline/.

49. Misty L. Heggeness, "Improving Child Welfare in Middle Income Countries: The Unintended Consequence of a Pro-Homemaker Divorce Law and Wait Time to Divorce," *Journal of Development Economics* 143 (March 1, 2020): 102405, https://doi.org/10.1016/j.jdeveco.2019.102405.

50. Ho-Po Crystal Wong, "Credible Commitments and Marriage: When the Homemaker Gets Her Share at Divorce," *Journal of Demographic Economics* 82, no. 3 (2016): 241–79. https://doi.org/10.1017/dem.2016.9; Shelly Lundberg et al., "Do Husbands and Wives Pool Resources?," *Journal of Human Resources* 32, no. 3 (1996): 464–80. https://doi.org/10.2307/146179; Heggeness, "Improving Child Welfare"; Marcos A. Rangel, "Alimony Rights and Intrahousehold Allocation of Resources: Evidence from Brazil," *The Economic Journal* 116, no. 513 (2006): 627–58, https://doi.org/10.1111/j.1468-0297.2006.01104.x; Claudia Martínez, "Intrahousehold Allocation and Bargaining Power: Evidence from Chile," *Economic Development and Cultural Change* 61, no. 3 (2013): 577–605, https://doi.org/10.1086/669260; Alessandra Voena, "Yours, Mine, and Ours: Do Divorce Laws Affect the Intertemporal Behavior of Married Couples?," *American Economic Review* 105, no. 8 (2015): 2295–332, https://doi.org/10.1257/aer.20120234.

51. Katharine Bradbury and Jane Katz, "The Responsiveness of Married Women's Labor Force Participation to Income and Wages: Recent Changes and Possible Explanations," Federal Reserve Bank of Boston Working Paper No. 08–7, 2008, https://papers.ssrn.com/sol3/papers.cfm?abstract_id=1324339.

52. Justin Wolfers, "Did Unilateral Divorce Laws Raise Divorce Rates? A Reconciliation and New Results," *American Economic Review* 96, no. 5 (2006): 1802–20. https://doi.org/10.1257/aer.96.5.1802.

53. Wolfers, "Did Unilateral Divorce Laws Raise Divorce Rates?"; Betsey Stevenson and Justin Wolfers, "Bargaining in the Shadow of the Law: Divorce Laws and Family Distress," *Quarterly Journal of Economics* 121, no. 1 (February 2006): 267–88. www.jstor.org/stable/25098790; Imran Rasul, "Marriage Markets and Divorce Laws," *Journal of Law, Economics, and Organization* 22, no. 1 (2006): 30–69, https://doi.org/10.1093/jleo/ewj008; US Census Bureau, "The Upside of Divorce," December 2019, www.census.gov/library/stories/2019/12/the-upside-of-divorce.html.

54. "Life Chronology," Frances Perkins Center, https://francesperkinscenter.org/learn/life-chronology/.

55. "Life Chronology," Frances Perkins Center.

56. Claudia Goldin, *Career and Family: Women's Century-Long Journey Toward Equity* (Princeton, NJ: Princeton University Press, 2021).

57. Betsey Stevenson and Justin Wolfers, "Trends in Marital Stability," in *Research Handbook on the Economics of Family Law*, ed. S. L. Schaeffer, 115–30 (Cheltenham, UK: Edward Elgar, 2011).

58. Goldin, *Career and Family*.

59. Sowards, *¡Sí, Ella Puede!*

1. Conçetta Ciarlo, "Beyoncé! Billie Eilish! Kelly Rowland! Inside Glamour's Women of the Year," *Vogue*, October 9, 2024, www.vogue.com/slideshow/glamour -women-of-the-year-2024; Sam Reed, "Glamour's Women of the Year 2024: Everything You Missed at This Year's Show," *Glamour*, October 9, 2024, www.glamour .com/story/women-of-the-year-2024-recap.

2. Samantha Barry, "They Raised the World's Biggest Superstars. Now They're Telling Their Own Stories," *Glamour*, www.glamour.com/story/tina-knowles -maggie-baird-mandy-teefey-donna-kelce-women-of-the-year-2024.

3. Barry, "They Raised the World's Biggest Superstars."

4. Natasha Dye and Julie Jordan, "Rihanna Is Pregnant with Second Baby, Reveals Bump During Super Bowl 2023 Halftime Show," *People*, February 12, 2023, https://people.com/parents/super-bowl-2023-rihanna-reveals-shes-pregnant-with -second-baby-during-super-bowl-halftime-show/.

5. Nelisa Msila Hamilton (@Nelisa_Msila), "Wait Rihanna is pregnant again?," Twitter (now X), March 13, 2023, https://x.com/Nelisa_Msila/status/163533250001 5960067?s=20.

6. Wyndi Kappes, "Rihanna Says Her Super Bowl Bump Debut Wasn't Planned," The Bump, December 21, 2023, www.thebump.com/news/rihanna -baby-two.

7. Michael Gracey, P!nk, Remi Bakkar, Khasan Brailsford, and Eva Gardner, dirs., *P!nk: All I Know So Far*, 2021, Amazon Prime.

8. Pauline Villegas, "Pink Says Her 11-Year-Old Daughter Will Have a 'Minimum Wage' Job on Her Upcoming Tour," Business Insider, February 21, 2023, www .businessinsider.com/pink-daughter-tour-job-minimum-wage-2023-2.

9. Hanna Fillingham, "Beyoncé's Family Share Proud Blue Ivy Update That Sparks Mass Reaction from Fans," *Hello!*, September 17, 2023, www.hellomagazine .com/healthandbeauty/mother-and-baby/502643/beyonce-family-share-pride -blue-ivy-update-sparks-reaction-fans/.

10. Blue Ivy Carter, "My Power/Black Parade," Renaissance World Tour, Kansas City, 2023, www.youtube.com/watch?v=N5W1NN3iylE.

11. Sam Brief, "Allyson Felix Launches First-Ever Olympic Village Nursery for Paris 2024," NBC Olympics, July 12, 2024, www.nbcolympics.com/news /allyson-felix-launches-first-ever-olympic-village-nursery-paris-2024.

12. Sheryl Sandberg, *Lean In: Women, Work, and the Will to Lead* (New York: Knopf, 2013).

13. Misty L. Heggeness, "The Missing Link to Understanding Today's Care Economy: Data and Statistics," The Brookings Institution, forthcoming.

14. YoonKyung Chung et al., "The Parental Gender Earnings Gap in the United States," Working Paper No. 17–68, Center for Economic Studies, US Census Bureau, 2017, https://ideas.repec.org/p/cen/wpaper/17-68.html.

15. Claudia Goldin, *Career and Family: Women's Century-Long Journey Toward Equity* (Princeton, NJ: Princeton University Press, 2021).

16. Misty L. Heggeness, "The Girly Economics of Care Work: Implications for Economic Statistics," *AEA Papers and Proceedings* 113: 632–36, 2023, https://doi .org/10.1257/pandp.20231108.

17. Author's calculations using the American Time Use Survey, US Census Bureau, ipums.org.

18. *Scary Mommy* (blog), www.scarymommy.com/; Jon Lucas and Scott Moore, dirs., *Bad Moms*, STX Entertainment, 2016, www.imdb.com/title/tt4651520/.

19. Tess McClure, "Jacinda Ardern Resigns as Prime Minister of New Zealand," *The Guardian*, January 19, 2023, www.theguardian.com/world/2023/jan/19 /jacinda-ardern-resigns-as-prime-minister-of-new-zealand; "Serena Williams's Farewell to Tennis—In Her Own Words," *Vogue*, August 9, 2022, www.vogue.com /article/serena-williams-retirement-in-her-own-words.

20. Anne-Marie Slaughter, "Why Women Still Can't Have It All," *The Atlantic*, June 13, 2012, www.theatlantic.com/magazine/archive/2012/07/why-women-still -cant-have-it-all/309020/.

21. Interview with Eve Rodsky, September 20, 2023.

22. Ella Braidwood, "US Players Won Their Equal Pay Fight. Their Rivals Took Notes," *New York Times*, October 10, 2022, www.nytimes.com/2022/10/10/sports /soccer/uswnt-equal-pay.html.

23. Brooks Barnes, "'Barbie' Reaches $1 Billion at the Box Office, Studio Says," *New York Times*, August 6, 2023, www.nytimes.com/2023/08/06/movies/barbie-1 -billion-box-office.html.

24. Barnes, "'Barbie' Reaches $1 Billion."

25. Barnes, "'Barbie' Reaches $1 Billion."

26. Madeline Berg and Samantha Grindell, "Taylor Swift Shook Off Publishers for Her New Book. That Could Spell Trouble for the Rest of the Industry," Business Insider, www.businessinsider.com/taylor-swift-disrupt-publishing-industry -eras-tour-book-2024-10.

27. Emily Peck, "Return of Working Moms Defies Pandemic Expectations," Axios, May 25, 2023, www.axios.com/2023/05/25/working-moms-covid-recovery; Misty L. Heggeness, "Why Is It So Hard to Understand Women and Work?," *Random Thoughts; Important Things*, Substack newsletter, May 15, 2021, https:// mistyheggeness.substack.com/p/why-is-it-so-hard-to-understand-women.

28. Misty L. Heggeness, "Estimating the Immediate Impact of the COVID-19 Shock on Parental Attachment to the Labor Market and the Double Bind of Mothers," *Review of Economics of the Household* 18, no. 4 (December 2020): 1053–78, https://doi.org/10.1007/s11150-020-09514-x.

29. Katherine Riley and Stephanie Stamm, "Nearly 1.5 Million Mothers Are Still Missing From the Workforce," *Wall Street Journal*, April 27, 2021, www.wsj .com/articles/nearly-1-5-million-mothers-are-still-missing-from-the-workforce -11619472229.

30. Claire Cain Miller, "The Pandemic Has Been Punishing for Working Mothers. But Mostly, They've Kept Working," *New York Times*, May 11, 2022, www .nytimes.com/2022/05/11/upshot/pandemic-working-mothers-jobs.html; Claire

Cain Miller, "The 'Silver Lining to the Pandemic' for Working Mothers," *New York Times*, October 28, 2023, www.nytimes.com/2023/10/28/upshot/mothers-remote-work-pandemic.html.

31. Heather Boushey, *Finding Time: The Economics of Work-Life Conflict* (Cambridge, MA: Harvard University Press, 2016).

32. US Bureau of Labor Statistics, "Employment Characteristics of Families Summary," news release, April 24, 2024, www.bls.gov/news.release/famee.nr0.htm.

33. Jason Furman et al., "The Role of Childcare Challenges in the US Jobs Market Recovery During the COVID-19 Pandemic," Working Paper No. 28934, National Bureau of Economic Research, June 2021, https://doi.org/10.3386/w28934.

34. "Minnesota Issues Resources Guides: Minneapolis Interstate 35W Bridge Collapse," Minnesota Legislature, October 2022, www.lrl.mn.gov/guides/guides?issue=bridges.

35. David Schaper, "10 Years After Bridge Collapse, America Is Still Crumbling," NPR, August 1, 2017, www.npr.org/2017/08/01/540669701/10-years-after-bridge-collapse-america-is-still-crumbling.

36. Schaper, "10 Years After Bridge Collapse."

37. Personal communication, Claire Cain Miller, May 7, 2024.

38. Melinda Wenner Moyer, "Pods, Microschools and Tutors: Can Parents Solve the Education Crisis on Their Own?," *New York Times*, July 22, 2020, www.nytimes.com/2020/07/22/parenting/school-pods-coronavirus.html.

39. Scott Daewon Kim and Petra Moser, "Women in Science: Lessons from the Baby Boom," Working Paper No. 29436, National Bureau of Economic Research, October 2021, https://doi.org/10.3386/w29436.

40. Jennifer Siebel Newsom, dir., *Fair Play*, 2022, www.fairplaylife.com/documentary.

41. *Scary Mommy* (blog), https://www.scarymommy.com/; The Holderness Family, https://theholdernessfamily.com/.

42. Girls Who Code, "50 Prominent Women Run Full Page Ad in *The New York Times* Calling on President Biden to Implement Marshall Plan for Moms in First 100 Days," PR Newswire, January 26, 2021, www.prnewswire.com/news-releases/50-prominent-women-run-full-page-ad-in-the-new-york-times-calling-on-president-biden-to-implement-marshall-plan-for-moms-in-first-100-days-301214913.html.

43. "Marshall Plan (1948)," Milestone Documents, National Archives, www.archives.gov/milestone-documents/marshall-plan.

44. Samantha Field, "Women's Labor Force Participation Rate Reaches an All-Time High," Marketplace, June 2, 2023, www.marketplace.org/2023/06/02/womens-labor-force-participation-rate-hits-an-all-time-high/.

45. Federal Reserve Economic Data (FRED), Federal Reserve Bank of St. Louis, https://fred.stlouisfed.org/series/LRAC25FEUSM156S.

46. Taylor Nicole Rogers, "American Mothers Re-Enter the Workforce at High Rates," *Financial Times*, August 27, 2023, www.ft.com/content/deb96102-06f1-4c3c-aabc-84b135c4b673; Brendan M. Price and Melanie Wasserman, "The Sum-

mer Drop in Female Employment," *Review of Economics and Statistics* (2024): 1–46, https://doi.org/10.1162/rest_a_01469.

47. Lauren Bauer and Sarah Yu Wang, "Prime-Age Women Are Going Above and Beyond in the Labor Market Recovery," Brookings Institution, August 30, 2023, www.brookings.edu/articles/prime-age-women-labor-market-recovery/.

48. The White House, "Fact Sheet: American Rescue Plan Funds Provided a Critical Lifeline to 200,000 Child Care Providers—Helping Millions of Families to Work," October 21, 2022, https://bidenwhitehouse.archives.gov/briefing-room/statements-releases/2022/10/21/fact-sheet-american-rescue-plan-funds-provided-a-critical-lifeline-to-200000-child-care-providers-helping-millions-of-families-to-work; American Rescue Plan Act of 2021, Pub. L. No. 117-2, 132 Stat. 4-245 (2021).

49. "Child Tax Credit," US Department of the Treasury, https://home.treasury.gov/policy-issues/coronavirus/assistance-for-american-families-and-workers/child-tax-credit.

50. Claire Thornton, "'The Streak Is Not Broken': US Poverty Rate over Time Shows Spike in 2022 Levels," *USA Today*, September 12, 2023, www.usatoday.com/story/news/nation/2023/09/12/us-poverty-rate-2022-increase/70775443007/.

7. SELF-INVESTMENT

1. The 19th*, https://19thnews.org/.

2. Bill & Melinda Gates Foundation, "Statement from CEO Mark Suzman About Melinda French Gates," May 13, 2024, www.gatesfoundation.org/ideas/media-center/press-releases/2024/05/melinda-french-gates; Karne Mizoguchi, "Bill and Melinda Gates Announce Divorce: 'We No Longer Believe We Can Grow Together as a Couple,'" *People*, May 3, 2021, https://people.com/human-interest/bill-gates-melinda-gates-announce-divorce-after-27-years-of-marriage/.

3. Anupreeta Das and Santul Nerkar, "Melinda French Gates to Resign from Gates Foundation," *New York Times*, May 13, 2024, www.nytimes.com/2024/05/13/business/melinda-gates-resigns-gates-foundation.html; "Pivotal Ventures, a Melinda French Gates Company," Pivotal Ventures, www.pivotalventures.org/.

4. Melinda French Gates, "The Enemies of Progress Play Offense. I Want to Help Even the Match," *New York Times*, May 28, 2024, www.nytimes.com/2024/05/28/opinion/melinda-french-gates-reproductive-rights.html.

5. "Melinda French Gates Announces $1B Commitment to Advance Women's Power Globally," Pivotal Ventures, December 11, 2024, www.pivotalventures.org/articles/melinda-french-gates-announces-1billion-commitment-to-advance-women-globally. Katie Kindelan, "Melinda Gates Announces $100 Million Investment in Women's Health Research," ABC News, September 10, 2025, https://abcnews.go.com/GMA/Wellness/melinda-gates-announces-100m-investment-womens-health-research/story?id=125409962.

6. "Forbes Profile: MacKenzie Scott," *Forbes*, August 7, 2024, www.forbes.com /profile/mackenzie-scott/.

7. Caleb Naysmith, "Jeff Bezos's Ex-Wife MacKenzie Scott Has Given over $16 Billion to Charity Since Her Divorce as Jeff Bezos Adds Another $100 Million Yacht to His Fleet," Yahoo! Finance, January 29, 2024, https://finance.yahoo.com /news/jeff-bezoss-ex-wife-mackenzie-203010406.html; MacKenzie Scott, "384 Ways to Help," Medium, December 15, 2020, https://mackenzie-scott.medium .com/384-ways-to-help-45d0b9ac6ad8.

8. Lacey Rose, "Mega-Mansions, MacKenzie Scott and 'Hot Ones': Inside Maya Rudolph's Billionaire Spoof 'Loot,'" *Hollywood Reporter*, June 23, 2022, www .hollywoodreporter.com/feature/maya-rudolphs-billionaire-spoof-loot-apple -tv-1235169751/.

9. Female Founders Fund, https://femalefoundersfund.com/; Intercontinental Exchange, "Women on Wall Street," www.ice.com/about/corporate-responsibility /diverse-leadership/women-on-wall-street.

10. Interview with Anu Duggal, October 23, 2024.

11. "Partners," The Care Summit, www.thecaresummit.com/sponsors#sponsors.

12. Jane Thier, "Sallie Krawcheck Reveals How She Came Up with Ellevest, and How She's Redefining Investing for Women," *Fortune*, June 27, 2024, https:// fortune.com/2024/06/27/sallie-krawcheck-ellevest-ceo-secrets-to-success/; "Ellevest," Ellevest, https://www.ellevest.com/magazine.

13. Sarah Lacy, "Making Room at the Table: Interview with Sallie Krawcheck," Startups.com, April 27, 2021, www.startups.com/library/founder-stories/sallie -krawcheck.

14. "Learn," Acorns, https://www.acorns.com/learn/.

15. Claire Wasserman, *Ladies Get Paid: The Ultimate Guide to Breaking Barriers, Owning Your Worth, and Taking Command of Your Career* (New York: Gallery Books, 2021).

16. "Mrs. Dow Jones," www.mrsdowjones.com/.

17. Taylor Lorenz, "Smashing the Finance Patriarchy with Memes," *New York Times*, December 24, 2019, www.nytimes.com/2019/12/24/style/finance-memes.html.

18. "A Timeline of Contraception," PBS American Experience, www.pbs.org /wgbh/americanexperience/features/pill-timeline/.

19. *Roe v. Wade*, 410 US 113 (1973).

20. Claudia Goldin and Lawrence F. Katz, "The Power of the Pill: Oral Contraceptives and Women's Career and Marriage Decisions," *Journal of Political Economy* 110, no. 4 (2002): 730–70, https://doi.org/10.1086/340778; Martha J. Bailey, "More Power to the Pill: The Impact of Contraceptive Freedom on Women's Life Cycle Labor Supply," *Quarterly Journal of Economics* 121, no. 1 (2006): 289–320, www.jstor .org/stable/25098791; Caitlin Myers, "Forecasts for a Post-Roe America: The Effects of Increased Travel Distance on Abortions and Births," *Journal of Policy Analysis and Management* 43, no. 1 (2024): 39–62, https://doi.org/10.1002/pam.22524.

21. Caitlin Myers and Anjali Srinivasan, "Brief of *Amici Curiae* Economists in Support of Respondents in *Dobbs v. Jackson's Women's Health Organization*," Per-

spectives on Sexual and Reproductive Health 56, no. 3 (2024): 211–21, https://doi.org/10.1111/psrh.12268.

22. Myers and Srinivasan, "Brief of *Amici Curiae* Economists."

23. Goldin and Katz, "The Power of the Pill"; Bailey, "More Power to the Pill."

24. Lindsey Bever, "After Social Media Outcry, CDC Tells Doctors to Better Manage IUD Pain," *Washington Post*, August 8, 2024, www.washingtonpost.com/wellness/2024/08/08/iud-pain-cdc/.

25. Grace Snelling, "Scientists Designed This New Copper IUD to Be Less Painful," *Fast Company*, March 11, 2025, www.fastcompany.com/91292010/miudella-hormone-free-iud-less-pain.

26. Justin Wolfers, "Did Unilateral Divorce Laws Raise Divorce Rates? A Reconciliation and New Results," *American Economic Review* 96, no. 5 (2006): 1802–20, https://doi.org/10.1257/aer.96.5.1802.

27. Misty L. Heggeness, "Improving Child Welfare in Middle Income Countries: The Unintended Consequence of a Pro-Homemaker Divorce Law and Wait Time to Divorce," *Journal of Development Economics* 143 (March 1, 2020): 102405, https://doi.org/10.1016/j.jdeveco.2019.102405.

28. "About," The Care Summit," www.thecaresummit.com/about.

29. Vanessa Romo, "Women's NCAA Championship TV Ratings Crush the Men's Competition," NPR, April 10, 2024, www.npr.org/2024/04/10/1243801501/womens-ncaa-championship-tv-ratings.

30. Home Depot (@homedepot), "Your Guide to Home Improvement," TikTok, May 5, 2023, www.tiktok.com/@homedepot/video/7232319734702771499.

31. Ted Jenkin, "Women Are Gaining Power When It Comes to Money—Here's Why That's a Big Deal," CNBC, May 3, 2022, www.cnbc.com/2022/05/03/money-decisions-by-women-will-shape-the-future-for-the-united-states.html.

32. Tracy Grant, "Marissa Mayer and Telecommuting: Yahoo CEO Got It Right," *Washington Post*, March 4, 2013; Bonnie Fuller, "Marissa Mayer Shouldn't Be Criticized for Building an Office Nursery," Huffington Post, February 26, 2013, www.huffpost.com/entry/marissa-mayer-office-nursery_b_2769296.

33. Jessica Gross, "Sheryl Sandberg's 'Lean In' Circles Completely Miss the Point on Workplace Maternity," Slate, February 22, 2013, https://slate.com/human-interest/2013/02/sheryl-sandberg-and-the-lean-in-movement-what-lean-in-circles-misunderstand-about-maternity-policy.html.

34. "House Approves Paid Parental Leave for Federal Employees," Women's Congressional Policy Institute, www.wcpinst.org/source/house-approves-paid-parental-leave-for-federal-employees/.

35. "Duckworth's FAM Act to Help Nursing Mothers Signed into Law," press release, October 9, 2018, www.duckworth.senate.gov/news/press-releases/duckworths-fam-act-to-help-nursing-mothers-signed-into-law; Jocelyn Frye and Tammy Duckworth, "A Conversation with Senator Tammy Duckworth," keynote conversation, Brookings Institution, Washington, DC, June 10–11, 2024.

36. Richard Fry, "Women Now Outnumber Men in the US College-Educated Labor Force," *Pew Research Center* (blog), September 26, 2022, www.pewresearch

.org/short-reads/2022/09/26/women-now-outnumber-men-in-the-u-s-college
-educated-labor-force/; Michael T. Nietzel, "Women Continue to Outpace Men in
College Enrollment and Graduation," *Forbes*, www.forbes.com/sites/michaeltnietzel
/2024/08/07/women-continue-to-outpace-men-in-college-enrollment-and
-graduation/.

8. NEGOTIATION AND PLANNING

1. Beyoncé and the Dixie Chicks, "Daddy Lessons (Live at CMA Awards 2016)," 2016, www.youtube.com/watch?v=85Ksi-uzuIg.

2. Adell Platon, "Beyoncé & Dixie Chicks Duet, One of CMA Awards' Buzziest Moments, Absent from Show's Website—Update," *Billboard*, November 3, 2016, www.billboard.com/music/rb-hip-hop/beyonce-dixie-chicks-cma-awards-website
-social-media-7565538/.

3. Sam Adams, "The Dixie Chicks Just Recognized Beyoncé's 'Daddy Lessons' as a Country Song. Will Country Radio?," Slate, May 2, 2016, https://slate.com
/culture/2016/05/the-dixie-chicks-just-recognized-that-beyonce-s-daddy-lessons-is
-a-country-song-will-country-radio.html.

4. David Brooks, "The Nuclear Family Was a Mistake," *The Atlantic*, February 10, 2020, www.theatlantic.com/magazine/archive/2020/03/the-nuclear-family-was-a
-mistake/605536/; Joanna Rostek, *Women's Economic Thought in the Romantic Age: Towards a Transdisciplinary Herstory of Economic Thought* (New York: Routledge, 2021).

5. Katie Nodjimbadem, "The Lesser-Known History of African-American Cowboys," *Smithsonian*, February 13, 2017, www.smithsonianmag.com/history
/lesser-known-history-african-american-cowboys-180962144/.

6. Erin Blakemore, "Meet Stagecoach Mary, the Daring Black Pioneer Who Protected Wild West Stagecoaches," History, August 11, 2023, www.history.com
/news/meet-stagecoach-mary-the-daring-black-pioneer-who-protected-wild
-west-stagecoaches.

7. Cecilia Gutierrez Venable and Jessica Brannon-Wranosky, "The Life of Johanna 'Chona' Phillips: A Black Seminole Legacy," Texas State Historical Association, May 28, 2020, www.tshaonline.org/handbook/entries/july-johanna.

8. Rivea Ruff, "Meet the Black Country Artists Featured on Beyoncé's 'Cowboy Carter,'" *Essence*, April 3, 2024, www.essence.com/gallery/black-country-artists
-beyonce-cowboy-carter/; Randy Savvy, "Beyoncé and the Heritage of the Black Cowboy: A Recognition Whose Time Has Come," *Los Angeles Magazine*, February 25, 2024, https://lamag.com/opinion/beyonce-country-music-texas-hold-em-black
-cowboys; Curatorial Intern, "Black on the Range: African American Cowboys of the 19th Century," Rancho Los Cerritos, August 13, 2021, www.rancholoscerritos
.org/black-on-the-range-african-american-cowboys-of-the-19th-century/.

9. Andy Greene, "Beyoncé's 'Cowboy Carter' Started with This CMA Performance," *Rolling Stone*, March 27, 2024, www.rollingstone.com/music/music-features
/beyonce-the-chicks-cmas-performance-cowboy-carter-1234995125/.

10. Dom Hines, "Beyoncé Slams 'Award Shows, Record Labels and Radio' After 'Preconceived' Cowboy Carter Backlash," *Us Weekly*, April 2, 2024, www.usmagazine.com/entertainment/news/beyonce-slams-award-shows-and-radio-after-cowboy-carter-backlash/.

11. "Netflix NFL Christmas Gameday Reaches 65 Million US Viewers," Netflix, https://about.netflix.com/news/netflix-nfl-christmas-gameday-reaches-65-million-us-viewers.

12. Daysia Tolentino, "Why Was Beyoncé Snubbed by the Country Music Association Awards? Experts Cite a Few Reasons," NBC News, September 11, 2024, www.nbcnews.com/news/nbcblk/beyonce-cma-snub-cowboy-carter-experts-rcna170480.

13. "Beyoncé Becomes First Black Woman to Win Grammy for Best Country Album with 'Cowboy Carter,'" Grammy.com, www.grammy.com/news/beyonce-first-black-woman-best-country-album-win-2025-grammys-cowboy-carter.

14. Rakesh Kochhar, "The Enduring Grip of the Gender Pay Gap," *Pew Research Center* (blog), March 1, 2023, www.pewresearch.org/social-trends/2023/03/01/the-enduring-grip-of-the-gender-pay-gap/.

15. John Hanna and David A. Lieb, "They Don't Define DEI, but Kansas Lawmakers Are Attacking It Like GOP Colleagues Elsewhere," AP News, March 21, 2024, https://apnews.com/article/diversity-equity-inclusion-universities-ban-kansas-69ba2c0492944b76772353289e565b19.

16. Brittany S. Cassidy and Anne C. Krendl, "A Crisis of Competence: Benevolent Sexism Affects Evaluations of Women's Competence," *Sex Roles* 81 (2019): 505–20, https://doi.org/10.1007/s11199-019-1011-3.

17. Nikolay Angelov et al., "Parenthood and the Gender Gap in Pay," *Journal of Human Resources* 50, no. 1 (2015): 123–55, www.journals.uchicago.edu/doi/10.1086/684851.

18. Steven D. Levitt, "Nobel Laureate Claudia Goldin on 'Greedy Work' and the Wage Gap," *Freakonomics* (blog), https://freakonomics.com/podcast/bonus-nobel-laureate-claudia-goldin-on-greedy-work-and-the-wage-gap/.

19. Kochhar, "The Enduring Grip of the Gender Pay Gap."

20. "State Candidates and the Use of Campaign Funds for Childcare Expenses," Center for American Women and Politics (CAWP), https://cawp.rutgers.edu/election-watch/state-candidates-and-use-campaign-funds-childcare-expenses.

21. "Campaign Funds for Childcare: Where We Stand," Vote Mama Foundation, www.votemamafoundation.org/cfccstates.

22. Kristy Buzard et al., "Who You Gonna Call? Gender Inequality in External Demands for Parental Involvement," *The Quarterly Journal of Economics*, 2025, qjaf027, https://doi.org/10.1093/qje/qjaf027.

23. Misty L. Heggeness, "From Warrior to Housemaid—How the Pandemic Changed Me," *The Shadow* (blog), May 29, 2021, https://medium.com/the-shadow/from-warrior-to-housemaid-how-the-pandemic-changed-me-2342622ac81e.

24. "Moms First," Moms First, https://momsfirst.us/; "Caring Across," Caring Across Generations, https://caringacross.org/.

25. "Developing Policy Solutions," National Domestic Workers Alliance, www.domesticworkers.org/programs-and-campaigns/developing-policy-solutions/.

26. Lucia Foster et al., "Early Career Paths of Economists Inside and Outside of Academia," *Journal of Economic Perspectives* 37, no. 4 (2023): 231–50, https://doi.org/10.1257/jep.37.4.231.

27. Scott Daewon Kim and Petra Moser, "Women in Science: Lessons from the Baby Boom," Working Paper No. 29436, National Bureau of Economic Research, October 2021, https://doi.org/10.3386/w29436.

28. Kim and Moser, "Women in Science."

29. Heather Antecol et al., "Equal but Inequitable: Who Benefits from Gender-Neutral Tenure Clock Stopping Policies?," *American Economic Review* 108, no. 9 (2018): 2420–41, www.doi.org/10.1257/aer.20160613.

30. Buzard et al., "Who You Gonna Call?"

31. Claire Cain Miller, "Young Men Embrace Gender Equality, but They Still Don't Vacuum," *New York Times*, February 11, 2020, www.nytimes.com/2020/02/11/upshot/gender-roles-housework.html.

32. Misty L. Heggeness, "The Girly Economics of Care Work: Implications for Economic Statistics," *AEA Papers and Proceedings* 113: 632–36, 2023, https://doi.org/10.1257/pandp.20231108.

33. Heggeness et al., "Reinvention: The Path to Career and Life Fulfillment Is Non-Linear," unpublished manuscript, June 2025.

34. Georgie Hewson, "How Simone Biles Overcame 'the Twisties' to Compete for Olympic Gold," ABC News, July 30, 2024, www.abc.net.au/news/2024-07-30/what-are-twisties-and-how-did-simone-biles-get-them/104159056.

35. Greg Whiteley, dir., *Simone Biles Rising*, Netflix, 2022.

36. Lindsay Kimble, "Simone Biles Ends Her 2024 Olympic Games with Four Medals: 'I've Accomplished Way More Than My Wildest Dreams,'" *People*, August 5, 2024, https://people.com/simone-biles-wins-four-medals-2024-olympics-8690143.

37. "Beyoncé Introduces Team USA, from Simone Biles to Noah Lyles: Paris Olympics," NBC Sports, 2024, www.youtube.com/watch?v=wa7HpWw7DEk.

38. Kari Anderson, "Women Earned the Majority of Gold Medals for Team USA in Paris—Here's a List of Every American Woman Who Won Gold," Yahoo Sports, August 12, 2024, https://sports.yahoo.com/women-earned-the-majority-of-gold-medals-for-team-usa-in-paris—heres-a-list-of-every-american-woman-who-won-gold-171156767.html.

39. Hanna Barton, "Biles, Chiles, Finish Their Paris 2024 Runs with Silver and Bronze," TeamUSA.com, www.teamusa.com/news/2024/august/05/biles-chiles-finish-their-paris-2024-run-with-silver-and-bronze.

40. Caroline Criado Perez, *Invisible Women: Data Bias in a World Designed for Men* (New York: Harry N. Abrams, 2021).

41. Claudia Goldin, "Federal Support for Childcare in Four Acts and 90 Years," presentation at the conference "The Care Economy: Connections, Challenges, and Opportunities," Brookings Institution, June 10, 2024.

42. Anne-Marie Slaughter, "Why Women Still Can't Have It All," *The Atlantic*, June 13, 2012, www.theatlantic.com/magazine/archive/2012/07/why-women-still -cant-have-it-all/309020/.

43. Natalie Robehmed, "Jennifer Lawrence Speaks Out on Making Less Than Male Co-Stars," *Forbes*, October 13, 2015, www.forbes.com/sites/natalierobehmed /2015/10/13/jennifer-lawrence-speaks-out-on-making-less-than-male-co-stars; Debra Birnbaum, "'Shameless' Star Emmy Rossum Resolves Pay Dispute, Setting Path for Season 8," *Variety*, December 14, 2016, https://variety.com/2016/tv/news /shameless-star-emmy-rossum-pay-disparity-season-8-1201942219/.

44. Laura Clancy and Anna Jackson, "About 1 in 3 UN Member States Have Ever Had a Woman Leader," *Pew Research Center* (blog), October 3, 2024, www .pewresearch.org/short-reads/2024/10/03/women-leaders-around-the-world/.

45. Tomás Mier, "Beyoncé Attends Taylor Swift's 'Eras Tour' Film Premiere: 'An Actual Fairytale,'" *Rolling Stone* (blog), October 12, 2023, www.rollingstone.com /music/music-news/beyonce-attends-taylor-swift-eras-tour-film-premiere -1234852419/; Larisha Paul, "Taylor Swift Supports Beyoncé at 'Renaissance' Docu-mentary Concert Film Premiere in London," *Rolling Stone* (blog), November 30, 2023, www.rollingstone.com/music/music-news/taylor-swift-attends-beyonce -renaissance-film-london-premiere-1234906237/; Maddie Ellis, "Taylor Swift Attends Beyoncé's 'Renaissance' Film Premiere in London," Today, December 1, 2023, www.today.com/popculture/music/taylor-swift-beyonce-renaissance -premiere-london-rcna127407.

46. Stephanie H. Murray, "How the Pandemic Could Finally End the Mommy Wars," *Time*, December 29, 2021, https://time.com/6130336/mommy-wars -pandemic/.

47. "Get To Know Us: History & Inception," 'me too.' Movement, https:// metoomvmt.org/get-to-know-us/history-inception/.

48. Personal communication, Claire Cain Miller, May 7, 2024.

49. "Child Tax Credit," US Department of the Treasury, https://home.treasury. gov/policy-issues/coronavirus/assistance-for-american-families-and-workers/child -tax-credit.

50. Personal communication, Claire Cain Miller.

51. Rory Jiwani, "The Women Trailblazers for Sporting Gender Equality," Olympics.com, March 2, 2021, www.olympics.com/en/news/top-10-moments -gender-equality-in-sport-intl-equal-pay-day.

52. "Kansas City Current Announce Patrick Mahomes as New Club Co-Owner," Kansas City Current, January 10, 2023, www.kansascitycurrent .com/news/kansas-city-current-announce-patrick-mahomes-as-new-club-co -owner.

53. *Time* (@TIME), "'I'd like to raise a glass to a new era in sports. An era when the women's game is finally getting the attention it deserves,' said Patrick Maho-mes," X, May 13, 2024, https://x.com/TIME/status/1790035119870263685? lang=en.

1. Claudia Goldin, "Why Women Won," Working Paper No. 31762, National Bureau of Economic Research, October 2023, https://doi.org/10.3386/w31762.

2. Toluse Olorunnipa and Patrick Svitek, "Biden Makes Stunning Decision to Pull Out of 2024 Race," *Washington Post*, July 21, 2024, www.washingtonpost.com /politics/2024/07/21/joe-biden-drops-out/.

3. Michael Scherer, Gerrit De Vynck, and Maeve Reston, "Historic Flood of Cash Pours into Harris Campaign and Allied Groups," *Washington Post*, July 23, 2024, www.washingtonpost.com/politics/2024/07/23/kamala-harris-donations -election/.

4. Errin Haines and Jennifer Gerson, "Four Hours, 44,000 Black Women and One Zoom Call," The 19th*, July 23, 2024, https://19thnews.org/2024/07 /win-with-black-women-zoom-call-harris-organizers/.

5. Holly Ramer, "'We Were Built for This Moment': Black Women Rally Around Kamala Harris," AP News, July 23, 2024, https://apnews.com/article/kamala- harris-president-black-women-support-bddoba0a19697c7cd2f183773e97aa6e; Zoe G. Phillips, "Zooms for Kamala Harris Draw Six-Digit Attendance, Break Records and Raise Millions," *Hollywood Reporter*, July 25, 2024, www.hollywoodreporter.com /news/politics-news/kamala-harris-zooms-celebrities-raise-millions-1235958582/; Jennifer Gerson, "The Night White Women Raised Millions for Harris. And Broke Zoom," The 19th*, July 26, 2024, https://19thnews.org/2024/07/white-women-harris -broke-zoom/.

6. Andrea González-Ramírez, "Kamala Already Has the Swifties' Vote," *New York Magazine*, July 25, 2024, www.thecut.com/article/swifties-for-harris-ask-are -you-ready-for-it.html.

7. "Taylor Swift Endorses Kamala Harris after Presidential Debate," NBC News, September 11, 2024, www.nbcnews.com/politics/2024-election/taylor -swift-endorses-kamala-harris-rcna170547.

8. Molly Bohannon, "Vote.gov Had Nearly 406,000 Visitors After Taylor Swift's Endorsement," *Forbes*, www.forbes.com/sites/mollybohannon/2024/09/12 /votegov-had-nearly-406000-visitors-after-taylor-swifts-endorsement/.

9. "Women in the US Congress 2025," Center for American Women and Politics (CAWP), https://cawp.rutgers.edu/facts/levels-office/congress/women-us -congress-2025.

10. Katherine Schaeffer, "The Data on Women Leaders," Pew Research Center fact sheet, September 27, 2023, www.pewresearch.org/social-trends/fact-sheet /the-data-on-women-leaders/.

11. Jessica Grose, "Opinion: The Hope at the Bottom of the 'Child Care Cliff,'" *New York Times*, September 20, 2023, www.nytimes.com/2023/09/20/opinion /child-care-cliff.html.

12. "Fact Sheet: Obama Administration Auto Restructuring Initiative— General Motors," Obama White House Archives, https://obamawhitehouse .archives.gov/realitycheck/the-press-office/fact-sheet-obama-administration-auto

-restructuring-initiative-general-motors.; Paul Kiel, "The Bailout Was 11 Years Ago. We're Still Tracking Every Penny," ProPublica, October 3, 2019, www.propublica .org/article/the-bailout-was-11-years-ago-were-still-tracking-every-penny; David Shepardson, "US Airlines to Defend $54 Billion COVID-19 Government Lifeline," Reuters, December 15, 2021, www.reuters.com/business/aerospace-defense /us-airlines-defend-54-billion-covid-19-government-lifeline-2021-12-15/.

13. Nancy Folbre, *The Invisible Heart: Economics and Family Values* (New York: The New Press, 2002).

14. Markus Goldstein, "Does It Matter for the Kids If We Give a Cash Transfer to the Woman or the Man in the Household?," *World Bank Blogs*, September 9, 2021, https://blogs.worldbank.org/en/impactevaluations/does-it-matter-kids -if-we-give-cash-transfer-woman-or-man-household.

15. "How to Get Dads to Take Parental Leave? Seeing Other Dads Do It," *Morning Edition*, NPR, February 8, 2016, www.npr.org/2016/02/08/465726445 /how-to-get-dads-to-take-parental-leave-seeing-other-dads-do-it.

16. Misty L. Heggeness, Joseph Bommarito, and Lucie Prewitt, The Care Board: Version 1.0 (dataset), Kansas Population Center, 2025, https://thecareboard.org.

17. Heggeness et al., The Care Board (dataset).

18. "Supreme Court Overturns Roe v. Wade, Ending Right to Abortion Upheld for Decades," *All Things Considered*, NPR, June 24, 2022, www.npr.org/2022 /06/24/1102305878/supreme-court-abortion-roe-v-wade-decision-overturn.

SELECTED BIBLIOGRAPHY

Acharya, Dev R., Jacqueline S. Bell, Padam Simkhada, Edwin R. van Teijlingen, and Pramod R. Regmi. "Women's Autonomy in Household Decision-Making: A Demographic Study in Nepal." *Reproductive Health* 7 (2010): 15. https://doi.org/10.1186/1742-4755-7-15.

Aizer, Anna. "The Gender Wage Gap and Domestic Violence." *American Economic Review* 100, no. 4 (2010): 1847–59. https://doi.org/10.1257/aer.100.4.1847.

Akerlof, George A. "Sins of Omission and the Practice of Economics." *Journal of Economic Literature* 58, no. 2 (2020): 405–18. https://doi.org/10.1257/jel.20191573/.

Altindag, Duha T., J. Nunley, and A. Seals. "Child-Custody Reform and the Division of Labor in the Household." *Review of Economics of the Household* 15, no. 3 (2017): 833–56. https://doi.org/10.1007/s11150-017-9374-7.

Anderson, Siwan, and Mukesh Eswaran. "What Determines Female Autonomy? Evidence from Bangladesh." *Journal of Development Economics* 90, no. 2 (2009): 179–91. www.sciencedirect.com/science/article/abs/pii/S0304387808001089.

Andrasfay, Theresa, and Noreen Goldman. "Reductions in 2020 US Life Expectancy Due to COVID-19 and the Disproportionate Impact on the Black and Latino Populations." *Proceedings of the National Academy of Sciences* 118, no. 5 (February 2, 2021): e2014746118. https://doi.org/10.1073/pnas.2014746118.

Angelov, Nikolay, Per Johansson, and Erica Lindahl. "Parenthood and the Gender Gap in Pay." *Journal of Human Resources* 50, no. 1 (2015): 123–55. www.journals.uchicago.edu/doi/10.1086/684851.

Antecol, Heather, Kelly Bedard, and Jenna Stearns. "Equal but Inequitable: Who Benefits from Gender-Neutral Tenure Clock Stopping Policies?" *American Economic Review* 108, no. 9 (2018): 2420–41. www.doi.org/10.1257/aer.20160613.

Auriol, Emmanuelle, Guido Friebel, Alisa Weinberger, and Sascha Wilhelm. "Underrepresentation of Women in the Economics Profession More Pronounced in the United States Compared to Heterogeneous Europe." *PNAS* 119, no. 16 (2022): e2118853119. https://doi.org/10.1073/pnas.2118853119.

Bailey, Martha J. "More Power to the Pill: The Impact of Contraceptive Freedom on Women's Life Cycle Labor Supply." *Quarterly Journal of Economics* 121, no. 1 (2006): 289–320. www.jstor.org/stable/25098791.

Bailey, Martha J., Lea Bart, and Vanessa Wanner Lang. "The Missing Baby Bust: The Consequences of the COVID-19 Pandemic for Contraceptive Use, Pregnancy, and Childbirth Among Low-Income Women." *Population Research and Policy Review* 41, no. 4 (August 2022): 1549–69. https://doi.org/10.1007/s11113-022-09703-9.

Bailey, Martha J., Janet Currie, and Hannes Schwandt. "The COVID-19 Baby Bump in the United States." *Proceedings of the National Academy of Sciences* 120, no. 34 (August 22, 2023): e2222075120. https://doi.org/10.1073/pnas.2222075120.

Baker, Peter. "The Women Who Are Reshaping Economics." *New York Times*, January 10, 2018. www.nytimes.com/2018/01/10/us/politics/women-economics.html.

Basu, Bharati, and Pushkar Maitra. "Intra-Household Bargaining Power and Household Expenditure Allocation: Evidence from Iran." *Review of Development Economics* (2020). https://doi.org/10.1111/rode.12636.

Becker, Gary S. *The Economics of Discrimination*. Chicago: University of Chicago Press, 1957.

Becker, Gary S. "Altruism in the Family and Selfishness in the Market Place." *Economica* 48, no. 189 (1981): 1–15.

Becker, Gary S. *A Treatise on the Family*. Cambridge, MA: Harvard University Press, 1993.

Bee, Michele, and Maxime Desmarais-Tremblay. "The Birth of *Homo economicus*: The Methodological Debate on the Economic Agent from J. S. Mill to V. Pareto." *Journal of the History of Economic Thought* 45, no. 1 (2022): 1–26. https://doi.org/10.1017/S1053837221000535.

Bell, Carolyn Shaw. "Report of the Committee on the Status of Women in the Economic Profession." *American Economic Association* 63, no. 2 (1973): 508–11.

Berik, Günseli, Yana van der Meulen Rodgers, and Stephanie Seguino. "Feminist Economics of Inequality, Development, and Growth." *Feminist Economics* 15, no. 3 (July 1, 2009): 1–33. https://doi.org/10.1080/13545700903093524.

Bittman, Michael, Paula England, Liana Sayer, Nancy Folbre, and George Matheson. "When Does Gender Trump Money? Bargaining and Time in Household Work." *American Journal of Sociology* 109, no. 1 (2003): 186–214. https://doi.org/10.1086/378340.

Bound, John, and Harry J. Holzer. "Industrial Shifts, Skills Levels, and the Labor Market for White and Black Males." Working Paper No. 3715, National Bureau of Economic Research, May 1991. https://doi.org/10.3386/w3715.

Boushey, Heather. *Finding Time: The Economics of Work-Life Conflict*. Cambridge, MA: Harvard University Press, 2016.

Bradbury, Katharine, and Jane Katz. "The Responsiveness of Married Women's Labor Force Participation to Income and Wages: Recent Changes and Possible Explanations." Federal Reserve Bank of Boston Working Paper No. 08–7, 2008. https://papers.ssrn.com/sol3/papers.cfm?abstract_id=1324339.

Bridgman, Benjamin, Andrew Craig, and Danit Kanal. "Accounting for Household Production in the National Accounts: An Update 1965–2020." *BEA Survey of*

Current Business 102, no. 2 (2022). https://apps.bea.gov/scb/issues/2022/02
-february/pdf/0222-household-production.pdf.

Burke, Jeremy, and Amalia R. Miller. "The Effects of Job Relocation on Spousal Careers: Evidence from Military Change of Station Moves." *Economic Inquiry* 56, no. 2 (2018): 1261–77. https://doi.org/10.1111/ecin.12529.

Buzard, Kristy, Laura Gee, and Olga Stoddard. "Who You Gonna Call? Gender Inequality in External Demands for Parental Involvement." *The Quarterly Journal of Economics*, 2025, qjaf027, https://doi.org/10.1093/qje/qjaf027.

Calarco, Jessica. *Holding It Together: How Women Became America's Safety Net.* New York: Portfolio, 2024.

Campbell, Elizabeth L., and Oliver Hahl. "Stop Undervaluing Exceptional Women." *Harvard Business Review*, July 22, 2022. https://hbr.org/2022/07/stop-undervaluing-exceptional-women.

Cassidy, Brittany S., and Anne C. Krendl. "A Crisis of Competence: Benevolent Sexism Affects Evaluations of Women's Competence." *Sex Roles* 81 (2019): 505–20. https://doi.org/10.1007/s11199-019-1011-3.

Chari, Anusha. "Report on the Committee on the Status of Women in the Economics Profession." *AEA Papers and Proceedings* 113 (2023): 815–39.

Chetty, Raj, John N. Friedman, and Emmanuel Saez. "Using Differences in Knowledge Across Neighborhoods to Uncover the Impacts of the EITC on Earnings." *American Economic Review* 103, no. 7 (2013): 2683–721. https://doi.org/10.1257/aer.103.7.2683.

Chetty, Raj, John N. Friedman, Emmanuel Saez, Nicholas Turner, and Danny Yagan. "Income Segregation and Intergenerational Mobility Across Colleges in the United States." *Quarterly Journal of Economics* 135, no. 3 (2020): 1567–633. https://doi.org/10.1093/qje/qjaa005.

Chung, YoonKyung, Barbara Downs, Danielle H. Sandler, and Robert Sienkiewicz. "The Parental Gender Earnings Gap in the United States." Working Paper No. 17–68, Center for Economic Studies, US Census Bureau, 2017. https://ideas.repec.org/p/cen/wpaper/17-68.html.

Ciscato, Edoardo, and Simon Weber. "The Role of Evolving Marital Preferences in Growing Income Inequality." *Journal of Population Economics* 33, no. 1 (2020): 307–47. https://doi.org/10.1007/s00148-019-00739-4.

Cortés, Patricia, and Jessica Pan. "Children and the Remaining Gender Gaps in the Labor Market." *Journal of Economic Literature* 61, no. 4 (2023): 1359–409. https://doi.org/10.1257/jel.20221549.

Coser, Lewis A. "Greedy Organizations." *European Journal of Sociology* 8, no. 2 (1967): 196–215. www.jstor.org/stable/23998539.

Coser, Rose Laub, and Gerald Rokoff. "Women in the Occupational World: Social Disruption and Conflict." *Social Problems* 18, no. 4 (1971): 535–54. https://doi.org/10.2307/799727.

Criado Perez, Caroline. *Invisible Women: Data Bias in a World Designed for Men.* New York: Harry N. Abrams, 2021.

Darity, William A., Jr., Darrick Hamilton, and James B. Stewart. "A Tour de Force in Understanding Intergroup Inequality: An Introduction to Stratification

Economics." *Review of Black Political Economy* 42 (2015): 1–6. https://doi .org/10.1007/s12114-014-9201-2.

Dinner, Deborah. "The Universal Childcare Debate: Rights Mobilization, Social Policy, and the Dynamics of Feminist Activism, 1966–1974." *Law and History Review* 28, no. 3 (2010): 577–628. https://doi.org/10.1017/S0738248010000581.

Doepke, Matthias, Markus Tertilt, and Alessandra Voena. "The Economics and Politics of Women's Rights." *Annual Review of Economics* 4 (2012): 339–72. https://doi.org/10.1146/annurev-economics-080511-110928.

Dong, Xinwei. "Intrahousehold Property Ownership, Women's Bargaining Power, and Family Structure." *Labour Economics* 78 (2022): Article C. https://doi .org/10.1016/j.labeco.2022.102235.

Downey, Kirstin. *The Woman Behind the New Deal: The Life and Legacy of Frances Perkins—Social Security, Unemployment Insurance, and the Minimum Wage.* New York: Anchor, 2010.

Duflo, Esther. "Women Empowerment and Economic Development." *Journal of Economic Literature* 50, no. 4 (2012): 1051–79. https://doi.org/10.1257/jel.50.4.1051.

Fairlie, Robert W., and Bruce D. Meyer. "Trends in Self-Employment Among White and Black Men During the Twentieth Century." *Journal of Human Resources* 35, no. 4 (2000): 643–69. https://doi.org/10.2307/146366.

Fernández-Kranz, Daniel, and Jennifer Roff. "The Effect of Alimony Reform on Married Women's Labor Supply: Evidence from the American Time Use Survey." IZA Discussion Paper No. 14949. Institute of Labor Economics (IZA), 2021.

Ferrie, Joseph P., Claudia Goldin, and Claudia Olivetti. "Mobilizing the Manpower of Mothers: Childcare Under the Lanham Act During WWII." Working Paper No. 32755, National Bureau of Economic Research, July 2024. www.nber.org /papers/w32755.

Fofana, Namizata Binaté, Gerrit Antonides, Anke Niehof, and Johan A. C. van Ophem. "How Microfinance Empowers Women in Côte d'Ivoire." *Review of the Economics of the Household* 13 (2015): 1023–41. https://doi.org/10.1007 /s11150-015-9278-6.

Folbre, Nancy. *The Invisible Heart: Economics and Family Values.* New York: The New Press, 2002.

Foster, Lucia, Erika McEntarfer, and Danielle H. Sandler. "Early Career Paths of Economists Inside and Outside of Academia." *Journal of Economic Perspectives* 37, no. 4 (2023): 231–50. https://doi.org/10.1257/jep.37.4.231.

Furman, Jason, Melissa Schettini Kearney, and Wilson Powell. "The Role of Childcare Challenges in the US Jobs Market Recovery During the COVID-19 Pandemic." Working Paper No. 28934, National Bureau of Economic Research, June 2021. https://doi.org/10.3386/w28934.

Gabriel, Mary. *Madonna: A Rebel Life.* New York: Little, Brown, 2023.

Gillen, Martie, and Hyungsoo Kim. "Older Women and Poverty Transition." *Journal of Applied Gerontology* 28, no. 3 (2009): 320–41. https://doi.org/10.1177 /0733464808326953.

Goldin, Claudia. *Career and Family: Women's Century-Long Journey Toward Equity*. Princeton, NJ: Princeton University Press, 2021.

Goldin, Claudia. "Why Women Won." Working Paper No. 31762, National Bureau of Economic Research, October 2023. https://doi.org/10.3386/w31762.

Goldin, Claudia. "Nobel Lecture: An Evolving Economic Force." *American Economic Review* 114, no. 6 (2024): 1515–39. https://doi.org/10.1257/aer.114.6.1515.

Goldin, Claudia, and Lawrence F. Katz. "The Power of the Pill: Oral Contraceptives and Women's Career and Marriage Decisions." *Journal of Political Economy* 110, no. 4 (2002): 730–70. https://doi.org/10.1086/340778.

Grigoryeva, Angelina. "Own Gender, Sibling's Gender, Parent's Gender: The Division of Elderly Parent Care Among Adult Children." *American Sociological Review* 82, no. 1 (2017): 116–46. https://doi.org/10.1177/0003122416686521.

Heath, Rachel, and Seema Jayachandran. "The Causes and Consequences of Increased Female Education and Labor Force Participation in Developing Countries." Working Paper No. 22766, National Bureau of Economic Research, October 2016. www.nber.org/system/files/working_papers/w22766/w22766.pdf.

Heggeness, Misty L. "Improving Child Welfare in Middle Income Countries: The Unintended Consequence of a Pro-Homemaker Divorce Law and Wait Time to Divorce." *Journal of Development Economics* 143 (March 1, 2020): 102405. https://doi.org/10.1016/j.jdeveco.2019.102405.

Heggeness, Misty L. "Estimating the Immediate Impact of the COVID-19 Shock on Parental Attachment to the Labor Market and the Double Bind of Mothers." *Review of Economics of the Household* 18, no. 4 (December 2020): 1053–78. https://doi.org/10.1007/s11150-020-09514-x.

Heggeness, Misty L. "The Girly Economics of Care Work: Implications for Economic Statistics." *AEA Papers and Proceedings* 113: 632–36, 2023. https://doi.org/10.1257/pandp.20231108.

Heggeness, Misty L. "Swifties vs. NFL Fans: An Economist Explains What Happens When Two Rabid Fan Bases Collide." *Fast Company*, October 8, 2023. www.fastcompany.com/90962560/swifties-vs-nfl-fans-an-economist-explains-what-happens-when-two-rabid-fanbases-collide.

Heggeness, Misty L. "Taylor Swift Isn't the Economic Force. It's Her Fans." *Time*, April 18, 2024. https://time.com/6968040/taylor-swift-swifties-economic-force/.

Heggeness, Misty L. "Taylor Swift, Underdog Voices, and Women's Historical Right to 'Bolt.'" *Ms. Magazine*, May 7, 2024. https://msmagazine.com/2024/05/07/taylor-swift-the-bolter/.

Heggeness, Misty L., Joseph Bommarito, and Pilar McDonald. "The Challenge to Recognize 'Care Privilege' in the Field of Economics." *Oxford Review of Economic Policy*, forthcoming.

Heggeness, Misty L., Joseph Bommarito, and Pilar McDonald. "An Introduction to Care Privilege and Policymaking in the United States." *Applied Economic Perspectives and Policy*, forthcoming.

Heggeness, Misty, Boyeon Park, and Lucie Prewitt. "Reinvention: The Path to Career and Life Fulfillment Is Non-Linear." Unpublished manuscript, June 2025.

Heggeness, Misty, Lilly Springer, and Yurong Zhang. "New Parent Labor Supply in Adaptive Markets." January 18, 2025. https://papers.ssrn.com/sol3/papers.cfm?abstract_id=5102602.

Herbst, Chris M. "Universal Child Care, Maternal Employment, and Children's Long-Run Outcomes: Evidence from the US Lanham Act of 1940." *Journal of Labor Economics* 35, no. 2 (2017): 519–64. www.jstor.org/stable/26553263.

Hyland, Marie, Simeon Djankov, and Petra Koujianou Goldberg. "Gendered Laws and Women in the Workforce." *American Economic Review: Insights* 2, no. 4 (2020): 475–90. https://doi.org/10.1257/aeri.20190631.

Jefferson, Therese. "Women and Retirement Pensions: A Research Review." *Feminist Economics* 15, no. 4 (2009): 115–45. https://doi.org/10.1080/13545700903153963.

Juhn, Chinhui. "Labor Market Dropouts and Trends in the Wages of Black and White Men." *ILR Review* 56, no. 4 (July 1, 2003): 643–62. https://doi.org/10.1177/001979390305600406.

Kearney, Melissa Schettini, and Phillip Levine. "The US COVID-19 Baby Bust and Rebound." Working Paper No. 30000, National Bureau of Economic Research, April 2022. https://doi.org/10.3386/w30000.

Kim, Scott Daewon, and Petra Moser. "Women in Science: Lessons from the Baby Boom." Working Paper No. 29436, National Bureau of Economic Research, October 2021. https://doi.org/10.3386/w29436.

Klasen, Stephan, and Francesca Lamanna. "The Impact of Gender Inequality in Education and Labor Force Participation on Economic Growth: New Evidence for a Panel of Countries." *Feminist Economics* 15, no. 3: 91–132. https://doi.org/10.1080/13545700902893106.

Koppa, Vijetha. "Can Information Save Lives? Effect of a Victim-Focused Police Intervention on Intimate Partner Homicides." *Journal of Economic Behavior and Organization* 217 (January 2024): 756–82. https://doi.org/10.1016/j.jebo.2023.11.001.

Krouse, Sarah, and Anne Steele. "Women Own This Summer. The Economy Proves It." *Wall Street Journal*, August 10, 2023. www.wsj.com/economy/consumers/the-summer-women-flexed-their-spending-power-dc2ce92c.

Lansky, Sam. "2023 Person of the Year: Taylor Swift." *Time*, December 6, 2023. https://time.com/6342806/person-of-the-year-2023-taylor-swift/.

Levitt, Steven D., and Stephen J. Dubner. *Freakonomics: A Rogue Economist Explores the Hidden Side of Everything.* New York: HarperCollins, 2005.

Lundberg, Shelly, and Robert A. Pollak. "Separate Spheres Bargaining and the Marriage Market." *Journal of Political Economy* 101, no. 6 (1993): 988–1010. https://doi.org/10.1086/261912.

Lundberg, Shelly, and Robert A. Pollak. "Noncooperative Bargaining Models of Marriage." *American Economic Review* 84, no. 2 (1994): 132–37. www.jstor.org/stable/2117816.

Lundberg, Shelly, and Robert A. Pollak. "Bargaining and Distribution in Marriage." *Journal of Economic Perspectives* 10, no. 4 (1996): 139–58. https://doi.org/10.1257/jep.10.4.139.

Lundberg, Shelly, Robert Pollak, and Terry Wales. "Do Husbands and Wives Pool Resources?" *Journal of Human Resources* 32, no. 3 (1996): 464–80. https://doi.org/10.2307/146179.

Majlesi, Kaveh. "Labor Market Opportunities and Women's Decision Making Power Within Households." *Journal of Development Economics* 119 (March 1, 2016): 34–47. https://doi.org/10.1016/j.jdeveco.2015.10.002.

Marçal, Katrine. *Who Cooked Adam Smith's Dinner? A Story of Women and Economics*. Trans. Saskia Vogel. New York: Pegasus Books, 2016.

Martínez, Claudia. "Intrahousehold Allocation and Bargaining Power: Evidence from Chile." *Economic Development and Cultural Change* 61, no. 3 (2013): 577–605. https://doi.org/10.1086/669260.

Mas-Colell, Andreu, Michael D. Whinston, and Jerry R. Green. *Microeconomic Theory*. Oxford: Oxford University Press, 1995.

Myers, Caitlin. "Forecasts for a Post-Roe America: The Effects of Increased Travel Distance on Abortions and Births." *Journal of Policy Analysis and Management* 43, no. 1 (2024): 39–62. https://doi.org/10.1002/pam.22524.

Myers, Caitlin, and Anjali Srinivasan "Brief of *Amici Curiae* Economists in Support of Respondents in *Dobbs v. Jackson's Women's Health Organization*." *Perspectives on Sexual and Reproductive Health* 56, no. 3 (2024): 211–21. https://doi.org/10.1111/psrh.12268.

Nelson, Julie A. *Feminism, Objectivity, and Economics*. New York: Routledge, 1995.

Nelson, Julie A. *Economics for Humans*. Chicago: University of Chicago Press, 2006.

Osborne, Frances. *The Bolter: The Story of Idina Sackville, Who Ran Away to Become the Chief Seductress of Kenya's Scandalous "Happy Valley Set."* New York: Vintage, 2008.

Paull, Gillian. "Children and Women's Hours of Work." *The Economic Journal* 118, no. 526 (2008): F8–F27. https://doi.org/10.1111/j.1468-0297.2007.02114.x.

Pfleiderer, Paul. "Chameleons: The Misuse of Theoretical Models in Finance and Economics." *Economica* 87, no. 345 (2020): 81–107. https://doi.org/10.1111/ecca.12295.

Rangel, Marcos A. "Alimony Rights and Intrahousehold Allocation of Resources: Evidence from Brazil." *The Economic Journal* 116, no. 513 (2006): 627–58. https://doi.org/10.1111/j.1468-0297.2006.01104.x.

Rasul, Imran. "Marriage Markets and Divorce Laws." *Journal of Law, Economics, and Organization* 22, no. 1 (2006): 30–69. https://doi.org/10.1093/jleo/ewj008.

Reimers, Cordelia W. "Labor Market Discrimination Against Hispanic and Black Men." *Review of Economics and Statistics* 65, no. 4 (1983): 570–79. https://doi.org/10.2307/1935925.

Richter, David, Michael D. Krämer, Nicole K. Y. Tang, Hawley E. Montgomery-Downs, and Sakari Lemola. "Long-Term Effects of Pregnancy and Childbirth on

Sleep Satisfaction and Duration of First-Time and Experienced Mothers and Fathers." *Sleep* 42, no. 4 (2019): 1–10. https://doi.org/10.1093/sleep/zsz015.

Romer, Paul. "Mathiness in the Theory of Economic Growth." *American Economic Review* 105, no. 5 (2015): 89–93. http://doi.org/10.1257/aer.p20151066.

Rostek, Joanna. *Women's Economic Thought in the Romantic Age: Towards a Transdisciplinary Herstory of Economic Thought.* New York: Routledge, 2021.

Roth, Guenther. Review of *Greedy Institutions: Patterns of Undivided Commitment*, by Lewis A. Coser. *American Political Science Review* 71, no. 2 (1977): 632–34. https://doi.org/10.2307/1978360.

Samuelson, Paul A. "Social Indifference Curves." *Quarterly Journal of Economics* 70 (February 1956): 1–22. https://doi.org/10.2307/1884510.

Sandberg, Sheryl. *Lean In: Women, Work, and the Will to Lead.* New York: Knopf, 2013.

Seidu, Abdul-Aziz, Richad Gyan Aboagye, Joshua Okyere, et al. "Women's Autonomy in Household Decision-Making and Safer Sex Negotiation in Sub-Saharan Africa: An Analysis of Data from 27 Demographic and Health Surveys." *SSM-Population Health* 14 (2021): 100773. https://doi.org/10.1016/j.ssmph.2021.100773.

Slaughter, Anne-Marie. "Why Women Still Can't Have It All." *The Atlantic*, June 13, 2012. www.theatlantic.com/magazine/archive/2012/07/why-women-still-cant-have-it-all/309020/.

Smarsh, Sarah. *Heartland: A Memoir of Working Hard and Being Broke in the Richest Country on Earth.* New York: Scribner / Simon & Schuster, 2018.

Smith, Adam. *The Wealth of Nations.* 5th ed. London: W. Strahan and T. Cadell, 1789.

Smith, James P., and Finis R. Welch. "Chapter 7: Black/White Male Earnings and Employment: 1960–70." In *The Distribution of Economic Well-Being*, ed. F. Thomas Juster, 233–302. Cambridge, MA: National Bureau of Economic Research, 1977. www.nber.org/chapters/c4374.

Sowards, Stacey K. *¡Sí, Ella Puede! The Rhetorical Legacy of Dolores Huerta and the United Farm Workers.* Austin: University of Texas Press, 2019.

Stansbury, Anna, and Robert Schultz. "The Economics Profession's Socioeconomic Diversity Problem." *Journal of Economic Perspectives* 37, no. 4 (Fall 2023): 207–30. https://doi.org/10.1257/jep.37.4.207.

Stevenson, Betsey, and Justin Wolfers. "Bargaining in the Shadow of the Law: Divorce Laws and Family Distress." *Quarterly Journal of Economics* 121, no. 1 (February 2006): 267–88. www.jstor.org/stable/25098790.

Stevenson, Betsey, and Justin Wolfers. "Marriage and Divorce: Changes and Their Driving Forces." *Journal of Economic Perspectives* 21, no. 2 (2007): 27–52. www.aeaweb.org/articles?id=10.1257/jep.21.2.27.

Stevenson, Betsey, and Justin Wolfers. "Trends in Marital Stability." In *Research Handbook on the Economics of Family Law*, ed. S.L. Schaeffer, 115–30. Cheltenham, UK: Edward Elgar, 2011.

Stoltzfus, Emilie. "Child Care: The Federal Role During World War II." Congressional Research Service Report for Congress, RS20615. 2000.

Sullivan, Kelly. "Sleep Duration and Feeling Rested Are Differentially Associated with Having Children Among Men and Women (P3.060)." *Neurology* 88, no. 16 (2017). https://doi.org/10.1212/WNL.88.16_supplement.P3.060.

Thaler, Richard H. "From *Homo economicus* to *Homo sapiens*." *Journal of Economic Perspectives* 14, no. 1 (2000): 133–42. https://doi.org/10.1257/jep.14.1.133.

Thaler, Richard H. *Misbehaving: The Making of Behavioral Economics.* New York: W. W. Norton, 2015.

Uckat, Hannah. "Leaning In at Home: Women's Promotions and Intra-Household Bargaining in Bangladesh." Policy Research Working Paper No. 10370, World Bank, 2023. http://hdl.handle.net/10986/39586.

Voena, Alessandra. "Yours, Mine, and Ours: Do Divorce Laws Affect the Intertemporal Behavior of Married Couples?" *American Economic Review* 105, no. 8 (2015): 2295–332. https://doi.org/10.1257/aer.20120234.

Wang, Shing-Yi. "Property Rights and Intra-Household Bargaining." *Journal of Development Economics* 107 (March 1, 2014): 192–201. https://doi.org/10.1016/j.jdeveco.2013.12.003.

Waring, Marilyn. *If Women Counted: A New Feminist Economics.* San Francisco: Harper, 1990.

Wasserman, Claire. *Ladies Get Paid: The Ultimate Guide to Breaking Barriers, Owning Your Worth, and Taking Command of Your Career.* New York: Gallery Books, 2021.

Wolfers, Justin. "Did Unilateral Divorce Laws Raise Divorce Rates? A Reconciliation and New Results." *American Economic Review* 96, no. 5 (2006): 1802–20. https://doi.org/10.1257/aer.96.5.1802.

Wong, Ho-Po Crystal. "Credible Commitments and Marriage: When the Homemaker Gets Her Share at Divorce." *Journal of Demographic Economics* 82, no. 3 (2016): 241–79. https://doi.org/10.1017/dem.2016.9.

INDEX

Founded in 1893,
UNIVERSITY OF CALIFORNIA PRESS
publishes bold, progressive books and journals
on topics in the arts, humanities, social sciences,
and natural sciences—with a focus on social
justice issues—that inspire thought and action
among readers worldwide.

The UC PRESS FOUNDATION
raises funds to uphold the press's vital role
as an independent, nonprofit publisher, and
receives philanthropic support from a wide
range of individuals and institutions—and from
committed readers like you. To learn more, visit
ucpress.edu/supportus.

The book cover takes inspiration from the author's own pictures of friendship bracelets, using the theme as a hero image symbolizing Taylor Swift's fans and the fan-founded trade economy of the Eras Tour. The typeface is Adobe Caslon, an eighteenth-century typeface updated, redrawn, and digitized by a woman, Carol Twombly, for Adobe in the 1980s.